Droid™ 2

FOR

DUMMIES®

Droid™ 2
FOR
DUMMIES®

by Dan Gookin

WILEY

Wiley Publishing, Inc.

Droid™ 2 For Dummies®

Published by
Wiley Publishing, Inc.
111 River Street
Hoboken, NJ 07030-5774

www.wiley.com

Copyright © 2011 by Wiley Publishing, Inc., Indianapolis, Indiana

Published by Wiley Publishing, Inc., Indianapolis, Indiana

Published simultaneously in Canada

For general information on our other products and services, please contact our Customer Care Department within the U.S. at 877-762-2974, outside the U.S. at 317-572-3993, or fax 317-572-4002.

For technical support, please visit www.wiley.com/techsupport.

Wiley also publishes its books in a variety of electronic formats. Some content that appears in print may not be available in electronic books.

Library of Congress Control Number: 2010940232

ISBN: 978-1-118-00286-5

Manufactured in the United States of America

10 9 8 7 6 5 4 3 2 1

WILEY

About the Author

Dan Gookin has written more than 115 books about technology, many of them accurate. He is most famously known as the author of the original *For Dummies* book, *DOS For Dummies,* published in 1991. Additionally, Dan has achieved fame as one of the first computer radio talk show hosts, the editor of a computer magazine, a national technology spokesman, and an occasional actor on the community theater stage.

Dan still considers himself a writer and technology "guru" whose job it is to remind everyone that our electronics are not to be taken too seriously. His approach is light and humorous yet very informative. He knows that modern gizmos can be complex and intimidating but necessary to help people become productive and successful. Dan mixes his vast knowledge of all things high-tech with a unique, dry sense of humor that keeps everyone informed — and awake.

Dan's most recent books are *Word 2010 For Dummies, PCs For Dummies,* Windows 7 Edition, and *Laptops For Dummies,* 4th Edition. He holds a degree in communications/visual arts from the University of California, San Diego. Dan dwells in North Idaho, where he enjoys woodworking, music, theater, riding his bicycle, being with his boys, and fighting local government corruption.

Author's Acknowledgments

I would like to acknowledge Kelly Crummey and Megan Keefe, from WeberShandwick, for their helpful assistance.

Publisher's Acknowledgments

We're proud of this book; please send us your comments through our online registration form located at http://dummies.custhelp.com. For other comments, please contact our Customer Care Department within the U.S. at 877-762-2974, outside the U.S. at 317-572-3993, or fax 317-572-4002.

Some of the people who helped bring this book to market include the following:

Acquisitions and Editorial

Senior Project Editor: Paul Levesque

Acquisitions Editor: Katie Mohr

Copy Editor: Rebecca Whitney

Technical Editor: Paul Eastham

Editorial Manager: Leah Cameron

Editorial Assistant: Amanda Graham

Sr. Editorial Assistant: Cherie Case

Cartoons: Rich Tennant
(www.the5thwave.com)

Composition Services

Project Coordinator: Kristie Rees

Layout and Graphics: Carl Byers, Samantha K. Cherolis, Cheryl Grubbs, Joyce Haughey

Proofreader: Leeann Harney

Indexer: Infodex Indexing Services, Inc.

Publishing and Editorial for Technology Dummies

Richard Swadley, Vice President and Executive Group Publisher

Andy Cummings, Vice President and Publisher

Mary Bednarek, Executive Acquisitions Director

Mary C. Corder, Editorial Director

Publishing for Consumer Dummies

Diane Graves Steele, Vice President and Publisher

Composition Services

Debbie Stailey, Director of Composition Services

Contents at a Glance

Table of Contents

Introduction

Don't be fooled: Just because the Droid 2 is a *smartphone* doesn't mean that it's harboring some form of insidious intelligence. There's no alien brain in the device. It isn't going to take over the world, though it can intimidate you — that is, until you understand and accept that it's *your* phone. The Droid 2 is a gizmo that helps make your life a heck of a lot easier.

The key to understanding an amazing piece of technology such as the Droid 2 is understanding. To help you get there, I offer this book: your friendly, informative, relaxed, and often irreverent reference to the Motorola Droid 2 cell phone. Prepare to get more from your phone.

About This Book

This book is a reference. I don't intend for you to read it from cover to cover. Instead, you'll find each chapter to be its own, self-contained unit, covering a specific topic about using the Droid 2 phone. Each chapter is further divided into sections representing a task you perform with the phone or explaining how to get something done. Sample sections in this book include

- Typing on your Droid 2
- Phoning someone you call often
- Setting up Visual Voice Mail
- Sending a picture to Facebook
- Creating a 3G mobile hotspot
- Turning your phone into a deejay
- Dialing an international number
- Saving battery life

You have nothing to memorize, no mysterious utterances, no animal sacrifices, and definitely no PowerPoint presentations. Instead, every section explains a topic as though it's the first thing you read in this book. Nothing is assumed, and everything is cross-referenced. Technical terms and topics, when they come up, are neatly shoved to the side, where they're easily avoided. The idea here isn't to learn anything. This book's philosophy is to help you look it up, figure it out, and get back to your life.

How to Use This Book

This book follows a few conventions for using the Droid 2. The main way you interact with your phone is by using its *touchscreen,* which is the glassy part of the phone as it's facing you. Buttons also adorn the Droid 2, all of which are explained in Part I of this book.

You have various ways to touch the screen, which are explained and named in Chapter 3.

Chapter 4 discusses text input on the Droid 2, which involves using the Multi-Touch keyboard on the screen or the sliding keyboard. The Droid 2 also features the Swype onscreen keyboard for superfast text entry. And, when you tire of typing, you can always input text on your Droid 2 by dictation.

This book directs you to do things on your phone by following numbered steps. Each step involves a specific activity, such as touching something on the screen. For example:

3. Choose Downloads.

This step directs you to touch the text or item on the screen labeled Downloads. You might also be told to do this:

3. Touch Downloads.

 Some phone options can be turned off or on, as indicated by a gray box with a green check mark in it, as shown in the margin. By touching the box on the screen, you add or remove the green check mark. When the green check mark appears, the option is on; otherwise, it's off.

 The barcodes in the margins are there to help you install recommended apps. To install the app, scan the barcode using special software you install on the Droid 2. Chapter 20 discusses how to add software to your phone, and in Chapter 26 I discuss how to use the Barcode Scanner app to read barcodes.

Foolish Assumptions

Even though this book is written with the gentle handholding required by anyone who is just starting out, or who is easily intimidated, I have made a few assumptions. For example, I assume that you're a human being and not a robot from Venus.

My biggest assumption: You have a Droid 2 phone by Motorola. Though you can use this book generically with any Android phone, it's specific to the things the Droid 2 can do.

In the United States, cellular service for the Droid 2 is provided by Verizon. Many things that the Droid 2 can do are based on the services Verizon offers, such as Visual Voice Mail or Backup Assistant.

I also assume that you have a computer, either a desktop or laptop. The computer can be a PC or Windows computer or a Macintosh. Oh, I suppose it could also be a Linux computer. In any event, I refer to your computer as "your computer" throughout this book. When directions are specific to a PC or Mac, the book says so.

Programs that run on the Droid 2 are *apps*, which is short for *applications*. A single program is an app.

Finally, this book doesn't assume that you have a Google account, but already having one helps. Information is provided in Chapter 2 about setting up a Google account — an extremely important part of using the Droid 2. Having a Google account opens up a slew of useful features, information, and programs that make using your Droid 2 phone more productive.

How This Book Is Organized

This book has been sliced into six parts, each of which describes a certain aspect of the Droid 2 or how it's used.

Part I: Droid 2: The Sequel

This part of the book serves as your introduction to the Droid 2. Chapters cover setup and orientation and familiarize you with how the phone works. Part I is a good place to start, plus you discover things in this part that aren't obvious from just guessing how the phone works.

Part II: Phone 101

Nothing is more basic for a phone to do than make calls, which is the topic of the chapters in this part of the book. The Droid 2 can make calls, receive calls, and serve as an answering service for calls you miss. It also manages the names of all the people you know and even those you don't want to know but have to know anyway.

Part III: Beyond Telephone Communications

The Droid 2 is about more than just telephone communications. Part III of this book explores other ways you can use your phone to stay in touch with people, the Internet, and other gizmos such as your desktop computer or a Bluetooth headset. Chapters in this part explain how to use text messaging, send and receive email, browse the Web, use social networking, and set up your phone for networking, among other things.

Part IV: More than a Mere Mortal Cell Phone

This part of the book explores the nonphone things your phone can do. For example, your phone can find locations on a map, give you verbal driving directions, take pictures, shoot videos, play music, play games, and do all sorts of wonderful things that no one would ever think a phone can do. The chapters in this part of the book get you up to speed on those activities.

Part V: Hither and Thither

The chapters in this part of the book discuss a slate of interesting topics, from taking the phone overseas and making international calls to customizing it to the necessary chores of maintenance and troubleshooting.

Part VI: The Part of Tens

Finally, this book ends with the traditional *For Dummies* Part of Tens, where each chapter lists ten items or topics. For the Droid 2, the chapters include tips, tricks, shortcuts, and things to remember, plus a list of some of my favorite Droid 2 phone apps.

Icons Used in This Book

This icon flags useful, helpful tips or shortcuts.

This icon marks a friendly reminder to do something.

This icon marks a friendly reminder *not* to do something.

This icon alerts you to overly nerdy information and technical discussions of the topic at hand. Reading the information is optional, though it may win you a pie slice in *Trivial Pursuit*.

Where to Go from Here

Start reading! Observe the table of contents and find something that interests you. Or, look up your puzzle in the index. When those suggestions don't cut it, just start reading Chapter 1.

My email address is dgookin@wambooli.com. Yes, that's my real address. I reply to all the email I get, and you'll get a quick reply if you keep your question short and specific to this book. Although I do enjoy saying Hi, I cannot answer technical support questions, resolve billing issues, or help you troubleshoot your phone. Thanks for understanding.

You can also visit my Web page for more information or as a diversion: www.wambooli.com.

Enjoy this book and your Droid 2!

Part I
Droid 2: The Sequel

In this part . . .

1 t's a given that Hollywood sequels rarely live up to the quality of the original movies. That hard-and-fast rule among movie buffs ensures that the rare exceptions are well known: *The Godfather II, The Empire Strikes Back,* and *Toy Story 2.* Plus, a handful of others are often touted as being as good as or better than their originals. But normally, sequels suck.

That isn't the case with the Droid 2. Unlike a typical Hollywood spinoff, the Droid 2 is a great improvement upon its predecessor. All the things you might have admired about the first Droid are there, such as its compact size and sliding keyboard. Additionally, new features have been added — stuff you might not recognize. So whether you're an old hand or you're new to the Droid 2, you'll welcome the helpful orientation information found in this part of the book.

A Droid 2 of Your Own

In This Chapter

▶ Putting your phone together
▶ Charging the battery
▶ Identifying the phone's pieces parts
▶ Taking the phone with you
▶ Keeping the phone in one place

*N*o one ever asked what happened to R2D1, the lesser-known little brother of R2D2 from the *Star Wars* films. His real name was *R2D*. That was before the newer, improved R2D2 came along. Once the newer, improved model showed up, R2D became R2D1. He lost his luster and fame after the newer model showed up. That happens to all sorts of Droids all over the universe.

For your phone, the Droid 2 replaces the original Droid, which, as far as I know, is still named Droid and not Droid 1. Getting started with your Droid 2 begins with a basic familiarity of the hardware. This chapter helps you get to know your way around the Droid 2, by identifying its various parts, buttons, and sliding whatnot.

Initial Droid 2 Setup

Though it hasn't happened, it would be neat if your phone rang inside the box just as you were opening it. The ringing would certainly accelerate the tedious process of opening the box. Then imagine how much fun it would be to answer the phone and hear a cheerful yet robotic voice say, "Hello from your new Droid 2!" Yeah, that would be fun. Reality is different, as described in this section.

Looking in the box

Several items come in the Droid 2 box. Even though you've probably opened the box already and its contents are doubtless strewn across your desktop, I suggest that you take a moment to locate and identify each of the following goodies:

- Droid 2 phone
- Papers, instructions, warranty, and perhaps a booklet titled *Getting Started* or even *Los Primeros Pasos*
- The phone's battery, which might already be inside the phone
- The phone's back (battery) cover
- Charger/data cable, which is basically a USB cable
- Charger head, a wall adapter for the charger/data cable

The phone may ship with a clingy, static plastic cover over its screen. Another plastic cover may be clinging to the battery cover. The plastic thingies tell you where various features are located or how to install the battery. You can remove the plastic at this time.

An additional sheet of plastic may be found by sliding out the Droid 2 keyboard; flip the phone over and remove the plastic from the back of the touchscreen.

In addition to the items described in the preceding list, you might have been given a bonus package of goodies from whoever sold you the phone. If the outfit is classy, you have a handy little tote bag with perhaps the Verizon logo on it. Inside the bag, you might find these items:

- Smart-looking, leatherette belt-clip phone holster
- Micro-USB car charger
- Headphones
- Even more random pieces of paper

The most important doodad is the phone itself, which might require some assembly before you can use it; refer to the next section for assembly directions.

You can safely set aside all this stuff until you get the phone assembled. I recommend keeping the instructions and other information as long as you own the phone: The phone's box makes an excellent storage place for that stuff — as well as anything else you don't plan to use right away.

If anything is missing or appears to be damaged, contact the folks who sold you the phone.

Installing the phone's battery

Your phone might arrive in a disassembled state. If so, your first duty as a new Droid 2 owner is to install its battery. Your second duty is to charge the battery. Installing the battery is easy, and charging it doesn't require a lightning storm and a kite.

If the nice people who sold you the phone already installed the battery, the phone is ready for charging; see the next section. Otherwise, you can install the battery yourself by following these steps:

1. **Ensure that the phone is turned off.**

   There's no need to follow this step unless you got all excited and already turned on your phone. If so, see Chapter 2 for information on turning off the Droid 2.

2. **Flip over the phone so that the front (the glassy part) is facing away from you.**

   Don't remove the phone's cover when the phone is turned on. You should also disconnect any cables or the headset, if attached.

3. **If the battery isn't installed, you must remove the cover: Place both thumbs on the center part of the upper back cover.**

   Refer to Figure 1-1 for proper thumb placement.

4. **Gently slide the back cover downward using your thumbs.**

   A gentle push is all that's required; feel free to squeeze the phone as you push downward. The back cover slides down a wee bit, about ⅛-inch.

5. **Lift the phone's back cover and set it aside.**

Figure 1-1: Thumb-placement suggestion for removing back cover.

6. **If necessary, remove the battery from its plastic cocoon.**

   You can also remove the back cover from its plastic cocoon. You can also peel the plastic "sticky" from the back cover at this time.

7. **Orient the battery so that its metallic contacts are in the upper right corner as you're looking at the back of the phone.**

   The battery is shaped like a giant, square mint cookie. The battery doesn't taste like mint, so please do not eat it.

8. **Insert the battery, top edge first, and then lower the bottom edge like you're closing the lid on a tiny box.**

   Refer to Figure 1-2 for help in positioning and inserting the battery. The metal contacts on the battery should be on the upper right edge as you insert the battery into the phone, as illustrated in the figure.

   When it's fully inserted, the back of the battery is flush with the back of the phone; it cannot stick up, not one itty bit.

9. **Replace the phone's back cover.**

   The cover has four prongs that slide into four slots on the back of the phone. Position the cover over the slots and it falls into place. Then slide up the cover with your thumbs until it snaps into place.

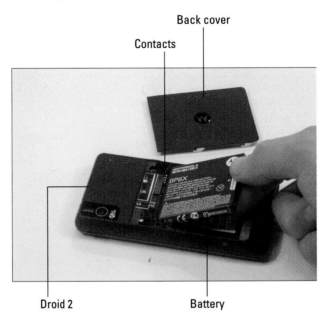

Figure 1-2: Inserting the phone's battery.

After the battery is installed, the next step is to charge the battery. Continue reading in the next section.

Charging the battery

After inserting the battery into your new phone, the next step is to charge it. It's cinchy:

1. **Connect the charger head (the plug thing) to the charger/data cable.**

   They connect only one way.

2. **Plug the charger head and cable into a wall socket.**

3. **Plug the phone into the charger/data cable.**

   The charger cord plugs into the micro-USB connector, found at the phone's left side. The connector plugs in only one way.

As the phone charges, the notification light on the phone's front side may light up. When the light is orange-yellow, the phone is charging. When the light is green, the phone is fully charged.

The phone may turn on when you plug it in for a charge. That's okay; but you need to read Chapter 2 to find out what to do the first time the Droid 2 turns on. You also may need to phone your cell provider for additional setup instructions before you turn on the phone.

- ✔ Wait until the notification light turns green before unplugging the phone from its power cable, especially the first time you charge the phone.

- ✔ The notification light uses three colors: amber for charging, green for fully charged, and red for warning that the battery is low.

- ✔ The notification light flashes whenever the phone requires your attention, such as when new email or a text message has been received. See Chapter 3 for information on reviewing notifications.

- ✔ You can use the phone while it's charging.

- ✔ The Droid 2 can use any standard cell phone charger, though I recommend using the equipment that came with the phone or is designed for a Droid 2.

- ✔ You can charge the Droid 2 in your car, using what was once called a "cigarette lighter." Simply ensure that your car cell phone charger features a micro-USB connector and that it's designed for use with the Droid 2.

- ✔ The phone also charges itself when plugged into a computer using either the USB cable that came with the phone or any micro-USB cable attached to a computer. The computer must be on for charging to work.

- ✔ The Droid 2 charges more quickly when it's plugged into the wall as opposed to a computer's USB port or a car adapter.

- ✔ A micro-USB connector is a standard USB connector, but one that features a teensy dongle that plugs into the left side of your Droid 2 phone. The connector has a flat, trapezoid shape, which makes it different from the *mini-USB connector*, which is squat and slightly larger, and used primarily on evil cell phones.

Droid 2 Orientation

Back in the old days, a telephone came with a rotary dial. When you *dialed* a phone, you were literally turning a dial on the phone. When you *hung up* the phone, you placed the headset on a hook. Not so with cell phones. For example, on the Droid 2 you use something called a *touchscreen* to dial the phone. In case you don't know what a touchscreen is, or what many of the other goobers are that festoon your phone, this section explains everything.

Knowing what's what on your phone

Like all other confusing things, the Droid 2 attempts to intimidate you with some new terms for its features, not to mention that you may not be aware of all the hardware features available. Fret not, gentle reader.

Figure 1-3 illustrates the names of all the useful knobs and doodads on the front of your Droid 2 phone. Figure 1-4 illustrates the same things, but for your phone's backside.

Figure 1-3: Your phone's face.

Power / Lock button
Headphone jack
5 megapixel camera
LED flash
Power / USB connector
Volume up
Volume down
Camera shutter button
Battery cover

Figure 1-4: Your phone's rump.

The terms referenced in Figures 1-3 and 1-4 are the same ones used else-where in this book as well as in whatever scant Droid 2 documentation exists.

In addition to a front and back, your phone has a middle part, which slides out. This teensy keyboard was added to the Droid 2 because of a shipping error from Lilliput. You slide the keyboard out to the left when facing the phone, as illustrated in Figure 1-5.

When you're done using the keyboard, you can slide it back into the phone, as shown in Figure 1-5.

- ✒ The phone's Power button, which turns the phone off or on, is found on top the phone, as shown in Figures 1-3 and 1-4.

- ✒ The main part of the phone is the touchscreen display. You use the touchscreen with one or more of your fingers to control the phone, which is where it gets the name *touch*screen.

- ✒ The soft buttons appear below the touchscreen, as shown in Figure 1-3. They have no function unless the phone is turned on.

- ✒ Yes, the main microphone is on the bottom of the phone. Even so, it picks up your voice loud and clear. There's no need to hold the phone at an angle for the microphone to work.

✔ The phone's volume is adjusted by using the volume buttons on the phone's left side, as shown earlier in Figure 1-3.

✔ Sliding out the keyboard wakes up the phone when it has been sleeping. Refer to Chapter 2 for more information on why the phone gets tired and falls asleep.

✔ Officially, the keyboard is the *sliding keyboard*. Notice that it's not a true QWERTY keyboard, like the one found on your computer. Chapter 4 covers using the sliding keyboard.

✔ When the keyboard is out, the phone's touchscreen display switches to landscape orientation. You can read more about the phone's ability to orient the display into landscape and portrait modes in Chapter 3.

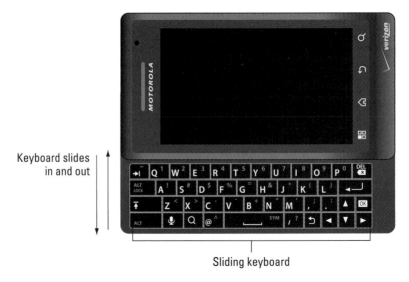

Keyboard slides in and out

Sliding keyboard

Figure 1-5: The Droid 2 secret keyboard.

Listening with earphones

The Droid 2 most likely didn't come with earphones. That's not a reason to give up on the concept. In fact, the nice people who sold you the Droid 2 might have tossed in a set of earbud-style earphones for you to use. If not, well then, they weren't that nice, were they?

You're probably familiar with the earbud type of earphone: The buds are set into your ears. The sharp, pointy end of the earphones, what you don't want to stick into your ear, plugs into the top of the phone.

Between the earbuds and the sharp, pointy thing is often found a doodle on which a button sits. The button can be used to mute the phone or to start or stop the playback of music when the Droid 2 is in its music-playing mode.

You can also use the doodle button to answer the phone when it rings.

There's usually a teensy hole on the back side of the doodle that serves as the phone's microphone. You can use the earphones as a hands-free headset with the Droid 2. Because I'm half Italian, I love this option.

✔ You can purchase any standard cell phone headset for use with the Droid 2.

✔ Some headsets feature extra doodle buttons. Those headsets work fine with the Droid 2, though the extra buttons may not do anything specifically with the Droid 2.

✔ The earbuds are labeled R for right and L for left. If not, the end with the shorter wire is placed in your right ear.

✔ You don't use the earphone's doodle to set the phone's volume, either in a call or while you're listening to music. Instead, the volume is set by using the volume control buttons, found on the side of the phone, as illustrated in Figures 1-3 and 1-4.

✔ See Chapter 18 for more information on using your Droid 2 as a portable music player.

✔ Be sure to fully insert the earphone connector into the phone. The person you're talking with can't hear you well when the earphones are plugged in only part of the way.

✔ You can also use a Bluetooth headset with your phone, to listen to a call or some music. See Chapter 14 for more information on Bluetooth attachments for the Droid 2.

✔ Fold the earphones when you don't need them, as opposed to wrapping them in a loop: Put the earbuds and connector in one hand and then pull the wire straight out with the other hand. Fold the wire in half, and then in half again. You can then put the earphones in your pocket or on a tabletop. By folding the wires, you avoid creating one of those Christmas-tree-light wire balls that would otherwise appear.

Exploring your phone's guts

Rarely do you need to examine the intricacies of your phone's innards. Still, unlike other cell phones, the Droid 2 is designed to let you easily access replaceable items inside the unit without having to sneak around behind the manufacturer's back and alerting the warranty police.

Specifically, you need to open your phone for only two reasons:

- To replace the battery
- To access the MicroSD memory card

When you need to access those items, you can obey these steps:

1. **Turn off your phone.**

   See the section "Turning off the phone," in Chapter 2, for more information.

2. **Flip the phone over.**

3. **Press down on the upper part of the back cover, using your thumbs as illustrated earlier, in Figure 1-1.**

   The back cover slides down.

4. **Set aside the back cover.**

   Use Figure 1-6 to identify the phone's battery and the MicroSD memory card.

   The battery is removed by lifting its bottom edge: Use your fingernail to lift beneath the label Battery Removal Here, as illustrated in Figure 1-6.

   To remove the MicroSD card, pull it downward using the tiny lip at the bottom of the card. It fits in there kind of tightly, so don't be shy about dragging it out. Pull out the card all the way until it's free.

   See Chapter 23 for more information on the Droid 2 battery.

   When you're done rummaging around inside your phone, you close things up:

5. **Set the back cover onto the phone; the little prongs on the back cover fit into four holes on either side of the phone.**

   The cover fits only one way.

6. **Slide the cover up until it snaps into position.**

   To access the MicroSD card, you must first remove its battery.

MicroSD card   Hardware reset switch

Lift the battery here   Battery

Figure 1-6: Stuff inside your phone.

You can turn on the phone again, after the cover is locked into place. See Chapter 2 for information on turning on your phone.

The Droid 2 does not have or use a SIM card. Other cell phones use the SIM card to access the cellular network. The SIM, which stands for Subscriber Identity Module, identifies the phone and does other things you need not care about.

Fashionable Droid 2 Accessories

The Droid 2 has available two accessories you can buy to enhance your mobile communications experience. They are the Multimedia Station and the Car Mount phone holder.

Using the Multimedia Station

In a nutshell, the *Multimedia Station* is a heavy base into which you can set your phone. The station features a USB connection so that the phone can recharge inside the Multimedia Station as well as communicate with a computer.

When the Droid 2 is set inside the Multimedia Station, it runs a special Clock home screen, which displays the current time and provides access to common phone features, as shown in Figure 1-7.

Figure 1-7: The Droid 2 in the Multimedia Station.

The Multimedia Station makes a great home for the phone (see the next section) and can be used as a bedside alarm or as a great way to access the phone when it's deskbound.

✔ The Multimedia Station can be purchased at the same place where you obtained your Droid 2 or at any location where cell phone goodies are sold.

✔ With the Multimedia Station, you get the handsome, high-tech-looking base and a USB cable, plus a power adapter.

✔ See Chapter 19 for more information about using your state-of-the-art cell phone as a digital clock.

✔ Chapter 18 covers playing music on the Droid 2.

✔ Playing slide shows and managing pictures with the Droid 2 are covered in Chapter 17.

Watching Your Droid 2 in Your Car

There's no point in fumbling with your phone while you're on the road. That's because the Droid 2 comes with a handy car mount. When the car mount is properly assembled, a suction cup on one end of it lets you stick your Droid 2 to any flat surface. Because it's a *car mount,* I assume that you'll suck it to the windshield or dashboard of your favorite auto and not your refrigerator or an elevator door.

When you stick the Droid 2 into the car mount, the phone automatically switches to the Car Home screen, shown in Figure 1-8. You can read more about the Car Home screen in Chapter 3, which is your basic Droid 2 orientation chapter.

Car Home notification icon   Map and navigation

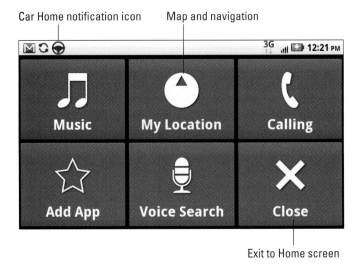

Exit to Home screen

Figure 1-8: The Car Home screen.

The Droid 2 also has a rapid car charger, which may come with the car mount or may be an extra purchase. The rapid car charger is one of those gizmos that plugs into the car's power adapter (née cigarette lighter). The other end of the rapid car charger plugs into the Droid 2, which can be nestled in the car mount or just rattling loose inside your vehicle.

- ✏ Yes, you can use the rapid car charger without having to use the car mount.

- ✏ To make the suction cup on the car mount work properly, you use a hard, smooth surface. An adhesive plastic disk comes with the car mount. Use the disk to ensure that the suction cup has something solid to suck on.

A Home for Your Phone

There was no point in finding a home for your phone back when the Telephone Company bolted the thing to the wall. I remember hunting all over the house for our family's first cordless phone. That was a pain when the batteries were dead and the phone's locator-ring trick didn't work. It was even more of a pain when you just *knew* that the phone was lost in the sofa cushions and Aunt Martha was pulling some *zzz*'s on the couch.

Your Droid 2 lives an untethered existence, so find it a permanent spot — even when you're carrying it around.

Carrying the Droid 2

The compact design of the Droid 2 is perfect for a pocket or even the teensi-est of party purses. It's well designed so that you can carry your phone in your pocket or handbag without the fear that something will accidentally turn it on, dial Sri Lanka, and run up a heck of a cell phone bill.

Because the Droid 2 features a proximity sensor, you can even keep the phone in your pocket while you're on a call. The proximity sensor disables the touchscreen, which ensures that nothing accidentally gets touched when you don't want it to be touched.

- ✏ Though it's okay to place the phone somewhere when you're making a call, be careful not to touch the phone's Power button (see Figure 1-3). Doing so may temporarily enable the touchscreen, which can hang up a call, mute the phone, or do any of a number of undesirable things.

✔ You can always store the Droid 2 in one of a variety of handsome carrying case accessories, some of which come in fine Naugahyde or leatherette.

✔ Don't forget that the phone is in your pocket, especially in your coat or jacket. You might accidentally sit on the phone, or it could fly out when you take off your coat. The worst fate for the Droid 2, or any cell phone, is to take a trip through the wash. I'm sure the phone has nightmares about that happening.

Storing the Droid 2

I recommend that you find a place for your phone when you're not taking it with you. Make the spot consistent: on top of your desk or workstation, in the kitchen, on the nightstand — you get the idea. Phones are as prone to being misplaced as are your car keys and glasses. Consistency is the key to finding your phone.

Then again, your phone does ring, so when you lose it, you can always have someone else call your cell phone to help you locate it.

✔ The Multimedia Station makes a handsome, permanent location for your Droid 2.

✔ I keep my Droid 2 on my desk, next to my computer. Conveniently, I have the charger plugged into the computer so that I keep the phone plugged in, connected, and charging when I'm not using it.

✔ Phones on coffee tables get buried under magazines and often squished when rude people put their feet on the furniture.

✔ Avoid putting the Droid 2 in direct sunlight; heat is a bad thing for any electronic gizmo.

✔ Do not put your phone in the laundry (see the preceding section). See Chapter 23 for information on properly cleaning the phone.

Initial Configuration

*T*he 20th century ushered in many amazing new inventions, just about none of which required any initial setup or configuration. When you bought a car, it was ready to run. When you bought a TV, you plugged it in and turned it on. When you bought a microwave oven, you searched for a tepid cup of coffee and then marveled at how the brew heated up — in its own mug, no less. Those were simple times.

Like most things in this 21st century world, your Droid 2 requires some initial configuration. It's unavoidable. Even if the Nice People In The Store set up your phone and did all the stuff they do (whatever it is), your phone needs input from you to complete the setup process. It's all part of the 21st century, and getting the most from your Droid 2.

Oh, this chapter also covers the official ways of turning your phone on and off, as well as putting the phone to sleep and waking it again.

Greetings, Human

One of the most basic operations for any gizmo is knowing how to turn it on. Don't bother looking: The Droid 2 doesn't have an on-off switch. Instead, it has a *Power* button. It can be used in several ways, which is why I had to write this section, to explain things.

The Droid 2 doesn't turn on unless its battery is installed and fully charged. Sure, you can try turning on the phone without a battery, but it takes forever. See Chapter 1.

Turning on the Droid 2 for the first time

Before turning on your Droid 2 for the first time, ensure that it has been configured. The folks at the store may have completed the configuration for you. If not, you may need to call your cell phone provider before you turn on the phone. A notice inside the box alerts you to the process.

To turn on the Droid 2 for the first time, press the Power button. You see the Motorola logo, the word *Droid,* and some fancy graphics and animation. After a moment, you hear the phone say, robotically, "Droid!" Don't be alarmed. Well, at least its response is better than the one you hear when you turn on one of those inexpensive phones, which greets you with the phrase "You cheap bastard."

When you turn on your phone for the first time, you have to do some setup. This step is required, and it may have been done by the folks who sold you the Droid 2. If not, you can follow along here when you first start the phone and see the Android character prompting you to get started:

1. **Obey the instructions on the touchscreen display and touch the Android icon.**

2. **If you're prompted, touch the Activate button to activate your phone.**

   The Activation notice doesn't appear when the nice people who sold you your phone configured it for you. So, when you buy your phone directly from Verizon or someone else on the Internet, you have to suffer through the activation process.

   If you don't need to activate your phone, skip to Step 5.

3. **Heed the directions of the robot.**

   Touch the Speaker button so that you can hear what the robot is saying and punch numbers into the dialpad on the touchscreen when necessary.

4. **Touch the Next button after activating your phone.**

   You're presented with a tutorial, which tells you about your Droid 2 and how it works.

5. **Touch the Begin button to view the tutorial.**

   Or, you can touch the Skip button to proceed with basic configuration.

   If you opt to continue with the tutorial, obey the directions on the screen. Remember that I offer, elsewhere in this book, detailed instructions for using the touchscreen and the Droid 2 keyboards.

6. **Touch the Next button.**

You should have a Google account with your phone, especially because it says "with Google™" on the back. If you don't already have a Google account, set one up right now.

Setting up a Google account using your computer is easier than using the phone. See the section "Account Creation and Synchronization Setup" for more information on using a Google account with the Droid 2.

If you have multiple Google accounts, sign in to the phone using the primary account or the one that has the calendar you use most often.

7. **Choose the Sign In button to sign in to your existing Google account.**

8. **Touch the first text field, where you enter your Google account name.**

A keyboard appears at the bottom of the touchscreen.

9. **Use the onscreen keyboard to type your Google account name.**

Feel free to use the phone's slider keyboard, if you prefer it, though I recommend first reviewing Chapter 4 to get comfortable with that keyboard. Otherwise, these steps assume that you're using the onscreen keyboard.

The Google account name is also the first part of your Gmail email account. For example, my Gmail account name is dan.gookin.

Touch the onscreen keyboard's Delete button to back up if you make a mistake.

10. **Touch the Password text box.**

11. **Type your Google account password.**

Each character in the password appears briefly as you type it, and then the character turns into a black dot. So pay attention to what you type!

Touch the onscreen keyboard's Shift key to display capital letters.

Touch the onscreen keyboard's Symbols key to see numbers and a smattering of other symbols that might dwell in your Google account password.

12. **Touch the Sign In button.**

If you can't see the Sign In button, touch the Done button on the keyboard or, if that's not available, touch the Back soft button, found at the bottom of the touchscreen (and shown in the margin).

13. **Ensure that a check mark appears by the option Back Up Data with My Google Account.**

By checking this option, you ensure that information you enter in your phone is always synchronized and backed up to your Google account on the Internet. It's a good idea.

14. **Touch the Next button.**

15. **Touch the Finish Setup button.**

You may be asked additional setup and configuration questions. Plow through them, if you will, or you generally have an option to skip things by touching the Skip button on the touchscreen.

If you find any option that perplexes you, use this book's Index to look up the item and glean more information.

After the initial setup, you're taken to the Home screen. Chapter 3 offers more Home screen information, which you should probably read right away before the temptation to play with the Droid 2 becomes unbearable.

- If you have more than one Google account, you have to manually add that account after you initially configure your Droid 2. See the later section "Setting up a Google account on your phone."

- The Droid 2 works closely with your Google account, sharing information you have on the Internet for your email and contacts on Gmail, appointments on the Google Calendar, plus other Google applications.

- A Google account is free. Google makes bazillions of dollars by selling advertising on the web, so they don't charge you for your Google account or any of the fine services they offer.

- You will find that your phone has automatically synched with your Google account after initial setup. Your contacts, calendar appointments, and Google Talk pals will already be configured for you on your Droid 2.

- When your various Google accounts (email messages and calendar appointments, for example) are holding a massive amount of information, the Droid 2 may take a while to fully synchronize everything. An appropriate message appears on the phone during these long waiting periods.

- You can also configure your phone to work with other information-sharing services, such as those offered by your company or organization. See the section "Configuring the Droid 2 for corporate use" later in this chapter.

Turning on the phone

Unlike turning the phone on for the first time, turning it on after that isn't that involved. In fact, normally you probably won't be turning the Droid 2 off that much. When you have turned the phone off, turning it on again is done by pressing and releasing the Power button, found atop the phone.

After pressing the Power button, the phone turns itself on. You'll see the Droid 2 logo and animation, and the phone may scream "Droid!" at you. Eventually you'll be plopped into an unlocking screen.

The primary unlocking screen is shown in Figure 2-1. To access your phone, use your finger to slide the padlock icon to the right.

Slide to the right to
unlock the phone

Slide to the left to
silence the phone

Figure 2-1: Unlocking the phone.

A second unlocking screen, shown in Figure 2-2, uses an unlock pattern to help prevent unauthorized access to your phone. Drag your finger over the dots on the screen, duplicating the pattern you've preset. Only after you drag over the dots in the proper sequence is the phone unlocked.

Additional security locking screens involve your punching in a numeric PIN to gain access to the phone or typing in a password. If you're prompted, use the onscreen keyboard to input the PIN or password to gain access to your phone.

Drag your finger from
one dot to another

Touch to make an
emergency call

Follow the pattern
you've already set

Figure 2-2: Tracing the phone's security pattern.

Eventually, you see the Home screen, which is where you control the phone, run applications, and do all sorts of interesting things. The Home screen is covered in Chapter 3.

- ✔ The locking pattern, PIN, and password screens appear only when you've configured those items on your Droid 2. They add a level of security that the normal locking screen (shown in Figure 2-1) doesn't provide. See Chapter 22.

- ✔ PIN stands for *p*ersonal *i*dentification *n*umber.

- ✔ After unlocking the phone, you may hear some alerts or see notifications. These messages inform you of various activities taking place in the phone, such as new email, scheduled appointments, updated apps, and more. See Chapter 3 for information on notifications.

- ✔ Even if the phone has a security pattern, PIN, or password, you can still make emergency calls: Touch the Emergency Call button, as illustrated in Figure 2-2.

- ✔ For information on turning off the phone, see the section "Turning off the phone," later in this chapter.

There's an Android in your phone

You might see or hear the term *Android* used in association with your phone. That's because your phone, like your computer, has an *operating system* — the main program in charge of a computer's hardware. The operating system controls everything. For the Droid 2, that operating system is *Android*.

The Android operating system was developed by Google. Well, actually, it was started by another company that Google gobbled. Anyway: Android is based on the popular Linux operating

system, used to power desktop computers and larger, more expensive, computers all over the world. Android offers a version of Linux customized for mobile devices, such as the Droid 2, but also for other cell phone brands that I can't recall right now.

Because the Droid 2 uses the Android operating system, your phone has access to thousands of software programs. The entire process is covered in Chapter 20.

Waking up the phone

Most of the time, you don't turn off your phone. Instead, the phone does the electronic equivalent of falling asleep. Either the phone falls asleep on its own (after you've ignored it for a while), or you can put it to sleep by singing it a lullaby or following the information in the section "Snoozing the phone," later in this chapter.

In Sleep mode, the phone is still on and it can still receive calls (as well as email and other notifications), but the touchscreen is turned off.

The phone wakes itself up whenever it receives a call; you see the unlock screen, similar to the one shown earlier, in Figure 2-1, though information about the person calling appears on the touchscreen: Slide the unlock tab to the right to unlock and answer the phone.

When the phone isn't ringing, you can wake it at any time by pressing the Power button. A simple, short press is all that's needed. The phone awakens, yawns, and turns on the touchscreen display, and you can then unlock the phone as described in the preceding section.

- ✔ Touching the touchscreen when the screen is off doesn't wake up the phone.

- ✔ Pressing the camera shutter button while the phone is sleeping doesn't wake up the phone.

- ✔ Loud noises will not wake up the phone.

- ✔ The phone doesn't snore while it's sleeping.

> ✔ See the section "Snoozing the phone," later in this chapter, for information on manually putting the phone to sleep.
>
> ✔ The pattern lock, PIN, and password prompts don't appear when you're answering the phone; only the sliding lock (see Figure 2-1) is used.

Account Creation and Synchronization Setup

After initially turning on your phone and getting things configured, you're ready to go. Well, that is, unless you opted to skip the account synchronization step or you just didn't get a chance to synchronize the proper accounts. Don't fret! The Droid 2 welcomes your ability to procrastinate by providing more account synchronization options, as described in this section.

Getting a Google account

It helps *immensely* to have a Google account to get the most from your Droid 2 phone. If you don't already have a Google account, run — don't walk or stroll — to a computer and follow these steps to create your own Google account:

1. **Open the computer's Web browser program.**

2. **Visit the main Google page at www.google.com.**

   Type **www.google.com** into the Web browser's Address box.

3. **Click the Sign In link.**

   Another page opens where you can log in to your Google account, but you don't have a Google account, so:

4. **Click the link to create a new account.**

   The link is typically found beneath the text boxes where you would log in to your Google account. As I write this chapter, the link is titled Create an Account Now.

5. **Continue heeding the directions until you've created your own Google account.**

Eventually, your account is set up and configured. I recommend that you log off and then log back on to Google, just to ensure that you did everything properly. Also create a bookmark for your account's Google page: Pressing Ctrl+D or Command+D does that job in just about any Web browser.

Continue reading in the next section for information on synchronizing your new Google account with the Droid 2 phone.

> ✔ The Google account gives you access to a wide array of free services and online programs. These include Gmail for electronic messaging, Calendar for scheduling and appointments, the online picture sharing program Picasa, and an account on YouTube, along with Google Finance, blogs, Google Buzz, and other features that are also instantly shared with your phone.

> ✔ Information on using the various Google programs on your phone is covered throughout this book; specifically, in Part IV.

Setting up a Google account on your phone

The only time you need to set up a Google account for your Droid 2 is when you neglected to initially set up the account when you first bought the phone, you postponed setup, or you're adding a second Google account you already have. If you have the Google account already set up, great: Just concentrate on working through the steps in this section.

If you haven't yet configured a Google account, though, follow the steps in the preceding section and then continue with these steps:

1. **Go to the Home screen.**

   The Home screen is the Droid 2's main screen. You can always get there by pressing the Home soft button, found at the bottom of the touchscreen.

2. **Touch the Launcher button.**

   The Launcher button is found at the lower center of the Home screen. Touching this button displays the Applications Tray, which lists icons representing every application installed on your phone.

3. **Scroll the list of program icons to locate the My Accounts icon.**

   Scroll the list by using your finger; touch the screen and slide your finger up, toward the top of the phone.

   The application icons are arranged in alphabetical order, so the My Accounts icon might be partway down the list.

4. **Touch the Add Account button.**

5. **Choose Google.**

6. **Read the screen and touch the Next button.**

7. **Because you've already read the preceding section and have created your Google account on a computer, touch the Sign In button.**

   Yes, you can create a Google account using your phone and not a computer. It's just easier to use a computer. Trust me.

8. **Touch the Username text box.**

   The onscreen keyboard appears.

9. **Use the onscreen keyboard to type your Google account username.**

10. **Touch the Password text box.**

11. **Type your Google account password.**

    Refer to the suggestions in Step 10 in the earlier section "Turning on the Droid 2 for the first time" for help with typing your Google password.

12. **Touch the Sign In button.**

    If you need to, touch the Done button on the onscreen keyboard so that you can find the Sign In button.

    Wait while Google contacts your account and synchronizes any information. It takes longer when you have more information to synchronize.

13. **If you're prompted to back up your data, ensure that a green check mark appears in the box.**

14. **Touch the Finish button.**

    You're done.

After you touch Finish, you return to the My Accounts window.

 You can touch the Home soft button to return to the Home screen.

- ✔ See Chapter 3 for more information about the Home screen and the Applications Tab.

- ✔ Refer to Chapter 12 for information on adding other accounts to your Droid 2, such as Facebook or Twitter.

Changing your Google password

Experts say that you should change your computer passwords often. How often? Well, I know some government agencies where the password changes every 90 seconds. You don't need to be that severe with your Google account password.

When you change your Google password, do so on your computer first. Then you have to inform the Droid 2 of the new password. If you don't, your phone complains that it cannot access Google to update and synchronize information. Follow these steps to reset your Google password:

1. **On your desktop computer, direct the Web browser to go to the main Google page:** www.google.com.

2. **From the top of the page, click the Settings link.**

   As I write this chapter, the link is found in the upper right part of the page.

3. **Choose Google Account Settings from the Settings link menu.**

4. **By the Security heading, click the link Change Password.**

5. **Obey the directions on the screen for setting a new password.**

   Now that the password is reset, you need to update the Droid 2 with that information. If you don't, the phone pesters you incessantly. Continue with these steps:

6. **Wake up or turn on your Droid 2.**

   In a few moments, your phone generates a notification. You see an Alert icon appear on the top of the phone's display, in the notification area.

7. **Slide down the notification area down by swiping it with your finger.**

   The specific instructions for performing this action are covered in Chapter 3.

8. **From the list of notifications, choose Alert.**

   The Alert message says Sign-In Error or Sign Into Your Account.

9. **Type the new Google password into the box that appears on the touch-screen display.**

   Refer to information in the earlier sections "Turning on the Droid 2 for the first time" as well as "Setting up a Google account on your phone" for more information on typing in your Google account password.

After entering the new password, the phone instantly becomes happy and continues to sync the Google account information.

Press the Home soft button to return to the Home screen.

Configuring the Droid 2 for corporate use

Whether you're a mind-numbed corporate robot or in complete denial regarding your menial status at a large organization, you may be required to set up your Droid 2 for synchronizing with your outfit's Exchange Server. The idea is to put your phone on speaking terms with your organization's email, calendar, contact, and other types of information.

First of all, if your company is *really* big, you'll probably have someone do all the account setup for you. In fact, that person might even apply special restrictions to the Droid 2, preventing such innocent diversions as playing your Santa Shoots the Monkey game or using the Maps app to locate a bookie. Regardless, those digital martinets will probably do the setup for you or at least have instructions ready. Defy those folks at your own peril.

To set up the Droid 2 on your own, follow these steps:

1. **From the Home screen, touch the Launcher button.**

2. **Touch the My Accounts icon.**

3. **Touch the Add Account button at the bottom of the screen.**

4. **Choose Corporate Sync.**

5. **If prompted, touch the check box by the text *I Agree* so that you can agree to the terms and conditions, and then touch the Next button.**

6. **Fill in the blanks with the information provided to you by your organization.**

   Touch each field to summon the onscreen keyboard and then type the information required: domain\username, password, email address, and server. You can also use the sliding keyboard, if you prefer.

7. **Touch the Next button.**

   You may have to touch the Done button on the onscreen keyboard so that you can see the Next button.

   The Droid 2 attempts to contact and chat with the server.

8. **Touch the Finish button.**

And you're done. Of course, other things may or may not happen at this point, depending on what is shared on your corporate network and how you use the Droid 2 to access that information.

You can press the Home soft button to return to the Home screen, from whence you may do other interesting things with your Droid 2.

Goodbye, Phone

You can dismiss your Droid 2 from existence in one of three ways. The first way is to put the phone to sleep, to *snooze* it. The second is to turn the phone off. The third involves a trained hypnotist, a pound of chicken feathers, and an industrial vat of mayonnaise. Because of space constraints, the third method is not covered in this edition of the book.

Snoozing the phone

To snooze the phone, press and release the Power button. No matter what you're doing, the phone's display turns off. The phone itself isn't off, but the touchscreen display turns off. The phone enters a low-power state to save battery life and also to relax.

- ✔ You can snooze the phone while you're making a call. Simply press and release the Power button. The call stays connected, but the display is turned off.

- ✔ The Droid 2 will probably spend most of its time in Snooze mode.

- ✔ Snooze mode allows you to keep talking on the phone while you put it in your pocket. In Snooze mode, your pocket is in no danger of accidentally hanging up or muting the phone in the middle of a call.

- ✔ Snoozing does not turn off the phone; you can still receive calls while the phone is somnolent.

- ✔ Any timers or alarms you set are still activated when the phone is snoozing. See Chapter 19 for information on setting timers and alarms.

- ✔ To wake up the phone, press and release the Power button. See the section "Waking up the phone," earlier in this chapter.

Controlling snooze options

There's no need to manually snooze your Droid 2. That's because it has a built-in timeout: After a period of inactivity, or boredom, the phone snoozes itself automatically — just like Grandpa Chester does when Grandma starts talking politics.

You have control over the snooze timeout value, which can be set anywhere from 15 seconds to 30 minutes. Obey these steps:

1. **From the Home screen, touch the Launcher button.**

2. **Touch the Settings icon to open the Settings window.**

3. **Choose Display.**

4. **Choose Screen Timeout.**

5. **Choose a timeout value from the list that's provided.**

   The standard value is 1 minute.

6. **Press the Home soft button to return to the Home screen.**

When you don't touch the screen, or you aren't using the phone, the sleep timer starts ticking. About ten seconds before the timeout value you set (refer to Step 5), the touchscreen dims. Then it goes to sleep. If you touch the screen before then, the sleep timer is reset.

Turning off the phone

To turn off your phone, follow these steps:

1. **Press and hold the Power button.**

   Eventually, you see the Phone Options menu, shown in Figure 2-3.

Figure 2-3: The Phone Options menu.

2. **Choose the Power Off item.**

   Off goes the phone, crying out "Droid" as it goes.

The phone doesn't receive calls when it's turned off. Those calls instead go to voicemail, either the voicemail you set up with the cellular service or to Visual Voicemail. See Chapter 7 for more information on voicemail.

 If you change your mind and don't want to shut down the phone, press the Back soft button to cancel.

3

The Droid 2 Tour

In This Chapter

- Working the touchscreen
- Changing the phone's volume
- Entering Vibration or Silence mode
- Using the phone horizontally
- Checking notifications
- Running applications and working widgets
- Finding lost applications
- Accessing recently used apps

The dumbest and simplest devices are the easiest to use. Because there's a simplicity in the design of a pencil, for example, just about anyone can pick it up and figure out how it works. The same design philosophy applies to a shovel or a hammer. The dumber the device, the easier it is to pick up and use right away. After all, you don't see the book *Scissors For Dummies* (at least not yet).

Complex devices can be frightening. That fear holds especially true for an advanced smartphone such as the Droid 2. The gizmo is identifiable to any denizen of the 21st century as a cell phone, but, really, *how* do you make it work? To help ease you on your way, I'm offering this chapter as a Droid 2 orientation and guide. You can read about your phone's interface, how it works, and how to get the most from your new phone experience.

Basic Droid 2 Operations

The Droid 2 is most likely different from any other phone you've owned. Even if you owned the original Droid, some things work differently on the Droid 2. To help familiarize yourself with how the phone works, this section covers some basic phone operations.

Using the soft buttons

Below the touchscreen are four buttons labeled with four icons. They're the *soft buttons,* and they perform specific functions no matter what you're doing with the phone. Table 3-1 lists the soft buttons' functions in order, from left to right.

Table 3-1		Droid 2 Soft Buttons		
Button	*Name*	*Press Once*	*Press Twice*	*Press and Hold*
◼◻◻◻	Menu	Display menu	Nothing	Nothing
⌂	Home	Go to Home screen	Voice command	Recent applications
↶	Back	Go back, close, dismiss keyboard	Nothing	Nothing
◯	Search	Open phone-and-Web search	Nothing	Voice Actions menu

Not every button always performs the actions listed in Table 3-1. For example, if there's no menu to open, pressing the Menu button does nothing. When a menu is visible, pressing the Menu soft button hides it.

The soft buttons can still be used when the sliding keyboard is extended. Also, buttons on the sliding keyboard duplicate the function of the Search and Back soft buttons.

You can control what happens when you press the Home soft button twice. The function, double-tap Home, is covered in Chapter 22.

Various sections throughout this book give examples for using the soft buttons. Their images appear in the book's margins where relevant.

Manipulating the touchscreen

The touchscreen works in combination with one or two of your fingers. You can choose which fingers to use, or whether to be adventurous and try using the tip of your nose, but touch the touchscreen you must. Choose from several techniques:

Touch: In this simple operation, you touch the screen. Generally, you're touching an object, such as a program icon, or a control, such as a gizmo you use to slide something around.

Double-tap: Touch the screen in the same location twice. A double-tap can be used to zoom in on an image or a map, but it can also zoom out. Because of the double-tap's dual nature, I recommend using the pinch or spread operation instead.

Long-press: Touch and hold part of the screen. Some operations on the Droid 2, such as moving an icon on the Home screen, begin with the long-press.

Swipe: When you swipe, you start with your finger in one spot and then drag it to another spot. Usually, a swipe is up, down, left, or right, which moves material displayed in the direction you swipe your finger. A swipe can be fast or slow. It's also called a *flick*.

Pinch: A pinch involves two fingers, which start out separated and then are brought together. The effect is used to reduce an image or a map. The pinch is used to zoom out.

Spread: In the opposite of a pinch, you start with your fingers together and then spread them. The spread is used to zoom in.

You cannot use the touchscreen while wearing gloves, unless they're gloves specially designed for using electronic touchscreens, such as the gloves that Batman wears.

Setting the volume

The phone's volume controls are found on the right side of the phone as it's facing you. Press the top part of the button to raise the volume. Press the bottom part of the button to lower the volume.

The volume controls work for whatever noise the phone is making at the time: When you're on the phone, the volume controls set the level of the phone call. When you're listening to music or watching a video, the volume controls set that media volume.

The volume can be preset for the phone, media, and notifications. See Chapter 22 for information.

"Silence your phone!"

You cannot be a citizen of the 21st century and not have heard the admonition "Please silence your cell phones." The quick way to obey that command with your Droid 2 phone is to keep pressing the Volume Down button until the phone vibrates. What you've done is set the phone into Silent-and-Vibrate mode.

The Droid 2 can also be silenced with a swipe of your finger by obeying these steps:

1. Wake up the phone.

Obviously, if the phone is turned off, you have no need to turn it on just to make it silent. So, assuming that your phone is snoozing, press the Power button to see the unlock screen (refer to Figure 2-1, in Chapter 2).

2. Slide the Silencer button over to the left.

You're good.

Finally, you can thrust the Droid 2 into Silence mode by pressing and holding the Power button. From the Phone Options menu, choose Silent mode.

✔ When the phone is silenced and in Vibration mode, the Vibration icon appears on the status bar, as shown in the margin.

✔ You make the phone noisy again by undoing any of the steps in this section, though the easiest method is to repeat Steps 1 and 2. In Step 2, the Silencer button is the un-Silencer button.

✔ Also see Chapter 22 for various other methods of silencing the phone.

Going horizontal

The Droid 2 features an *accelerometer* gizmo. It's used by various programs in the phone to determine in which direction the phone is pointed or whether you've reoriented the phone from an upright to a horizontal position.

The easiest way to see how the vertical-horizontal orientation feature works is to view a Web page on your Droid 2. Obey these steps:

1. **Touch the Browser application on the Home screen.**

   The Droid 2 launches its Web browser program, venturing out to the Internet. Eventually, the browser's first page, the *home page,* appears on the touchscreen.

2. **Tilt the Droid 2 to the left.**

   As shown in Figure 3-1, the Web page reorients itself to the new, horizontal way of looking at the Web. For some applications, it's truly the best way to see things.

3. **Tilt the phone upright again.**

   The Web page redisplays itself in its original, upright mode.

Portrait
orientation

Landscape
orientation

Figure 3-1: Vertical and horizontal orientations.

You can also tilt the phone to the right to view the touchscreen in Landscape mode. Either way, the phone displays a Web page horizontally.

Oh, and don't bother turning the phone upside down and expect the image to flip that way, though some applications may delight you by supporting this feature.

- ✔ Landscape mode is entered regardless of the phone's orientation when you extend the sliding keyboard. See Chapter 4 for more information on the sliding keyboard.

- ✔ See Chapter 11 for more information on using your phone to browse the Web.

- ✔ Some applications switch the view from portrait to landscape orientation when you tilt the phone. Most applications, however, are fixed to portrait orientation.

- ✔ Some applications present themselves only in Landscape view, such as the YouTube application when playing a video.

- ✔ A useful application for demonstrating the Droid 2 accelerometer is the game *Labyrinth*. It can be purchased at the Android Market, or a free version, *Labyrinth Lite,* can be downloaded. See Chapter 20 for more information on the Android Market.

There's No Screen Like Home

The first thing you see after you unlock your Droid 2 is the *Home screen,* illustrated in Figure 3-2. It's also the location you go to whenever you end a phone call or quit an application.

Here are the key items to notice on the Home screen, illustrated in Figure 3-2:

status bar: The top of the Home screen is a thin, informative strip that I call the status bar. It contains notification icons and status icons, plus the current time.

notification icons: These icons come and go depending on what happens in your digital life. For example, new icons appear whenever you receive a new email message or have a pending appointment. The section "Reviewing notifications," later in this chapter, describes how to deal with notifications.

status icons: These icons represent the phone's current condition, such as the type of network it's connected to, signal strength, and battery status, as well as whether the speaker has been muted or a Wi-Fi network connected, for example.

widgets: A widget is a teensy program that can display information, let you control the phone, or access features. Touching a widget can manipulate a phone feature, access a program, or do something purely amusing. You can read more about widgets in Chapter 22.

Widget

Status bar   Current time

Notifications   Phone status

Launcher

Phone Dialer   Contacts

Wallpaper   Application icons

Figure 3-2: The Home screen.

application icons: The meat of the meal on the Home screen plate are the application icons. Touching an icon runs its program.

Launcher: Touching the Launcher button displays the Applications Tray, a scrolling list of all applications installed on your phone. The section "The Applications Tray," later in this chapter, describes how it works.

And now, the secret: The Home screen is seven times wider than what you see on the front of your Droid 2. The Home screen has left and right wings, as illustrated in Figure 3-3.

To view the left or right side of the Home screen, swipe your finger across the touchscreen display to the left or right. The Home screen slides over one page in whichever direction you swipe.

Way too many widgets   Main Home screen   Way too many widgets

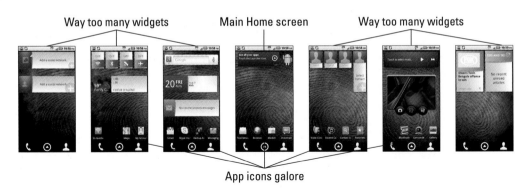

App icons galore

Figure 3-3: All the Home screens.

The wider Home screen gives you more opportunities to place applications and widgets. Also shown in Figure 3-3 are shortcut icons, widgets, and folders, which provide quick access to more of the phone's features and help to keep things organized.

▱ The Home screen is entirely customizable. You can add and remove icons from the Home screen, add widgets, shortcuts, even change the wallpaper images. See Chapter 22 for more information.

▱ Touching part of the Home screen that doesn't feature an icon or control doesn't do anything — that is, unless you're using the *live wallpaper* feature. In that case, touching the screen changes the wallpaper in some way, depending on the wallpaper that's selected. You can read more about live wallpaper in Chapter 22.

▱ The variety of notification and status icons is broad. You see the icons referenced in appropriate sections throughout this book.

▱ No matter which part of the Home screen you're viewing, the top part of the touchscreen stays the same, as do the display notification and status icons and the time.

▱ The bottom part of the Home screen always displays the Phone, Launcher, and Contacts icons. That is, unless you just swiped the screen left or right. In that case, you briefly see some icons that show you which specific part of the Home screen you're viewing.

 ▱ To return to the Home screen at any time, press the Home soft button.

I've Been Working on the Home Screen

I recommend getting to know three basic Home screen operations: reviewing notifications, starting programs, and accessing widgets.

Reviewing notifications

Notifications appear as icons at the top of the Home screen, as illustrated earlier, in Figure 3-2. To see what the notifications say, peel down the top part of the screen, as shown in Figure 3-4.

Notification icons

Touch here

Drag your finger down to
display the notifications

Figure 3-4: Accessing notifications.

The operation works like this:

1. **Touch the notification icons at the top of the touchscreen.**

2. **Swipe your finger all the way down the front of the touchscreen.**

   This action works like controlling a roll-down blind: You grab the top part of the touchscreen and drag it downward all the way. The notifications appear in a list, shown in Figure 3-5.

Drag the notification list all the way to the bottom of the touchscreen, to prevent it from rolling back up again. Use the notification panel control to pull the list all the way down, as shown in Figure 3-5.

3. Touch a notification to see what's up.

Touching a notification takes you to the program that generated the alert. For example, touching a Gmail notification displays a new message in the inbox.

Figure 3-5: The notification list.

If you choose not to touch a notification, you can "roll up" the notification list by sliding the panel control back to the top of the touchscreen.

- A notification icon disappears after you've chosen it.

- A notification icon also goes away when you start the program that generated the alert. For example, Gmail notifications disappear when you start Gmail and read pending messages.

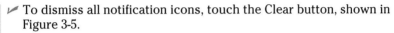

- To dismiss all notification icons, touch the Clear button, shown in Figure 3-5.

- When more notifications are present than can be shown on the status bar, you see the More Notifications icon displayed, as shown in the margin. The number on the icon indicates how many additional notifications are available.

- Dismissing notifications doesn't prevent them from appearing again later. For example, notifications to update your programs continue to appear, as do calendar reminders.

- Some programs, such as Facebook and the various Twitter apps, don't display notifications unless you're logged in. See Chapter 12.

- When new notifications are available, the Droid 2 notification light flashes. Refer to Chapter 1 for information on locating the notification light.

- See Chapter 19 for information on dismissing calendar reminders.

- Notification icons appear on the screen when the phone is locked. You must unlock the phone before you can drag down the status bar to display notifications.

Starting an application

It's cinchy to run an application on the Home screen: Touch its icon. The application starts.

- Not all applications appear on the Home screen, but all of them do appear when you display the Applications Tray. See the section "The Applications Tray," later in this chapter.

- When an application closes or you quit that application, you return to the Home screen.

- *Application* is abbreviated as *app*.

Accessing a widget

Widgets are teensy programs that "float" over the Home screen, as shown in Figure 3-3. To use a widget, simply touch it. What happens after that depends on the widget.

For example, touching the Weather widget displays a pop-up window with more weather information. Touching the Google widget displays the onscreen keyboard and lets you type, or dictate, something to search for on the Internet. The Power Control widgets turn off or on various phone features.

Information on these and other widgets appears elsewhere in this book. See Chapter 22 for information on working with widgets.

Using Car Home

The Droid 2 features an alternative Home screen, provided for the scary proposition of using your phone while driving an automobile. The Car Home screen, shown much earlier, in Figure 1-8, is designed to be easy to see at a glance and offers you access to the phone's more popular features without distracting you too much from the priority of piloting your car.

The Car Home screen appears automatically whenever your Droid 2 is nestled into the car mount phone holder accessory, discussed in Chapter 1. To see Car Home manually, you start the Car Dock app: Touch the Launcher button on the Home screen, scroll the list of applications, and touch the Car Dock icon.

- The Car Home screen features big, fat buttons linking to common tasks you'd need the phone for in a car, mostly to use maps and navigation, plus some basic phone features.

- You can add an app shortcut to the Car Home screen by touching the Add App button. Choose an app from the list that's displayed.

- To delete or replace an app shortcut that has already been added to the Car Home screen, press the Menu soft button and choose the Preferences command. Choose the Custom item on the Car Dock Setting screen to change the app shortcut on the Car Home screen.

- To return to the Droid 2's normal Home screen, touch the Close button on the Car Home screen.

The Applications Tray

The place where you find all applications installed on your Droid 2 is the *Applications Tray*. Though you may find shortcuts to applications (apps) on the Home screen, the Applications Tray is where you need to go to find *everything*.

Discovering all the apps on your phone

To start a program — an *app* — on the Droid 2, heed these steps:

1. **Touch the Launcher button at the bottom of the Home screen.**

   The Applications Tray appears, as shown in Figure 3-6. App icons are listed alphabetically, which still goes from *a* to *z,* as far as I can tell.

2. **Scroll the list of app icons by swiping your finger up or down.**

3. **Touch an icon to start that app.**

Applications

Swipe your finger up or down to scroll

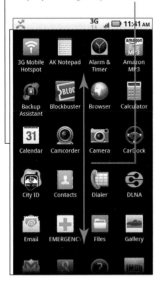

Figure 3-6: The Applications Tray shows your phone's apps.

The app that opens takes over the screen and does whatever good thing that program does.

The terms *program*, *application*, and *app* all mean the same thing.

Finding lost apps

The Droid 2 searching abilities can be used to find apps on your phone as well as lost contacts, music, and stuff on the Internet. The key is knowing how to use the Search command to locate an app. Follow these steps:

1. Press the Search soft button.

The Search screen appears. The Search text box appears atop the screen, and the phone's onscreen keyboard appears at the bottom.

2. Use your finger to type all or part of the app's name.

See Chapter 4 for more information on using the onscreen keyboard, as well as for using the sliding keyboard if you prefer real tiny buttons over virtual tiny buttons.

As you type, items whose names match the letters you've typed appear in the list. The word *Application* appears beneath the program name of any applications in the list.

3. **Scroll the list to explore the apps that have been found.**

   Use your finger to swipe the list up and down.

4. **Touch the name of the app you're looking for.**

   The app starts.

Searching for apps is a small part of searching for all kinds of information on the Droid 2, such as contact information, appointments, and email. Various chapters throughout this book describe other ways you can use the Droid 2 search function.

See Chapter 20 for information on how to use the Android Market to get more apps for your phone.

Reviewing your most recently used apps

 If you're like me, you probably use the same apps over and over, on both your computer and your phone. You can easily access that list of recent programs on the Droid 2 by pressing and holding the Home soft button. When you do, you see the eight most recently accessed programs, similar to the ones shown in Figure 3-7.

Figure 3-7: Recently used apps.

 To exit the list of recently used apps, press the Back soft button.

You can press and hold the Home soft button in any application at any time to see the recently used apps list.

 For programs you use all the time, consider creating shortcuts on the Home screen. Chapter 22 describes how to create shortcuts to apps, as well as shortcuts to people and shortcuts to instant messaging and all sorts of fun stuff.

4

Human-Droid Interaction

*I*t's the year 2134. You wake up in a pleasant though sterile room to the sound of soothing music. A door slides open and in walks a graceful mechanical being. It introduces itself as your personal Droid Z99, a descendant of what was originally a cell phone more than a century earlier. The Droid Z99 is your slave, dutifully obeying your every whim, supplying whatever you need. It seeks to fulfill any desire you have — as long as you never, ever, leave that room.

Though your introduction to the Droid 2 phone may not be as pleasant as a future introduction to a Droid Z99 robot, there's no risk to you that your phone will make you a prisoner. To get that message through to the phone, you should know how to use the numerous Droid 2 keyboards in addition to voice input. That information is covered in this chapter, which I recommend reading quickly, before your phone gets any wild ideas.

Keyboard Mania

You can choose one of three types of keyboard to input text information into the Droid 2: the onscreen keyboard that appears on the touchscreen, the sliding keyboard, and the onscreen Swype keyboard, designed for superfast typing. The decision to have multiple keyboards was obviously put forward to confound and confuse you.

The *onscreen* keyboard is a virtual keyboard. As such, you benefit from seeing different keys, depending on what the phone is doing. Therefore, it's more flexible, though not tactile.

The *sliding* keyboard is a teensy keyboard, similar to the one found on your computer, but made smaller. It allows you the luxury of having a physical keyboard on the Droid 2, which many folks find preferable over the onscreen keyboard.

The *Swype* keyboard looks like the onscreen keyboard, and can be used as such, but its strength lies in its ability to interpret as text the rapid squiggles and smears of your finger on the screen.

- ✐ This book holds no favor of one keyboard over another, though I must confess a personal preference for the onscreen keyboard.

- ✐ The following sections discuss the specifics of using each type of keyboard.

- ✐ Because using the Swype keyboard is much different from the hunt-and-peck nature of using either the onscreen or sliding keyboard, Swype is covered in its own section, later in this chapter.

- ✐ The Droid 2 also lets you dictate text into your phone. See the section "Voice Input," later in this chapter.

 ✐ The Droid 2 sliding keyboard started out full size. But then the scientists at Motorola zapped it using that huge shrinking machine the US government built under the Utah desert — you know, the same machine that shrunk Stephen Boyd and Raquel Welch in *Fantastic Voyage*.

Using the onscreen keyboard

The touchy-glassy way to input text information on your phone is to use the *onscreen keyboard*. It shows up anytime the phone demands text as input, such as when you're composing email, typing a text message, or composing a ransom note in Gmail.

Normally, the onscreen keyboard just pops up; for example, when you touch a text field or an input box on a Web page. Then you start typing with your finger or — if you're *really* good — with your thumbs.

The alphabetic version of the onscreen keyboard is shown in Figure 4-1. The keys a through z (lowercase) are there, plus a Shift/Caps Lock key, Delete key, Space key, and Period key.

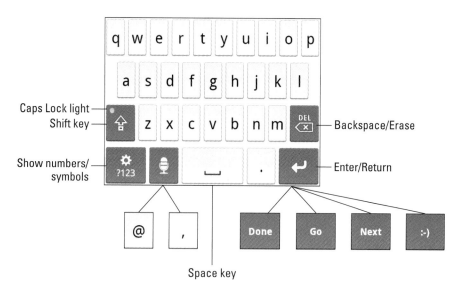

Figure 4-1: The onscreen keyboard.

The key in the lower right corner changes its look depending on what you're typing. The key has five variations, as shown in the figure. Here's what each one does:

Enter/Return: Just like the Enter or Return key on your computer keyboard, this key ends a paragraph of text. It's used mostly when filling in long stretches of text or when multiline input is available.

Done: Use this key to dismiss the onscreen keyboard and view the app full-screen. Normally, this key appears when you've finished typing text in the final field of a screen with several fields.

Go: This action key directs the app to proceed with a search, accept input, or perform another action.

Next: This key appears when typing information into multiple fields. Touching the key switches from one field to the next, such as when typing a username and password.

:-) The smiley face key inserts a smile icon into your text.

The key to the left of the Space key changes as well. It can be the @ symbol or a comma, depending on the app. In programs that accept voice input, a Microphone icon appears. Touching the Microphone icon button activates voice input, as covered later in this chapter.

 Touch the ?123 key to see the number keys as well as the various punctuation symbols shown in Figure 4-2.

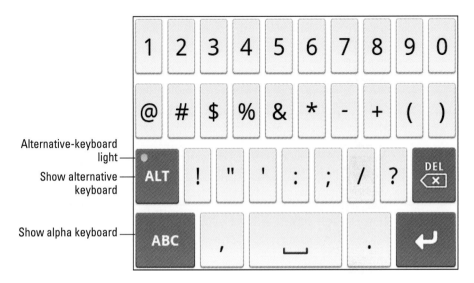

Figure 4-2: The number-and-symbol keyboard.

Pressing the Alt key on the number-and-symbol keyboard displays special symbols, as shown in Figure 4-3. When the Alt key has been pressed, its light turns on, as shown in the figure.

To return to the standard *alpha* keyboard (refer to Figure 4-1), touch the ABC key.

✔ If you detest the onscreen keyboard, you can always use the sliding keyboard. See the later section "Sliding out the sliding keyboard."

✔ Type with your finger first, and then eventually you get good enough to type with your thumbs. Or perhaps not; I still can't thumb-type well.

✔ Some applications show the keyboard when the phone is in landscape orientation. If so, the keyboard shows the same keys but offers more room for your stump-like fingers to type.

✔ Not every application features a horizontal keyboard, however, so you might be stuck using the narrower version of the keyboard.

✔ Alternative onscreen keyboards are available for use with your phone, such as the popular AnySoftKeyboard. See Chapter 20 for information on looking for apps in the Android Market.

✔ See Chapter 22 for information on how to adjust the onscreen keyboard.

Figure 4-3: Special characters on the Alt keyboard.

Sliding out the sliding keyboard

Like many popular cell phones, the Droid 2 features a real keyboard. The Droid 2 sliding keyboard is ensconced behind the touchscreen. You can slide out that keyboard (to the left as you face the phone) and use it if you prefer a physical keyboard for your cell phone typing chores.

Figure 4-4 illustrates a close-up of the sliding keyboard to call out its various parts.

Two sets of symbols share space on the sliding keyboard: one colored white and the other colored a pale blue. The pale blue characters are accessed by using the Alt and Alt Lock keys. See the later section "Typing on your Droid 2" for more information on typing with the sliding keyboard.

The sliding keyboard also features direction keys: up, down, right, and left, plus an OK key. Using these keys is covered later in this chapter, in the section "Text Editing."

Tab — 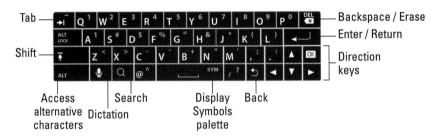 — Backspace / Erase
— Enter / Return
Shift —
— Direction keys

Access alternative characters   Dictation   Search   Display Symbols palette   Back

Figure 4-4: Keys on the sliding keyboard.

When you're done using the sliding keyboard, slide it back into the phone. The touchscreen may reorient itself back to Portrait mode when you do so, or the app may stay in its horizontal orientation.

Sliding the keyboard back into the phone doesn't turn off or sleep the Droid 2.

- ✔ The sliding keyboard features duplicates of the Search and Back soft buttons.

- ✔ You can still use the soft buttons on the front of the Droid 2 in addition to the soft buttons found on the sliding keyboard.

- ✔ Refer to Figure 1-5, in Chapter 1, for a full overview of the sliding keyboard.

- ✔ The sliding keyboard is one reason that the Droid 2 weighs considerably more than other, similar smartphones.

Droid 2 Hunt-and-Peck

Yes, typing on a cell phone is a skill set all its own. Sure, it has a dictation feature. When you're making a call, of course, you use your voice. But for many of the tasks you do on the Droid 2, you need to use a keyboard — either the onscreen keyboard or the sliding keyboard. The art of typing on those keyboards is covered in this section.

Typing on your Droid 2

Using the Droid 2 keyboards works just as you expect: Touch the key you want and that character appears in the program you're using. It's magic!

Typing can be quirky, depending on which keyboard you use, as covered in the sections that follow. For both keyboards, here are some helpful suggestions and thoughts:

- ✔ A blinking cursor on the touchscreen shows where new text appears, which is similar to how text input works on your computer.

- ✔ When you make a mistake, press the Del key to back up and erase.

- ✔ See the later section "Text Editing" for more details on editing your text.

- ✔ Above all, *type slowly* until you get used to the keyboard.

- ✔ You can produce an automatic period at the end of a sentence by pressing the Space key twice. In fact, pressing the Space key twice at any time changes the first space you typed into a period. As a bonus, the next character you type automatically appears in uppercase, to start a new sentence.

- ✔ People generally accept that composing text on a phone isn't perfect. Don't sweat it if you make a few mistakes as you type instant messages or email, though you should expect some curious replies from unintended typos.

- ✔ One way to get forgiveness for your typos is to include the signature *Sent from my DROID* in your email messages. See Chapter 10.

- ✔ When you type a password, the character you type appears briefly but, for security reasons, is then replaced by a black dot.

- ✔ When you tire of typing, you can always touch the Microphone key on the keyboard and enter Dictation mode. See the section "Voice Input," later in this chapter.

Onscreen keyboard typing

As you type on the onscreen keyboard, the button you touch appears enlarged on the screen, as shown in Figure 4-5. That's how you can confirm that your fingers are typing what you intend to type.

- ✔ To set the Caps Lock feature, press the Shift key twice. The little light highlighted in Figure 4-1 comes on, indicating that Caps Lock is on.

- ✔ Press the Shift key again to turn off Caps Lock.

- ✔ See the later section "Choosing a word as you type" to find out how to deal with automatic typo and spelling corrections.

Figure 4-5: Pressing the g key.

Sliding keyboard typing

Despite the capital letters on the sliding keyboard, the text you type appears in lowercase. To create a capital letter, you must press either Shift key (refer to Figure 4-4). Unlike using a computer keyboard, you don't need to hold down the Shift key; just press and release and then type a letter.

After the Shift key has been pressed, the cursor changes its appearance, as shown in the margin. It's your clue that the next letter typed will be in uppercase.

To activate Caps Lock, press the Shift key twice. The cursor changes its appearance, as shown in the margin. Press the Shift key again to release Caps Lock.

Access the light-blue symbol characters by pressing the Alt key. As with the Shift key, you don't need to press and hold the Alt key; just press and release. The cursor changes, as shown in the margin, to indicate that you're typing symbols and not the letter key.

To lock the symbols, press the Alt Lock key. The cursor changes again (as shown in the margin), and only the light-blue symbol characters are displayed as you type on the sliding keyboard. Press the Alt Lock key again to return to normal keyboard operation.

✔ You can also press the Alt key twice rather than press the Alt Lock key.

✔ The cursor may not change its appearance in every program you use. For example, in the Browser you may see only a vertical line for the cursor.

Accessing special characters

You can type more characters on your phone than are shown on either the onscreen or sliding keyboard. So don't think you're getting cheated when you don't see the key you want.

Onscreen keyboard special characters

On the onscreen keyboard, you access special characters by pressing and holding a specific key. When you do, a pop-up palette of options appears, from which you choose a special character.

To determine which keys on the onscreen keyboard sport extra characters, note the ellipsis that appear when you press the key, as shown in the margin. When you press and hold that key (a *long-press*), you see the pop-up palette of options, as shown in Figure 4-6. Choose the character you want from that palette or touch the X button to cancel.

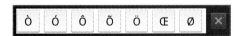

Figure 4-6: Optional characters on the O key.

Extra characters are available in uppercase as well; press the Shift key before you long-press on the onscreen keyboard.

Certain symbol keys on the onscreen keyboard also sport extra characters. For example, various currency symbols are available when you long-press the $ key, and a host of emoticons are available on the Smile key.

Sliding keyboard special characters

Accessing special characters on the sliding keyboard is done by pressing Alt and the Space key, where you find the letters *SYM* shown in light-blue text. What you see is a pop-up palette of symbols that, yes, you have to choose by touching them on the Droid 2 screen. Figure 4-7 shows the available symbols.

Figure 4-7: The SYM symbols on the sliding keyboard.

Despair not if you don't see the symbol or character you're looking for. Many more characters are available, but you have to know the press-and-hold trick on the sliding keyboard to see them.

To work the press-and-hold trick, press and hold the letter key that most resembles the symbol you want to type. For example, to type the ñ character, press and hold the N key. A palette of accented characters appears onscreen, from which you can choose ñ.

To produce a capital accented character, press the Shift key before you press and hold a letter key.

A palette of accented characters appears for most letter keys on the sliding keyboard; press and hold any key to see its palette onscreen. The vowel keys, specifically, have *many* characters available in their palettes.

Choosing a word as you type

As a "smart" phone, the Droid 2 makes a guess at the words you're typing as you type them. A list of suggestions appears above the onscreen keyboard, or at the bottom of the touchscreen when you're using the sliding keyboard. Choose a suggestion by touching it with your finger; the word instantly appears on the screen, saving you time (and potentially fixing your terrible spelling or typing, or both).

✔ One word guess appears highlighted in bold orange text. You can press the Space key to automatically choose that word.

✔ Though pressing the Space key to choose or correct a word is handy, it can also be the source of miscommunication when the phone guesses wrong.

✔ To fix an incorrectly chosen word, use the Del key to back up and erase. Type slower next time.

✔ You can disable the word suggestions and automatic error corrections. See Chapter 22.

Take a Swype at the Old Hunt-and-Peck

The Swype typing utility is designed to drastically improve your typing speed on a touchscreen phone, such as the Droid 2. The *Swype* secret is that you can type without lifting your finger from the keyboard; you literally swipe your finger over the touchscreen to rapidly type words.

Though Swype is an amazing tool, it's not for everyone. It appeals mostly to the younger crowd, which sends text messages like crazy. Still, Swype is a worthy alternative to using the normal onscreen keyboard, and it's definitely faster than using the sliding keyboard.

- ✔ Though Swype may be fast, it's not as fast as using dictation. See the later section "Voice Input."

- ✔ Don't confuse Swype with Skype, a utility you can use to place free phone calls and send instant text messages over the Internet.

Activating Swype

You can turn on Swype anytime you see the onscreen keyboard. Follow these steps:

1. **Press and hold the ?123 button to summon the Multi-Touch Keyboard menu.**

   Refer to Figure 4-1 for the key's location.

2. **Choose Input Method.**

3. **Choose Swype.**

   You may be given the option to view a Swype tutorial; do so, if you're prompted.

After switching to the Swype input method, you see a new keyboard, as shown in Figure 4-8. You're now ready to start using Swype for typing text. Or, rather, for *swyping* text.

Even though Swype is active, you can continue to use your finger (or thumbs) to touch-type on the onscreen keyboard, and the sliding keyboard remains active as well. Oh, and dictation still works, as shown in Figure 4-8.

- ✔ To view the Swype tutorial, press the Swype button on the keyboard (refer to Figure 4-8) and then touch the Tutorial button.

- ✔ See the later section "Deactivating Swype" when you want to return to the standard Droid 2 onscreen keyboard.

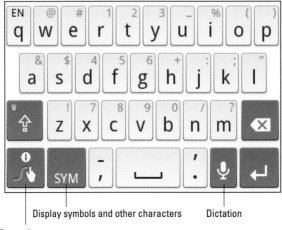

Figure 4-8: The Swype keyboard.

Using Swype to create text

The key to using Swype is not to lift your finger from the keyboard. The secret to learning Swype is to start slowly; don't worry that the teenager sitting next to you is "swyping" so fast that it looks like he's drawing Chinese characters on the phone.

Your first task in Swype is to learn how to type simple, short words: Keep your finger on the touchscreen and drag it over the letters in the word, such as the word *howdy*, shown in Figure 4-9. Lift your finger when you've completed the word, and the word appears in whichever app you're using.

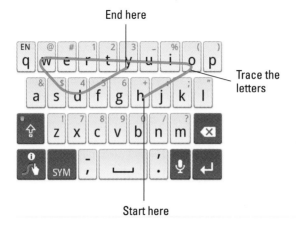

Figure 4-9: Swype the word *howdy*.

Capital letters are typed by dragging your finger above the keyboard after touching the letter, as shown in Figure 4-10 where *Idaho* was typed.

To produce a double letter, such as the *oo* in *book*, you add a little loop on that key. In Figure 4-11, the word *Hello* is typed, which uses both the capital-letter trick and the double-letter trick.

When Swype is confused about the characters you've typed, a pop-up window appears with word suggestions, as shown in Figure 4-12.

Choose a suggestion from the list or switch to the alternative suggestions, as illustrated in Figure 4-12.

Figure 4-10: Swyping a capital letter.

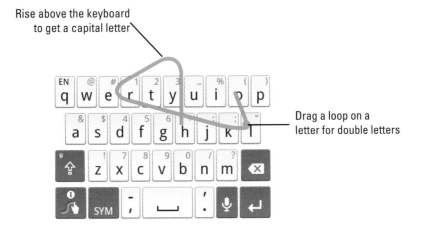

Rise above the keyboard to get a capital letter

Drag a loop on a letter for double letters

Figure 4-11: Swyping double letters.

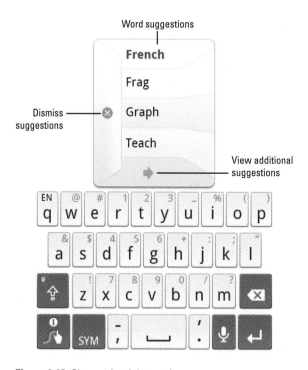

Figure 4-12: Choose the right word.

For more information on Swype typing tips, refer to the tutorial, found by touching the Swype button on the keyboard (refer to Figure 4-8).

✔ The Swype software interprets your intent as much as it does your accuracy. Even being close to the target letter is good enough; as long as you produce the pattern over the keyboard correctly, Swype usually displays the right word.

✔ Slow down and you'll get the hang of it.

Deactivating Swype

To return to the normal, onscreen keyboard and disable Swype, follow these steps:

1. From the Home screen, touch the Launcher button.

Up pops the list of applications on your phone.

2. Choose the Settings icon.

3. **Choose Language & Keyboard.**

4. **Choose Input Method.**

5. **Choose Multi-Touch Keyboard**

   The onscreen keyboard is activated.

You can press the Home soft button to return to the Home screen when you're done with the Language & Keyboard Settings window.

You can quickly switch keyboards by long-pressing any text field or area on the screen. From the menu that appears, choose Input Method and then choose the type of onscreen keyboard you want to use: Multi-Touch or Swype or whatever other options may appear.

Text Editing

I am but a fool to suggest that you'll be editing much text on your cell phone. For most people, the cry is, "Damn the typos, full speed ahead!" If you decide to edit your text, though, this section is worthy of a read.

Moving the cursor

The first part of editing text is to move the *cursor,* that blinking vertical line where text appears, to the correct spot. You can move the cursor in two ways.

The first way to move the cursor is simply to touch the part of the text where you want the cursor to blink. This method works, but because your finger is probably fatter than the spot where you want the cursor, it's not usually effective.

The second, and better, way to move the cursor is to use the direction keys, found on the sliding keyboard (refer to Figure 4-4). Pressing a direction key moves the cursor around the text in the direction of the arrow. It works just like pressing the arrow keys on a computer keyboard.

After you move the cursor, you can continue to type, use the Del key to back up and erase, or paste in text copied from elsewhere. See the later section "Cutting, copying, and pasting" for more information.

- When you touch the screen, you see a target icon appear in the text, as shown in the margin. That icon is used to help you select text, as covered in the following section.

- If you long-press on text, eventually you see a pop-up magnifying bubble, which you can use to carefully and precisely move the cursor.

✔ I use a combination of finger and direction key to move the cursor: Touch the screen first with your finger. Then use a direction key to make fine adjustments.

Selecting text

You may be familiar with selecting text in a word processor; selecting text on the Droid 2 works the same way. Well, *theoretically*, it works the same way: Selected text appears highlighted on the touchscreen. You can then delete, cut, or copy that block of selected text. It's the method of selecting text on a phone that's different.

Your phone has several methods for selecting text, as covered in the following sections.

After the text is selected, you can do four things with it: Delete it, replace it, copy it, or cut it. Delete the text by touching the Del key on the keyboard. Replace text by typing something new while the text is selected. The later section "Cutting, copying, and pasting text" describes how to cut or copy text.

Text selection with the sliding keyboard

The easiest way to select text is to use the sliding keyboard. It works like this:

1. **Extend the sliding keyboard.**

2. **Move the cursor to the location where you want to start selecting text.**

   You can use your finger, and then make fine adjustments, by using the direction keys on the sliding keyboard.

3. **Press and hold the Shift key.**

4. **Use the direction keys to extend the selection up, down, left, or right.**

   The selected text appears highlighted on the screen.

Text selection with your finger on the touchscreen

To quickly select a word, tap your finger twice on the touchscreen. The word becomes highlighted on the screen.

Pay heed to the start block and end block markers on either side of the selected word; they look like vertical bars with a triangle on the top or bottom. You can use your finger to drag those start and end markers around the screen, which extends the text selection, as shown in Figure 4-13.

Drag to set
block start

Drag to set
block end

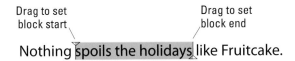

Nothing spoils the holidays like Fruitcake.

Figure 4-13: Selecting a block of text.

When dragging the start block or end block markers, keep your finger pressed against the screen: You jab at the marker and then drag your finger to move the marker around. As you drag, a pop-up magnifier bubble appears, to help you precisely locate where the block starts or ends.

Text selection using the Edit Text menu

Start selecting text by pressing and holding — a long-press — any part of a text screen or input box. When you do, the Edit Text menu appears, as shown in Figure 4-14.

⊙ Edit text
Select all
Select text
Cut all
Copy all
Paste
Input method
Add "fardel" to dictionary

Figure 4-14: The Edit Text selection menu.

The first two options on the Edit Text menu (refer to Figure 4-14) deal with selecting text:

Select All: Choose this option to select all text, whether it's in an input box or you've been entering or editing it in the current application.

Select Text: Choose this option to select a block of text starting at the cursor location. The operation then proceeds as described in the earlier section "Text selection with your finger on the touchscreen."

 To back out of the Edit Text menu, press the Back soft button.

You can cancel the selection of text by long-pressing the selected block and then choosing the Stop Selecting Text command from the menu that appears. See the later section "Cutting, copying, and pasting text."

The option to add a word to the dictionary (refer to the bottom of Figure 4-14) appears only when you're editing text from the onscreen keyboard.

Text selection on a Web page

When you're browsing the Web on your Droid 2, you select text by summoning a special menu item. Obey these steps:

1. **Press the Menu soft button to summon the Web browser's menu.**

2. **Choose the More command.**

3. **Choose Select Text.**

4. **Drag your finger over the text on the Web page you want to copy.**

5. **Lift your finger to complete selecting the text.**

When you finish selecting, the text is instantly copied. You can then paste the text into any application on your phone that accepts text input. See the next section.

Refer to Chapter 11 for more information on surfing the Web with your phone.

Cutting, copying, and pasting text

After selecting a chunk of text — or all the text — on the screen, you can then cut or copy that text and paste it elsewhere. Copying or cutting and then pasting text works just like it does on your computer.

Follow these steps to cut or copy text on your phone:

1. **Select the text you want to cut or copy.**

   Selecting text is covered earlier in this chapter.

2. **Long-press the selected text.**

   Touch the text on the touchscreen and keep your finger pressed down. You see a variant of the Edit Text menu, similar to the one shown in Figure 4-15.

Figure 4-15: The Edit Text cut-and-copy menu.

3. Choose Cut or Copy from the menu to cut or copy the text.

When you choose Cut, the text is removed; the cut-and-paste operation moves text.

4. If necessary, start the application you want to paste text into.

5. Choose the text box or text area where you want to paste the copied or cut text.

6. Move the cursor to the exact spot where the text will be pasted.

7. Long-press the text box or area.

8. Choose the Paste command from the Edit Text menu (refer to Figure 4-15).

The text you cut or copied appears in the spot where the cursor was blinking.

The text you paste can be pasted again and again. Until you cut or copy additional text, you can use the Paste command to your heart's content.

✔ You can paste text only into locations where text is allowed. Odds are good that if you can type, or whenever you see the onscreen keyboard, you can paste text.

✔ When you initially select text, the menu that opens (refer to Figure 4-14) contains two commands you can use to select *and* cut or copy text: Choose Cut All to cut all text in a box or an area. Choose Copy All to copy all text. You can then use the Paste command, described in this section, to paste that chunk of text.

Voice Input

One of the most amazing aspects of the Droid 2 is its uncanny ability to interpret your dictation as text. It pays almost as much attention to what you say as your spouse does, though for legal reasons I can't explain why that's relevant. Suffice it to say, diction is a boon to any cell phone user.

 Voice input is available whenever you see the Microphone icon, similar to the one shown in the margin. To begin voice input, touch the icon. A voice input screen appears, as shown in Figure 4-16.

Figure 4-16: The voice input thing.

When you see the text *Speak Now,* speak directly into the phone.

As you speak, the Microphone icon (refer to Figure 4-16) flashes. The flashing doesn't mean that the phone is embarrassed by what you're saying. No, the flashing merely indicates that the phone is listening, detecting the volume of your voice.

After you stop talking, the phone digests what you said. You see your voice input appear as a wavelike pattern on the screen. Eventually, the text you spoke — or a close approximation of it — appears on the screen. It's magical, and sometimes comical.

✔ The first time you try to use Voice Input, you might see a description displayed. Touch the OK button to continue.

✔ Also see Chapter 5 for information on dialing the phone by using your voice.

✔ A microphone key appears on both the onscreen and sliding keyboards, though the onscreen keyboard doesn't always sport a microphone key.

✔ The Microphone icon appears only when voice input is allowed. Not every application features voice input as an option.

✔ The better your diction, the better the results. Try to speak only a sentence or less.

- You can edit your voice input just as you edit any text. See the section "Text Editing," earlier in this chapter.

- You have to "speak" punctuation to include it in your text. For example, you say, "I'm sorry comma Belinda" to have the phone produce the text *I'm sorry, Belinda* (or similar wording.)

- Common punctuation marks that you can dictate include the comma, period, exclamation point, question mark, and colon.

- Pause your speech before and after speaking punctuation.

- Voice input may not function when no cellular data or Wi-Fi connection is available.

- The Droid 2 features a voice censor that replaces any naughty words you might utter with a series of pound (#) symbols. The phone knows a lot of blue terms, including the infamous "Seven Words You Can Never Say on Television," but apparently the terms *crap* and *damn* are fine. Don't ask me how much time I spent researching this topic.

Part II
Phone 101

In this part . . .

You remember going to the county fair? Remember the pitchmen? That was all part of the show. "It dices. It slices. It makes julienne fries!" Of course, the item they were huckstering cost twice as much as it did at the local store, and it broke after only a few uses. What's the old phrase — "jack-of-all-trades, master of none."

Your Droid 2 does a lot of useful things, and it handles them quite well for a jack-of-all-trades: photographs, videos, music, maps, email, and the Web. But at its core, your Droid 2 remains a phone. Its primary purpose, its *raison d'être,* is to make phone calls. That basic function is covered in this part of the book.

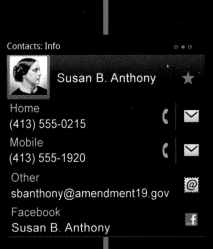

5

Yes, It's a Telephone

In This Chapter

▶ Calling someone

▶ Connecting with a contact

▶ Trying out voice dialing

▶ Getting a call

▶ Checking into a missed call

▶ Perusing the Recent call list

1 bought my first cell phone in 1993. It was a Motorola MicroTAC. I paid $600 for it. My cellular plan was horrendously expensive — something like $1.20 per minute for all calls. The sad part was that I didn't even receive a signal at my house. Still, I was mobile and the phone looked cool in its bulky pouch on my belt.

Technology has leapt forward greatly since 1993. Despite all the bells and whistles on the Droid 2, its main function is making and receiving phone calls. It does that quite well, and much better (not to mention cheaper) than the old MicroTAC.

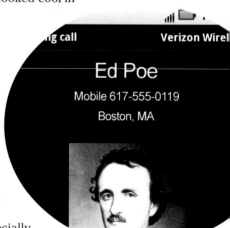

Reach Out and Touch Someone

It's the next best thing to being there, especially when your Uncle Roger is a fisherman and you detest the smell of bait. Oh, but it's good to hear his voice. Making that connection is simple on the Droid 2, especially after reviewing the information in this section.

Making a phone call

To place a call on your phone, heed these steps:

1. Touch the phone icon, found on the Home screen.

You see the Phone dialpad, similar to the one shown in Figure 5-1. If not, touch the Dialer tab, as indicated in the figure.

Figure 5-1: Dialing a phone number.

2. Input the number to call.

Touch the keys on the dialpad to input the number. If you make a mistake, use the Delete key, shown in Figure 5-1, to back up and erase.

As you dial, you may hear the traditional touch-tone sound as you input the number. The phone may also vibrate as you touch the numbers. These sound and vibration settings can be changed; see Chapter 22.

3. Touch the green phone button to make the call.

The phone doesn't make the call until you touch the green button.

As the phone attempts to make the connection, two things happen:

- First, the Call in Progress notification icon appears on the status bar. The icon is a big clue that the phone is making a call or is actively connected.

- Second, the screen changes to show the number you dialed, similar to the one shown in Figure 5-2. When the recipient is in your Contacts list, the name also appears, as shown in the figure. Further, if a picture is part of the person's contact information, the picture appears when the person answers the phone, as shown in Figure 5-2.

Phone number or
contact information

Phone call in progress

Call duration

| Connected | 00:24 Verizon Wireless |

Arnold Schwarzenegger

Work 916-445-2841

Sacramento, CA

Add call — Conference calling

End call — Hang up

Dialpad — Display the dialpad

Bluetooth — Activate Bluetooth headset

Mute — Turn off the microphone

Speaker — Put the call on speaker

Figure 5-2: Your call has gone through!

Even though the touchscreen is pretty, at this point you need to listen to the phone: Put it up to your ear or listen through the earphones or a Bluetooth headset.

4. When the person answers the phone, talk.

What you say is up to you, though I can recommend from experience that it's a bad idea to open your conversation with your girlfriend about the great dream you had about her last night until you're assured that you're talking with your girlfriend and not her mother.

Use the phone's Volume button (on the side of the Droid 2) to adjust the speaker volume during the call.

5. To end the call, touch the red End Call button.

The phone disconnects. You hear a soft *beep*, which is the phone's signal that the call has ended. The Call in Progress notification goes away.

 You can do other things while you're making a call on the Droid 2. Just press the Home button to run an application, read old email, check an appointment, or do whatever. Such activities don't disconnect you, though your cellular carrier may not allow you to do other things with the phone while you're on a call.

You can also listen to music while you're making a call, though I don't recommend it, because the music volume and call volume cannot be set separately.

To return to a call after doing something else, swipe down the notifications at the top of the screen and touch the notification for the current call. You return to the Connected screen, similar to the one shown in Figure 5-2. Continue yapping. (See Chapter 3 for information on reviewing notifications.)

- ✔ You can connect or remove the earphones at any time during a call. The call is neither disconnected nor interrupted by doing so.

- ✔ If you're using earphones, you can press the phone's Power button during the call to turn off the display and lock the phone. I recommend turning off the display so that you don't accidentally touch the Mute or End button during the call.

- ✔ You can't accidentally mute or end a call when the phone is placed against your face; a sensor in the phone detects when it's close to something and the touchscreen is automatically disabled.

- ✔ Don't worry about the phone being too far away from your mouth; it picks up your voice just fine.

 ✔ To mute a call, touch the Mute button, shown in Figure 5-2. A Mute icon, shown in the margin, appears as the phone's status (atop the touchscreen).

- Touch the Speaker button to be able to hold the phone at a distance to listen and talk, which allows you to let others listen and share in the conversation. The Speaker icon appears as the phone's status when the speaker is active.

- If you're wading through one of those nasty voicemail systems, touch the Dialpad button, shown in Figure 5-2, so that you can "Press 1 for English" when necessary.

- Don't hold the phone to your ear when the speaker is active.

- See Chapter 6 for information on using the Add Call button.

- When using a Bluetooth headset, connect the headset *before* you make the call.

- If you need to dial an international number, press and hold the 0 (zero) key until the plus-sign (+) character appears. Then input the rest of the international number. Refer to Chapter 21 for more information on making international calls.

- You hear an audio alert when the call is dropped or the other party hangs up on you. The disconnection can be confirmed by looking at the phone, which shows that the call has ended.

- You cannot place a phone call when the phone has no service; check the signal strength, as shown in Figure 5-1. Also see the nearby sidebar, "Signal strength and network information you don't have to read."

- You cannot place a phone call when the phone is in Airplane mode. See Chapter 21 for information.

- The Call in Progress notification icon (see Figure 5-2) is a useful thing. When you see this notification, it means that the phone is connected to another party. To return to the phone screen, swipe down the status bar and touch the phone call's notification. You can then press the End Call button to disconnect or just put the phone to your face to see who's on the line.

- You cannot, using current technology, browse the Internet or receive email (or other data) while you're making a call on the Droid 2. Future changes in technology or the cell network may change that condition.

Dialing a contact

Because your Droid 2 is also your digital Little Black Book, one of the easiest methods for placing a phone call is to simply dial one of the folks on your Contacts list. You have several ways to do it.

Signal strength and network information you don't have to read

Two technical-looking status icons appear to the left of the current time atop the Droid 2 screen. These icons represent the network the phone is connected to and the signal strength.

The Signal Strength icon displays the familiar bars, rising from left to right. The more bars you see, the better the signal. An extremely low signal is shown by zero bars; when there's no signal, you see an X over the bars.

When the phone is out of its service area but still receiving a signal, you see the Roaming icon, where an *R* appears near the bars. See Chapter 21 for more information on roaming.

To the left of the signal bar icon is the Network icon. No icon means that no network is available, which happens when the network is down or you're out of range. The icon might also disappear when you're making a call. Otherwise, you see an icon representing one of the different types of cellular data networks to which the Droid 2 can connect:

✔ The GPRS icon appears whenever the Droid 2 is connected to a 2G network using the General Packet Radio Service (GPRS) protocol.

✔ The EDGE icon shows up when the Droid 2 is connected to the EDGE 2G digital network. EDGE stands for *Enhanced Data Rates for GSM Evolution*, just in case you do crossword puzzles.

✔ The 3G icon appears when the Droid 2 is connected to a 3G network. (Figure 5-1 has the 3G icon on display.)

The Network icon animates whenever a signal is being transmitted.

Also see Chapter 14 for more information on the network connection and how it plays a role in your phone's Internet access.

Choosing a contact from the Contacts list

To phone up someone on your phone's Contacts list, follow these steps:

1. On the Home screen, touch the Contacts icon.

The icon appears in the lower right corner, next to the Launcher button, on the Home screen. After touching the icon, you see a list of contacts. Unless you've messed with the Contacts list, it's sorted alphabetically by first name, similar to the one shown in Figure 5-3.

2. Scroll the list of contacts to find the person you want to call.

To rapidly scroll, you can swipe the list with your finger or use the tab that appears on the right side of the list, as shown in Figure 5-3; drag the tab around using your finger.

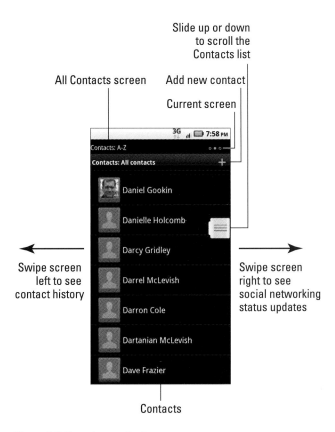

Slide up or down
to scroll the
Contacts list

All Contacts screen

Add new contact

Current screen

Swipe screen
left to see
contact history

Swipe screen
right to see
social networking
status updates

Contacts

Figure 5-3: Perusing contacts.

3. **Touch the contact you want to call.**

   The contact's detailed information appears.

4. **Choose the contact's phone number.**

   Touch the number to dial.

At this point, dialing proceeds as described earlier in this chapter.

See Chapter 8 for more information about the Contacts list.

Dialing a Quick Contact

Quick Contact information appears when you touch and hold a contact's photo, or the *silhouette placeholder,* in the Contacts list, as shown in Figure 5-4. After long-pressing the photo, you see the Quick Contact pop-up bubble, as shown in the figure. Touch the Phone/Dialpad icon to dial the contact.

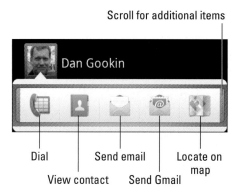

Scroll for additional items

Dan Gookin

Dial | Send email | Locate on map
View contact | Send Gmail

Figure 5-4: Quick Contact information.

Using a Contact Quick Task widget on the Home screen

The Droid 2 Home screen comes preconfigured with Contact Quick Task widgets. They're found on the first Home screen to the right of the main Home screen, and they're blank until you assign contacts to them.

After assigning a contact to a quick task widget, you can touch that quick task widget to instantly dial the contact. More information on how the Contact Quick Task widget is set up can be found in Chapter 8. See Chapter 22 for more information about widgets on the Home screen.

Phoning someone you call often

Because the Droid 2 is sort of a computer, it keeps track of your phone calls. Also, you can flag as favorites certain people whose numbers you want to keep handy. You can take advantage of these two features to quickly call the people you phone most often or to redial a number.

To use the call log to return a call, or to call someone right back, follow these steps:

1. **Touch the Phone icon on the Home screen.**

2. **Touch the Recent tab.**

   The tab is found at the top of the screen, to the right of the Dialer tab.

   The Recent tab displays a list of calls you've made and calls received. Though you can choose an item to see more information, to call someone back, it's just quicker to follow Step 3:

3. **Touch the green Phone icon next to the entry.**

   The Droid 2 dials the contact.

Where is that call coming from?

The Droid 2 displays the caller's location for both incoming and outgoing calls, similar to the ones shown in Figures 5-2 and 5-5. This feature happens courtesy of the City ID app.

City ID is a subscription service, though you can try the free 15-day trial on your Droid 2. After

that, you have to sign up to pay for the service. Though this tool may not help you identify callers you know, it's handy for gleaning information about unknown incoming calls.

Open the City ID app in the Applications Tray to find more information about City ID.

People you call frequently, or contacts you've added to the favorites list, can be accessed by heeding these directions:

1. **Touch the Phone icon on the Home screen.**

2. **Touch the Favorites tab.**

   The tab is found at the top of the screen, to the far right.

   The top part of the list contains *favorites,* contacts you've marked with a star. Below that you see a list of frequently called names and numbers.

3. **Scroll the list to find a contact.**

4. **Touch the contact to see that person's information, or touch the green Phone button to call the contact.**

Refer to Chapter 8 for information on how to make one of your contacts a favorite.

Using the Voice Dialer

The Droid 2 understands your speech, which means that you can not only dictate to the phone but also dial the phone using your voice and not your finger.

The quick-and-dirty way to dial the phone with your voice is to follow these steps:

1. **Press and hold the Search soft button.**

   You see the Microphone icon and the text *Speak Now.*

   When you first try this trick, you may see an introduction screen; touch the Speak Now button.

2. **Say the word *call* followed by the contact's name, or you can speak the phone number.**

When the contact name is recognized, the number is dialed immediately. Otherwise, you see a list of names to choose from — though that's not really in the spirit of voice dialing.

✔ You can quickly access the Droid 2 voice dialer function by touching the Voice Dial button, found on the Dialer screen (refer to Figure 5-1).

✔ Be precise! If the contact is named William Johnson, the Droid 2 may not dial it when you say "Bill Johnson."

✔ You have to be pretty dang fast to touch that Cancel button if the phone chooses the wrong contact to dial. Don't try this trick unless you can see the phone to confirm that it's dialing the proper number.

✔ The number dialed is the main, or *default*, number that's set up when you add the contact. See Chapter 8 for information on how to set the main number for a contact.

✔ See Chapter 4 for additional information on using the Droid 2 voice input ability.

Someone's Calling!

I believe that everyone enjoys getting a phone call. It's with a swift, confident motion that you reach for your cell phone, whipping it out to check the screen to see who's calling. Then comes either disgust as the call is banished to voicemail or feigned innocence as you mutter, "Hello," even though Caller ID has already clued you in to who's calling. Oh, I love the drama!

Receiving a call

Several things can happen when you receive a phone call on your Droid 2:

✔ The phone rings or makes a noise signaling you to an incoming call.

✔ The phone vibrates.

✔ The touchscreen reveals information about the call, as shown in Figure 5-5.

✔ The car in front of you explodes and your crazy passenger starts screaming in an incoherent yet comic manner.

The last item happens only in a Bruce Willis movie. The other three possibilities, or a combination thereof, are your signals that you have an incoming call. A simple look at the touchscreen tells you more information, as illustrated in Figure 5-5.

Figure 5-5 shows what an incoming call looks like when the Droid 2 is locked. If such is in fact the case, slide the green button to the right, which answers the phone.

Contact info (if available)

Incoming phone number

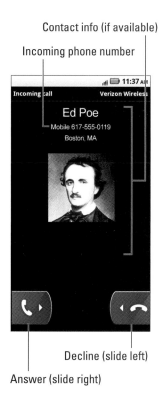

Decline (slide left)

Answer (slide right)

Figure 5-5: You have an incoming call.

When you're using your Droid 2 and a call comes in, you see a green Answer button. Touch that button to accept the call.

After answering the call, place the phone to your ear or use the headset, if one is attached.

To ignore the call, slide the red Decline button to the left (refer to Figure 5-5) or, if you're using the phone, touch the red Ignore button. The phone stops ringing and the call is immediately sent to voicemail.

You can also touch the Volume (Up or Down) button to silence the ringer.

 ✔ The contact picture, such as Mr. Poe in Figure 5-5, appears only when you've assigned a picture to that contact. Otherwise, the generic Android icon shows up.

 ✔ See Chapter 6 for information on how to deal with an incoming call when you're already on the phone.

  ✔ If you're using a Bluetooth headset, you touch the control on the headset to answer your phone. See Chapter 14 for more information on using Bluetooth gizmos.

  ✔ The sound you hear when the phone rings is known as the *ringtone*. You can configure the Droid 2 to play a number of ringtones, depending on who is calling, or you can set a universal ringtone. Ringtones are covered in Chapter 6.

Setting incoming call signals

Whether the phone rings, vibrates, or explodes depends on how you've configured the Droid 2 to signal you for an incoming call. Abide by these steps to set the various options (but not explosions) for your phone:

1. **On the Home screen, touch the Launcher button to view all apps on the phone.**

2. **Choose the Settings icon to open the phone's Settings screen.**

3. **Choose Sound.**

4. **Set the phone's ringer volume by touching Volume.**

5. **Manipulate the Ringtone slider left or right to specify how loud the phone rings for an incoming call.**

   After you release the slider, you hear an example of how loudly the phone rings.

6. **Touch OK to set the ringer volume.**

   If you'd rather just mute the phone, touch the Silent Mode option on the main Sound Settings screen.

7. **To activate vibration when the phone rings, touch Vibrate.**

8. **Choose a vibration option from the Vibrate menu.**

   For example, choose Always to always vibrate the phone or Only in Silent Mode so that the phone vibrates only when you've muted the volume.

9. **Touch the Home button when you're done.**

When the next call comes in, the phone alerts you using the volume setting or vibration options you've just set.

  ✔ See Chapter 3 for information on temporarily silencing the phone.

  ✔ Turning on vibration puts an extra drain on the battery. See Chapter 22 for more information on power management for your phone.

  ✔ Also refer to Chapter 22 for additional sound options on the Droid 2.

Who's Calling Who When?

Life got easier in my household when I got my Droid 2. Before the Droid 2, my son was the one who answered the old landline phone. He was terrible at remembering who phoned and when they called, let alone what message was left. With the Droid 2, however, I can instantly and boldly confirm who called, and when they called, and then call that person right back. Yes, indeed — another gizmo that the Droid 2 renders unnecessary is the common household teenager.

Dealing with a missed call

The notification icon for a missed call looming at the top of the screen means that someone called and you didn't pick up. Fortunately, the Droid 2 remembers all the details for you.

To deal with a missed call, follow these steps:

1. **Display the notifications.**

   See Chapter 3 for details on how to deal with notifications.

2. **Touch the Missed Call notification.**

   A list of missed calls is displayed. The list shows who called, with more information displayed when the phone number matches someone in your Contacts list. Also shown is the time they called.

3. **Touch the green Phone icon by an entry in the call log to return the call.**

Also see the next section for more information on the call log.

Reviewing recent calls

The Droid 2 keeps a record of all calls you make, incoming calls, and missed calls. Everything is listed on the Recent tab, shown in Figure 5-6. To see that list, touch the Phone icon on the Home screen and then choose the Recent tab, as shown in the figure.

The Recent tab shows a list of people who have phoned you or whom you have called, starting with the most recent call at the top of the list. An icon next to each entry describes whether the call was incoming, outgoing, or missed, as illustrated in the figure.

Touching an item in the call log displays contact information for the person who called, if that contact information exists. When contact information doesn't exist, you see a pop-up menu of options for returning the call, sending a text message, and so on.

Who called   Return call

Display call log

Missed call

Outgoing call

Incoming call

Figure 5-6: The call log.

To call someone back, touch the green Phone icon, shown in Figure 5-6.

The call log can become quite long. Use your finger to scroll the list.

 Using the call log is a quick way to add a recent caller as a contact. Simply touch an item in the list and choose Add to Contacts from the pop-up menu. See Chapter 8 for more information about contacts.

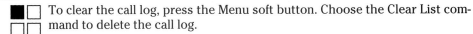 To clear the call log, press the Menu soft button. Choose the Clear List command to delete the call log.

Beyond the Basic Phone Stuff

In This Chapter

▷ Calling with speed dial

▷ Handing multiple incoming calls

▷ Setting up a conference call

▷ Configuring call forwarding options

▷ Banishing a contact forever to voicemail

▷ Finding a better ringtone

▷ Assigning ringtones to your contacts

▷ Using your favorite song or sound as a ringtone

*O*riginally, Alexander Graham Bell hired teenage boys to be phone operators. They proved unreliable. The boys were replaced by young women. Eventually, they too were replaced, when telephones came supplied with dials. That way, everyone became their own phone operator. It wasn't a hefty chore to dial a phone, mostly because the dial had no Enter key, but also because all the old telephone did was send and receive calls. Things are different today.

Your phone does more than make phone calls, of course. Still, it can likely do more with the basic phone call than any other phone you've owned. Most people don't bother with extra phone features. You can ignore the features as well, or you can choose to read this chapter and discover what your Droid 2 can do beyond the basic phone stuff.

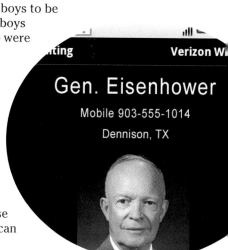

ting   Verizon W

Gen. Eisenhower
Mobile 903-555-1014
Dennison, TX

Speed Dial

How fast can you dial a phone? Pretty fast — specifically, for ten of the friends or folks you phone most often. The feature is *speed dial*. To set it up on your Droid 2, follow these steps:

1. **From the Home screen, touch the Phone button.**

   The Phone button is found to the left of the Launcher, at the bottom of the Home screen, or on the left of the Home screen when the sliding keyboard is extended.

2. **Press the Menu soft button.**

3. **Choose Speed Dial Setup.**

   The first speed-dial number is already configured to your carrier's voicemail system. The remaining numbers, 2 through 9, are blank.

4. **Touch a blank item in the list.**

   The blank lines contain the text *Add Speed Dial.* To the left of the blank item is the speed dial number, 2 through 9.

5. **Choose a contact to speed-dial.**

6. **When a contact has multiple phone numbers, you see a menu from which you can choose the specific phone number to speed-dial.**

7. **Repeat Steps 4 and 5 to add more speed-dial numbers.**

When you're done adding numbers, press the Back or Home button to exit the Speed Dial Setup screen.

Using speed dial is simple: Summon the phone dialer (refer to Figure 5-1, in Chapter 5), and then press and hold *(long-touch)* a number on the dialpad. When you release your finger, the speed-dial number is dialed.

To remove a speed-dial number, follow Steps 1 through 3 in this section. Touch the minus (–) button to the left of the speed-dial number to remove the number. You can then add another speed-dial number in that slot or just leave it empty.

To add a recent caller to the speed-dial list, long-press the recent caller from the Recent call log. Choose the option Add to Speed Dial from the menu that appears. This trick works only when you have an available slot for speed-dial numbers. See Chapter 5 for more information on the Recent call log.

Multiple Call Mania

A human being can hold only one conversation at a time. I remember hearing that theory in a lecture, but then the guy next to me started talking and I couldn't focus on what the speaker was saying. So I'll never know for certain. I do, however, know that the Droid 2 is capable of handling more than one call at a time. This section explains how it works.

Receiving a new call when you're on the phone

You're on the phone, chatting it up. Suddenly, someone else calls you. What happens next?

The Droid 2 alerts you to a new call. The phone may vibrate or make a sound. Look at the front of the phone to see what's up with the incoming call, as shown in Figure 6-1.

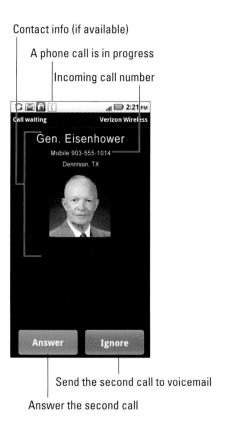

Contact info (if available)

A phone call is in progress

Incoming call number

Send the second call to voicemail

Answer the second call

Figure 6-1: Suddenly, there's an incoming call!

You have three options:

Answer the call. Touch the green Answer button to answer the incoming call. The call you're on is placed on hold.

Send the call directly to voicemail. Touch the Ignore button. The incoming call is sent directly to voicemail.

Ignore the call. Do nothing. The call eventually goes into voicemail.

When you choose to answer the call and the call you're on is placed on hold, you return to the first call when you end the second call. Or, you can manage the multiple calls as described in the next section.

Juggling two calls

After you answer a second call, as described in the preceding section, your Droid 2 is now working with two calls at a time. In this particular situation, you can speak with only one person at a time; juggling two calls is not the same thing as a conference call.

To switch between callers, touch the green Switch Calls button that appears on the touchscreen. Every time you touch the Switch Calls button, the conversation moves to the other caller.

To end a call, touch the End Call button, just as you normally would. Both calls might appear to have been disconnected, but that's not the case: In a few moments, the call you didn't disconnect "rings" as though the person called you back. They didn't call you back, though: The Droid 2 is simply returning you to that ongoing conversation.

> ✔ The number of different calls your phone can handle depends on your carrier. For most of us, that's only two calls at a time. In that case, a third person who calls you either hears a busy signal or is sent right into voicemail.

> ✔ Put the phone where you can see the touchscreen when you work with multiple calls. That way, you can see who's on the line, who is waiting, and how long they've been waiting.

> ✔ If the person on hold hangs up, you may hear a sound or feel the phone vibrate when the call is dropped.

Making a conference call

Unlike someone interrupting a conversation with an incoming call, a *conference call* is something you set out to do intentionally: You make one call and then *add* a second call. Touch a button on the Droid 2 touchscreen and then everyone is talking. Here's how it works:

1. **Phone the first person.**

   Refer to Chapter 5 if you need to bone up on your Droid 2 phone-calling skills.

2. **After your phone connects and you complete a few pleasantries, touch the Add Call button.**

   The first person is put on hold.

3. **Dial the second person.**

   You can use the dialpad or choose the second person from your Contacts list or Recent call log.

   Say your pleasantries and inform the party that the call is about to be merged.

4. **Touch the Merge Calls button.**

   The two calls are now joined: The touchscreen says *Conference Call,* and the End Last Call button appears. Everyone you've dialed can talk to and hear each other.

5. **Touch the End Call button to end the conference call.**

   All calls are disconnected.

When several people are in a room and want to participate in a call, you can always put the phone in Speaker mode: Touch the Speaker button.

Send a Call Elsewhere

Banishing an unwanted call on the Droid 2 is relatively easy. You can dismiss the phone from ringing by touching the Volume button. Or, you can send the call scurrying off into voicemail by sliding the red Ignore button to the left, as described in the section in Chapter 5 about receiving a call.

Other options exist for the special handling of incoming calls. They're the forwarding options, described in this section.

Forwarding phone calls

Call-forwarding is the process by which you take a phone call coming into your Droid 2 and send it elsewhere. For example, you can send all calls you receive to your office when you're on vacation. Then you have the luxury of having your cell phone and still making calls but freely ignoring anyone who calls you.

The options for call forwarding on the Droid 2 are set by the cell phone carrier, and not by the phone itself. In the United States, using Verizon as your cellular provider, the call forwarding options work as described in Table 6-1.

Table 6-1	Verizon Call Forwarding Commands	
To Do This	*Input First Number*	*Input Second Number*
Forward unanswered incoming calls	*71	Forwarding number
Forward all incoming calls	*72	Forwarding number
Cancel call forwarding	*73	None

For example, to forward all calls to (714) 555-4565, you input ***727145554565** and touch the green Dial button on the Droid 2. You hear just a brief tone after dialing, and then the call ends. After that, any call coming into your phone rings at the other number.

✔ You must disable call forwarding on your Droid 2 to return to normal cell phone operations. Dial *73.

✔ The Droid 2 doesn't even ring when you forward a call using *72. Only the phone number you've chosen to forward to rings.

✔ You don't need to input the area code for the forwarding number when it's a local call. In other words, if you only need to dial 555-4565 to call the forwarding number, you need to input only ***725554565** to forward your calls.

✔ The Android operating system has forwarding features that are unavailable on the Droid 2, though they might be made available in the future. If so, you can find them on the Settings screen: Choose Call Settings, and then choose Call Forwarding.

Sending a contact directly to voicemail

You can configure the Droid 2 to forward any of your cell phone contacts directly to voicemail. This is a great way to deal with a pest! Follow these steps:

1. **Touch the Contacts icon on the Home screen.**

   The Contacts list opens.

2. **Choose a contact.**

   Use your finger to scroll the list of contacts until you find the annoying person you want to eternally banish to voicemail.

3. **Touch the Menu soft button.**

4. **Choose Edit.**

5. **Choose Additional Info.**

   You may need to scroll to the bottom of the Edit Contact screen to find the Additional Info bar. When you do, touch the Triangle button on the right end of the bar to display the additional information.

6. **Touch the square next to the Send Straight to Voicemail? option.**

   A green check mark appears in the square, indicating that all calls from the contact (no matter which of their phone numbers they use) are sent directly into voicemail.

7. **Touch the Save button.**

To unbanish the contact, repeat these steps but in Step 6 touch the square to remove the green check mark.

> ✔ This feature is one reason why you might want to retain contact information for someone with whom you never want to have contact.
>
> ✔ See Chapter 8 for more information on contacts.
>
> ✔ Also see Chapter 7, on voicemail.

Fun with Ringtones

I confess: Ringtones can be lots of fun. They uniquely identify your phone's ring, especially when you forget to mute your phone and you're hustling to turn the thing off because everyone in the room is annoyed by your ringtone choice of *It's a Small World*.

On the Droid 2, you can choose which ringtone you want for your phone. You can create your own ringtones or use snippets from your favorite tunes. You can also assign ringtones for individual contacts. This section explains how it's done.

Choosing the phone's ringtone

To select a new ringtone for your phone, or to simply confirm which ringtone you're using already, follow these steps:

1. **From the Home screen, touch the Launcher button.**

2. **Choose Settings.**

3. **Choose Sound.**

4. **Choose Phone Ringtone.**

If you have a ringtone application, you may see a menu that asks you which source to use for the phone's ringtone. Choose Android System.

5. **Choose a ringtone from the list that's displayed.**

   Scroll the list. Tap a ringtone to hear a preview.

6. **Touch OK to accept the new ringtone or touch Cancel to keep the phone's ringtone as is.**

You can also set the ringtone used for notifications: In Step 4, choose Notification Ringtone instead of Phone Ringtone.

Setting a contact's ringtone

Ringtones can be assigned by contact so that when your annoying friend Larry calls, you can have your phone yelp like a whiny puppy. Here's how to set a ringtone for a contact:

1. **Touch the Contacts icon on the Home screen.**

2. **From the list, choose the contact to which you want to assign a ringtone.**

3. **Touch the Menu soft button.**

4. **Choose Edit.**

5. **Touch the Triangle button on the Additional Info bar to display more options.**

6. **Scroll down and press the Triangle button by Call Handling.**

7. **Choose a ringtone from the list.**

   It's the same list that's displayed for the phone's ringtones.

8. **Touch OK to assign the ringtone to that contact.**

9. **Touch the Save button to confirm your choice.**

Whenever that contact calls, the Droid 2 rings using the ringtone you've specified.

To remove a specific ringtone for a contact, repeat the steps in this section but choose the ringtone named Default Ringtone. That option sets the contact's ringtone to be the same as the phone's ringtone.

Using music as a ringtone

You can use any tune from the Droid 2 music library as the phone's ringtone. The first part of the process is finding a good tune to use. Follow along with these steps:

1. **Touch the Applications button on the Home screen to display all apps on the phone.**

2. **Touch Music to open the music player.**

3. **Choose a tune to play.**

    See Chapter 18 for specific information on how to use the Music application and use your Droid 2 as a portable music player.

    The song you want must either appear on the screen or be playing for you to select it as a ringtone.

4. **Press the Menu soft button.**

5. **Choose Use As Ringtone.**

    The song — the entire thing — is set as the phone's ringtone. Whenever you receive a call, that song plays.

The song you've chosen is added to the list of ringtones. It plays — from the start of the song — when you have an incoming call and until you answer the phone, send the call to voicemail, or choose to ignore the call and eventually the caller goes away and the music stops.

You can add as many songs as you like by repeating the steps in this section. Follow the steps in the earlier section "Choosing the phone's ringtone" for information on switching between different song ringtones. Refer to the steps in the earlier section "Setting a contact's ringtone" to assign a specific song to a contact.

A free app at the Android Market, Zedge, has oodles of free ringtones available for preview and download, all shared by Android users around the world. See Chapter 20 for information about the Android Market and how to download and install apps such as Zedge on your phone.

Creating your own ringtones

You can use any MP3 or WAV audio file as a ringtone for the Droid 2, such as a personalized message, a sound you record on your computer, or an audio file you stole from the Internet. As long as the sound is in the MP3 or WAV format, it can work as a ringtone on your phone.

The secret to creating your own ringtone is to transfer the audio file from your computer to the Droid 2. That topic is covered in Chapter 13, on synchronizing music between your computer and phone. After the audio file is in the phone's music library, you can choose the file as a ringtone in the same way you can assign any music on the Droid 2 as a ringtone, as described in the preceding section.

At the Sound of the Tone . . .

In This Chapter

▶ Configuring basic voicemail

▶ Retrieving messages

▶ Setting up Visual Voice Mail

▶ Reviewing Visual Voice Mail messages

*V*oicemail can prove to be handy in so many ways. First, and most obviously, voicemail exists for missed phone calls. When you're not available or you're on the other line, someone can leave you a message. Second, voicemail exists as a sort of digital hell to whence you can banish unwanted calls from annoying pests. Finally, voicemail exists as an excuse: You can dismiss anyone by simply claiming that you've yet to check your voicemail for messages. If only our ancestors had it so good.

Carrier Voicemail

The most basic, and most stupid, form of voicemail is the free voicemail service provided by your cell phone company. It's a standard feature with few frills and nothing that stands out differently, especially for such a nifty phone as the Droid 2.

Carrier voicemail picks up missed calls and calls you thrust into voicemail. The Droid 2 alerts you to a missed call by displaying the Missed Call notification (shown in the margin). You then dial the voicemail system, listen to your calls, and use the phone's dialpad to delete messages or repeat messages or use other features you probably don't know about because no one ever pays attention.

Harry Houdini
8/28/2010 8:32 PM

✔ The Missed Call icon does not appear when you've sent a call to voicemail.

  ✔ The meat of voicemail on the Droid 2 is *Visual Voice Mail,* covered later in this chapter. Even so, this section covers the basic instructions for using generic carrier voicemail, which you must configure before you can use Visual Voice Mail.

Setting up carrier voicemail

If you haven't yet done it, you need to set up voicemail on your phone. Even if you believe it to be set up and configured, consider churning through these steps, just to be sure:

1. **From the Home screen, press the Menu soft button.**

2. **Choose Settings.**

    The Settings screen appears.

3. **Choose Call Settings.**

4. **Choose Voicemail Service.**

5. **Choose My Carrier, if it isn't chosen already.**

    When My Carrier is already chosen, the phone is configured to use your cell service provider's voicemail service. You're done. Otherwise, continue:

6. **Back on the Call Settings screen, choose Voicemail Settings.**

    The number that's shown should be the one for your carrier's voicemail service. For example, on Verizon in the United States, the number is *86. If you need to change the number, read the next section.

Phone your carrier voicemail after the initial setup, which completes the configuration. On my carrier (Verizon), I configured my language, set a voicemail password, and then recorded a greeting, following the steps offered by the cheerful Verizon robot. Complete those steps even if you plan to use Visual Voice Mail, covered later in this chapter.

Don't forget to complete your voice mailbox setup by creating a customized greeting. When you don't, you may not receive voicemail messages, or people may believe that they've dialed the wrong number.

Changing the carrier voicemail number

When you need to change your voicemail number, follow Steps 1 through 3 in the preceding section and choose Voicemail Settings. If necessary, choose the Voicemail Number option. Type the proper voicemail number, as shown in Figure 7-1.

Current voicemail number

Choose a contact

Punch in a new voicemail number

Figure 7-1: Setting the carrier voicemail number.

If you touch the Contact icon, shown in Figure 7-1, you see the Droid 2 Contacts list, from which you can pluck a contact to use for voicemail. That option is intended for special voicemail services, such as Google Voice, which you can choose for the Droid 2. I recommend not using Aunt Linda's cell phone number as your voicemail service.

Getting your messages

To access carrier voicemail on the Droid 2, you manually dial into the voicemail service. For Verizon in the United States, it's *86. Or, if you haven't yet set up Visual Voicemail, you can open the Voicemail app and touch the Call Voicemail button.

What happens after the voicemail system is dialed depends on your carrier. I'm using Verizon in the United States, so I have to input my password and press the # key. Then any new messages are automatically played.

Table 7-1 lists the commands for using Verizon voicemail service (current at the time this book went to press). These commands may change later.

Table 7-1	Verizon Voicemail System Commands
Dial	**What You Can Do**
*	Go to the Main menu or, if you're at the Main menu, disconnect from voicemail
1	Listen to messages
2	Send a message to another phone number on the Verizon system
4	Review or change your personal options, such as the message greeting
5	Restart the session
7	Delete the message you just heard
88	After listening to a message, call the sender
9	Save the message you just heard
#	End input

✔ The easiest way to start the Voicemail app is to touch the Voicemail button, found on the dialpad window. (Refer to Figure 5-1, in Chapter 5.)

✔ You don't have to venture into carrier voicemail just to see who called you. Instead, check the call log to review recent calls. Refer to Chapter 5 for information on reviewing the call log.

✔ Calls you exile into voicemail are not flagged as Missed in the Recent call log.

✔ See Chapter 3 for more information on reviewing notifications.

Visual Voice Mail

A better option than carrier voicemail is to set up and use Visual Voice Mail. *Visual Voice Mail* is simply an interface into your existing carrier voicemail. This feature on the Droid 2 provides more flexibility when dealing with boring, old carrier voicemail. For example, using Visual Voice Mail, you can choose which messages to listen to and pause or replace messages.

The only drawback to using Visual Voice Mail is that it costs extra. You must subscribe to the service, which runs $2.99 per month as this book goes to press.

Setting up Visual Voice Mail

To configure Visual Voice Mail to work on your Droid 2, first set up carrier voicemail as covered earlier in this chapter.

After you get carrier voicemail up and running, and especially after you set your password or PIN, follow these steps:

1. **Touch the Launcher button to pop up the list of all apps installed on your phone.**

2. **Choose the Voicemail app.**

   A shortcut to the Voicemail app is also found on the main Home screen.

3. **Touch the Subscribe to Visual Voice Mail button.**

4. **Touch the Accept button after you've ignored the end user license agreement.**

5. **Type your current voicemail password into the text box.**

   See? That's why I recommend that you set up carrier voicemail first.

6. **Touch the Login button.**

   And you're done. The Visual Voice Mail inbox appears on the screen, listing any lingering messages in your voicemail inbox.

Your Voicemail app may need upgrading before you can access Visual Voice Mail. If so, touch the Upgrade button and use the Android Market app to upgrade and install the Visual Voice Mail program. After the program upgrade is installed, run the Visual Voice Mail app and follow the directions on the touchscreen to set things up.

Refer to Chapter 20 for more information on using the Android Market to install new applications on your Droid 2.

Accessing Visual Voice Mail

Visual Voice Mail serves as your access to all voicemail left on your phone. After Visual Voice Mail is configured (see the preceding section), you never need to dial carrier voicemail again. Simply pull down a Visual Voice Mail notification or start the Voicemail app, and all your messages are instantly available on the screen.

 When new voicemail arrives, you see a notification icon, as shown in the margin. To access your message, pull down the notifications and choose New Voicemail. You see your voicemail inbox, which lists all pending messages. Also shown are any messages you've already listened to but have not deleted.

Touch an item in the Voicemail inbox to review the message. You see a screen similar to the one shown in Figure 7-2. Use the controls on the screen to review or delete the message or to call the person back, or press the Back soft button to return to the Voicemail inbox.

Contact info (if available)

Date and time of voicemail

Mailbox stats

Play message

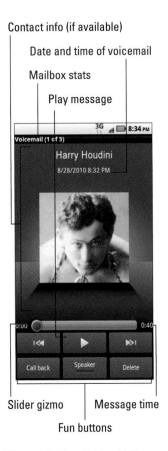

Slider gizmo   Message time

Fun buttons

Figure 7-2: Visual Voice Mail.

Choose the message you want to listen to, and then touch the Play button, shown in Figure 7-2. You can pause a message as it's playing by touching the Pause button, which replaces the Play button.

Visual Voice Mail uses the same greeting that was set when you first config-ured carrier voicemail. To change the greeting, you have to dial carrier voice-mail and follow the menus.

8

The People in Your Phone

In This Chapter

▶ Using the Contacts list

▶ Finding contacts

▶ Creating new contacts

▶ Getting a contact from a map search

▶ Putting a picture on a contact

▶ Working with favorites

▶ Deleting contacts

*A*dmit it: You find it difficult to remember important information about people, such as birthdays for people in your family. Yes, it's tough. My mom (to this day) writes everyone's birthdates on my kitchen calendar. Every year, she just copies over the birthdays, month by month, except for people who have died. For phone numbers, lots of people had phone books or used the Yellow Pages to jot down numbers. That's so 20th century.

Here in the Digital Age, we have remarkable gizmos that help you keep track of all sorts of vital information about the people you know. And, what better place to put that information than in your phone? It just makes sense.

Some applications access or affect the Contacts list maintained in your Droid 2. You're alerted to any such applications when they're installed on the phone. See Chapter 20 for more information on the Android Market.

Folks You Know

The name of the program on your phone that stores information about people you know is Contacts. I would normally write a contact lens joke here, but I just can't seem to be pithy enough, so I'll leave it at that.

Presenting the Contacts list

To peruse your phone's address book, touch the Contacts icon, found at the bottom of the Home screen, just to the right of the Launcher button. You see a list of all contacts on your phone, organized alphabetically by first name, similar to the list shown in Figure 8-1.

Touch to see more information.

Individual contact (no picture)

First name index letter

Long-press to see Quick Contact

Thumb tab

Contacts

Figure 8-1: The Contacts list.

Scroll the list by swiping with your finger. You see a thumb tab, shown in Figure 8-1, which you can use to quickly navigate up and down through your contacts. A large letter appears, telling you where you are in relation to the first names in the list.

To do anything with a contact, you first have to choose it: Touch a contact name and you see more information, as shown in Figure 8-2.

Figure 8-2: More detail for a contact.

You can do a multitude of things with the contact after it's displayed, as shown in Figure 8-2:

Make a phone call. To call the contact, touch one of the contact's phone entries, such as Home or Mobile. See Chapter 5.

Send a text message. Touch the Text Message icon (see Figure 8-2) to open the Text Messaging app and send that contact a message. See Chapter 9 for information on text messaging on your Droid 2.

Compose an email message. Touch the Email link to compose an email message to the contact. When the contact has more than one email address, you can choose to which one you want to send the message. Chapter 10 covers using email on your phone.

Locate your contact on map. When the contact has a home or business address, you can touch the little doohickey next to the address, shown in Figure 8-2, to summon the Maps application. Refer to Chapter 15 for all the fun stuff you can do with Maps.

Oh, and if you have birthday information there, you can view it as well. Singing "Happy Birthday" is something you have to do on your own.

Finding your Me account

Looking for yourself? Your contact information on the Droid 2 is listed under the Me account. Sure, you may have another account, but the Droid 2 automatically sets up your main account on the phone as *Me*.

You can scroll the Contacts list to find the Me account or, when viewing the Contacts list, you can follow these quick steps:

1. **Press the Menu soft button.**

2. **Choose My Info.**

   To combine the Me account with your Gmail (or another) account you have in the Contacts list, you *link* the accounts. After locating your Me account (refer to Steps 1 and 2), continue with these steps:

3. **Press the Menu soft button.**

4. **Choose Link Account.**

5. **Choose your other account from the Contacts list.**

   Scroll the list up and down, and then touch your other account name to select it. The two accounts are now linked, and the Me account — as well as your other account — show up together.

You can link any accounts in the Contacts list, such as people who have duplicate accounts for Facebook or Twitter or even on the phone but who may be listed under different names or organizations.

Information about linked contacts appears at the bottom of the contact's information, as shown in Figure 8-2. Touch the Triangle button in that gray area to see the additional, linked accounts.

To unlink an account, press the Menu soft button while viewing the contact information. Choose Unlink Contact. Then pluck the contact information you want to separate from the menu list that's displayed.

Searching contacts

You can have a massive number of contacts. For example, I have 414 on my phone. I started out with just 80 contacts that I imported from Gmail; I added the rest as I phoned or met people. The problem: It can take a while to wade through that list.

Rather than scroll the Contacts list with angst-riddled desperation, press the Search soft button. A Search All Contacts window appears. Type a few letters from the contact's name and quickly you see the list of contacts narrowed to the few who match the letters you type. Touch a name from the search list to view the contact's information.

You can also voice-search for a contact: After opening the Search All Contacts window, touch the Microphone icon on the onscreen keyboard and then speak the contact's name when you see the Speak Now prompt. The sounds you utter appear in the Search text box, which you can then use to search the list.

✔ See Chapter 5 for information on voice dialing.

✔ The later section "A New Contact Is Born" tells you how to deal with adding new contacts. It's next.

✔ No, there's no correlation between the number of contacts you have and the number of bestest friends you have — none.

Using a Contact Quick Task widget

Motorola (or Verizon — I mean, who really knows?) preconfigured your Droid 2 with some Contact Quick Task widgets on the Home screen, just to the right of the main Home screen. Four are available, as shown in Figure 8-3.

When you touch a blank widget (refer to Figure 8-3), the full Contacts list is displayed. Choose a contact to assign to the widget, and then touch various contact options — phone, text message, email — to place on the widget.

The first time you touch a widget with a phone number, you're asked whether you want to activate one-touch calling. After that, touching the widget, or the phone part of a widget, instantly calls that contact.

Resize controls

Blank contact

Phone the contact

Text message

Long-press to move/resize

Figure 8-3: Quick Task widgets.

Contacts can have multiple quick tasks assigned: To create more tasks, resize the widget to allow for more buttons. After you see the Add button, the widget is large enough to sport another quick task.

Refer to Chapter 22 for information on adding a Contact Quick Task widget. They're found in the Motorola widget category.

Chapter 22 also contains information on removing the widgets, in case you find them crowding your Home screen.

Special and funky contact numbers

Even if you have no friends, or you have friends but don't want them, a smattering of entries appears in your Contacts list — for one, the Me account, which represents you. Beyond Me (you), you may find some of these curious and interesting accounts to "dial":

#BAL: Receive a free text message indicating your current cell phone charges as well as any previous payments you've made.

#DATA: Receive a free text message indicating your text message or data usage.

#MIN: Receive a free text message indicating the minutes you've used on the Droid 2, including peak, off-hour, or weekend or whatever other categories for cell phone minutes they have.

#PMT: Make a payment using your Droid 2. This operation works only when you've configured your account to make payments via the phone.

#Warranty Center: Contact Verizon for troubleshooting and warranty issues regarding your Droid 2.

Customer Care: Contact Verizon support for your phone. (It's a shortcut for the number 611, which is the support number for your Droid 2 cell phone.)

See Chapter 9 for more information about reading text messages on the Droid 2.

A New Contact Is Born

You have many ways to get contact information into your phone. You can build them all from scratch, but that's tedious. More likely, you collect contacts as you use your phone. Or, you can borrow contacts from your Gmail contacts. In no time, you'll have a phone full of contact information.

Making a new contact

You can make a new contact for your Droid 2 phone in many ways.

Add a contact from the recent call log

One of the quickest ways to build up your Contacts list is to add people as they phone you — assuming that you've told them about your new phone number. After someone calls, you can use the Recent call log to add the person to your Contacts list. Obey these steps:

1. **From the Home screen, touch the Phone icon.**

2. **Choose the Recent tab.**

3. **Choose the phone number you want to create a contact for.**

4. **Choose Add to Contacts.**

5. **Choose New to make a new contact for that number.**

You can also choose Existing to add the phone number to an existing contact — for example, when Julie finally discloses that second cell phone number she never told you about. In that case, locate Julie's (or whoever's) contact in the list and then skip to Step 7.

6. **Fill in the contact's information.**

   Use either of the Droid 2 keyboards to fill in the blanks, as many as you know about the caller: given name and family name, for example, and other information, if you know it.

   For a business, use only the Family Name field for the business name.

   If you don't know any additional information, that's fine; just filling in the name helps clue you in to who is calling the next time that person calls (using that same number).

   Use the Next button on the onscreen keyboard to hop between the various text fields for the contact.

   Use the arrow keys on the sliding keyboard to hop between the text fields.

7. **Touch the Save button.**

   You're done.

Create a new contact from scratch

Sometimes, it's necessary to create a contact when you actually meet another human being in the real world. In that case, you have more information to input, and it starts like this:

1. **Touch the Contacts icon on the Home screen to access the Contacts list.**

2. **Press the Menu soft button.**

3. **Choose Add Contact.**

4. **Fill in the information on the Add Contact screen as best you can.**

   Fill in the text fields with the information you know: Given Name and Family Name, for example.

   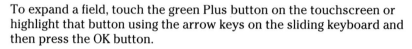

   To expand a field, touch the green Plus button on the touchscreen or highlight that button using the arrow keys on the sliding keyboard and then press the OK button.

   Touch the gray button to the left of the phone number or email address to choose the location for that item, such as Home, Work, or Mobile.

   Touch the Triangle button next to Additional Info at the bottom of the list to add *even more* information!

5. **Touch the Save button to complete editing and add the new contact.**

The new contact is automatically synced with your Google account on the Internet. That's one beauty of the Droid 2: You don't need to duplicate your efforts; the phone automatically updates all your Google account information on both the Droid 2 and the Internet.

Make a contact in Gmail on the Internet

One of the easiest ways to build up new contacts is to use your Gmail Contacts list on the Internet. It's easy because you're using a computer with a real keyboard and mouse to help you input the information. That method generally works better than typing with your thumbs on the Droid 2.

To add a new Gmail contact, follow these steps:

1. **On a computer, browse to your Google Gmail account at** http://gmail.google.com.

2. **Log in, if necessary.**

3. **Choose Contacts from the links listed on the left side of the page.**

4. **Click the New Contact button.**

5. **Fill in the contact information on the screen.**

   Use the Add links to add more than one email address, phone number, or address or other information, for example, when a contact has both home and work addresses.

6. **Click the Save button to save the contact information.**

   You can repeat Steps 4 through 6 to create additional contacts.

Because the Droid 2 stays in sync with your Google account, any new contacts you create on the Internet are automatically updated on your phone.

Build up contacts from your social networking sites

After you tell the phone which social networking sites you use, the Droid 2 scours your friends and followers for information. New contacts are built from that information and automatically placed into your phone's Contacts list. Even the avatar images associated with the accounts are saved on the Droid 2 Contacts list.

The key to pulling in contacts from your social networking sites is to use the Social Networking app on the Droid 2. Using this app is covered in Chapter 12.

Find a new contact by using a Maps location

When you use the Maps application to locate a restaurant, an apothecary, or a dirty book store, you can quickly create a contact for that location. Here's how:

1. **After searching for your location, touch the cartoon bubble that appears on the map.**

   For example, in Figure 8-4, Angelo's Ristorante has been found.

Figure 8-4: A business has been located.

2. **Scroll to the bottom of the information summary for the business and choose the item Add As a Contact.**

   The information from the Maps application is copied into the proper fields for the contact, including the address and phone number, plus other information (if available).

3. **Touch the Save button.**

   The new contact is created.

See Chapter 15 for detailed information on how to search for a location using the Maps application.

Editing a contact

When things change for a contact, or perhaps your thumbs were a bit too big when you created the contact while riding a bus during an earthquake, you can edit the contact information. Aside from just editing existing information or adding new items, you can also do a smattering of interesting things, as covered in this section.

⬐ See Chapter 6 for information on configuring a contact so that all their incoming calls go to voicemail.

⬐ Also refer to Chapter 6 on how to set a contact's ringtone.

⬐ Contact information can come from multiple sources, so editing information for a contact on your phone doesn't change its original source. That is, unless the source is your Gmail Contacts list, in which case the Droid 2 synchronizes your edits on the phone with the Contacts list on the Internet and vice versa.

Make basic changes

To make minor touch-ups on any contact, start by locating and displaying the contact's information. Press the Menu soft button and choose Edit. You can then add any new information by touching a field and typing on either the onscreen keyboard or the sliding keyboard. You can edit information as well: Touch the field to edit and change whatever you want.

Chapter 4 contains information on how to edit text on the Droid 2.

When you're done editing, touch the Save button.

Add a picture to a contact

It's so much nicer to have a contact with a pretty picture instead of that boring silhouette icon. Well, unless your contact is really a two-dimensional silhouette.

To add a picture to your contact, it helps to already have the picture stored on the phone. You can transfer the picture from a computer (covered in Chapter 13), or you can snap a shot with the phone anytime you see the contact or a person or an object that resembles the contact.

After the contact's photo, or any other suitable image, is stored on the phone, follow these steps to update the contact's information:

1. **Locate and display the contact's information.**

2. **Press the Menu soft button.**

3. **Choose Edit.**

4. **Touch the Add Picture icon.**

    The icon is found to the left of the contact's First Name field, where the contact's picture would normally appear.

5. **Choose the option Use Existing Photo.**

6. **Choose Gallery.**

    The Droid 2 photo gallery is displayed. It lists all photos and videos stored on your phone.

7. **Browse the gallery to look for a suitable image.**

   See Chapter 17 for more information on using the Gallery.

8. **Touch the image you want to use for the contact.**

9. **Select the size and portion of the image you want to use for the contact.**

   Use Figure 8-5 as your guide. You can choose which portion of the image to use by moving the cropping box, and you can resize the cropping box to select more or less of the image.

Figure 8-5: Choosing a contact's image.

10. **Touch Save to assign the image to the contact.**

11. **Touch Save to complete editing the contact.**

    The image is now assigned, and it appears whenever the contact is referenced on your Droid 2.

You can add pictures to contacts on your Google account using any computer. Just visit your Gmail Contacts list to edit a contact. You can then add to that contact any picture stored on your computer. The picture is eventually synced with the same contact on your Droid 2.

⮞ Pictures can also be added by your Gmail friends and contacts when they add their own images to their accounts.

⮞ Using a Picasa picture for a contact may not work on your phone. See Chapter 17 for more information on Picasa.

⮞ To remove or change a contact's picture, follow Steps 1 through 5 in the preceding step list and choose Remove Photo from the menu that pops up.

Set the default phone number and email address

When a contact has multiple phone numbers or email addresses, you can choose which one becomes the *default*. That default number or address is used by the Quick Contact feature to let you easily phone or send the contact a message. Here's how to set a contact's default phone number or email address:

1. **Display the contact's information.**

2. **Long-press the phone number you want to use as the main number.**

   Touch and hold the phone number until the Options menu pops up.

3. **Choose Make Default Number.**

   The phone number is appended with a tiny white check mark.

4. **Long-press the email address you want as the contact's primary email contact.**

5. **Choose Make Default Email.**

   As with the phone number, the email address entry grows a tiny white check mark.

See Chapter 5 for details about Quick Contact information.

Make a favorite

A *favorite* contact is someone you stay in touch with most often. It doesn't have to be someone you like — just someone you (perhaps unfortunately) phone often, such as your bail bondsman.

The list of favorite contacts is kept on the Phone apps' Favorites tab (refer to Figure 5-1, in Chapter 5). Touching that tab is the way to see your list of favorites. The top part of the list shows contacts you've flagged as favorites. The bottom part of the list displays numbers you frequently call.

To add a contact to the Favorites list, display the contact's information and touch the Star button in the contact's upper right corner, as shown in Figure 8-2. When the star is red, as shown in the figure, the contact is one of your favorites.

To remove a favorite, touch the contact's star again and it loses its color. Removing a favorite doesn't delete the contact, but it does remove it from the Favorites list.

- Occasionally peruse the names in the bottom part of the Favorites list, the frequent callers. You might consider promoting some of them to your favorites.

- The contact has no idea whether they're one of your favorites, so don't believe that you're hurting anyone's feelings by not making them a favorite.

Sharing a contact

You know Mary? I know Mary, too! But you don't have her contact information? Allow me to share that with you. Here's what I do:

1. **Summon the contact you want to share from your Contacts list.**
2. **Press the Menu soft button.**
3. **Choose Share Name Card.**
4. **Choose the items you want to share about the contact.**

   All the items have green check marks by them. Touch a green check mark to deselect an item you don't want to share about the contact.

5. **Touch the Send button.**
6. **Choose how to send the information: Bluetooth, Email, Gmail, Text Messaging, or whatever else might be displayed.**

   After choosing a method, the appropriate app appears for sharing the contact's name card. For Bluetooth, see Chapter 14; for Email and Gmail, see Chapter 10; for text messaging see Chapter 9.

In a few Internet moments, the email message will be received.

What you're sending is a *vCard,* a common type of file used by databases and personal information software to exchange contact information. You can use the vCard, for example, to import information into your computer's email program.

Removing a contact

Every so often, consider reviewing your phone's contacts. Purge those folks whom you no longer recognize or you've forgotten. It's simple:

1. **Locate the contact in your Contacts list and display the contact's information.**
2. **Press the Menu soft button.**
3. **Choose Delete Contact.**

   A warning may appear, depending on whether the contact has information linked from your social networking sites. If so, dismiss the warning.

4. **Touch OK to remove the contact from your phone.**

Because the Contacts list is synchronized with your Gmail contacts for your Google account, the contact is also removed there.

For some linked accounts, such as Facebook, deleting the account from your phone doesn't remove the human from your Facebook account. The warning that appears (before Step 4 in the preceding list) explains as much.

Part III
Beyond Telephone Communications

The 5th Wave   By Rich Tennant

"You can do a lot with a Droid, and I guess dressing one up in G.I. Joe clothes and calling it your little desk commander is okay, too."

You might believe that the plain old telephone service, commonly called POTS, was good only for making phone calls. It was all about verbal communication — talking with someone across town or across the country. Then again, the POTS was also used for computer communications, thanks to dial-up modems. And, though crude and not widely popular, video phones are out there.

Communication on your Droid 2 doesn't end with phone calls, and it isn't as limited as on the POTS. You have many ways to keep in touch on your Droid 2 with friends and family flung far and wide: text messaging, email, social networking, and even communications between your phone and other electronic devices. It's all covered in this part of the book.

9

The 21st Century Telegram (Texting)

In This Chapter

▶ Creating a text message

▶ Getting a text message

▶ Texting pictures, videos, and media items

▶ Managing your text messages

*T*exting is the cell phone feature that lets you choose to type, rather than talk, to exchange information. It's like turning the phone into a telegraph machine but without the tedium of having to learn Morse code. No, it's just the tedium of having to use your thumbs to type a message rather than your voice to speak that I find curious. Despite that, texting is extremely popular: It's a way to communicate quickly, to exchange information without an obtrusive interruption.

The process of texting need not be explained to anyone under the age of 25. Those kids text all the time. Heck, texting is a major moneymaker for the cellular companies. For the rest of us, texting is something you can do from time to time to stay in touch. It's handy. It might even be considered fun.

Message for You!

The common term for using a cell phone to send a text message to another cell phone is *texting*. I prefer to say it as "sending a text message." The program that handles this job on your Droid 2 is Text Messaging.

✔ Some Android applications can affect messaging. You're alerted to whether the program affects messaging before it's installed. See Chapter 20.

✔ Your cellular service plan may charge you per message for every text message you send. Some plans feature a given number of free messages per month. Other plans, favored by teenagers (and their parents), feature unlimited texting.

✔ Though using the Skype mobile app isn't exactly the same as sending a text message, it does let you send instant messages to folks. The person you're chatting with should have Skype installed, on either a PC or a mobile phone. Unlike text messages, Skype messages are free.

✔ The nerdy term for texting is *SMS*, which stands for Short Message Service.

Composing a new text message to a contact

Because most cell phones sport a text messaging feature, you can send a text message to just about any mobile number. It works like this:

1. **Open the Contacts icon on the Home screen.**

2. **Choose a contact, someone to whom you want to send a text message.**

3. **Touch the Message icon next to the contact's mobile number.**

   The Message icon looks like an envelope (refer to Figure 8-2, in Chapter 8).

   A message composition window appears, which also tracks your text conversation, similar to the one shown in Figure 9-1.

4. **Type the message text.**

   Be brief. A text message has a 160-character limit. You can check the screen to see how you're doing on that limit (refer to Figure 9-1). To help you stay under the limit, see the later sidebar "Common text-message abbreviations," for some common and useful text message shortcuts and acronyms.

5. **Touch the Send button.**

   The message is sent instantly. Whether the contact replies instantly depends. When the person replies, you see the message displayed (refer to Figure 9-1).

6. **Read the reply.**

7. **Repeat Steps 4 through 6 as needed — or eternally, whichever comes first.**

Stuff they've typed

Stuff you've typed

The contact you're texting

Voice input   Type here Smileys

Number of characters left to type

Figure 9-1: Typing a text message.

There's no need to continually look at your phone while waiting for a text message. Whenever your contact chooses to reply, you see the message recorded as part of an ongoing conversation. See the later section "Receiving a text message."

   ✔ You can send text messages only to cell phones. Grandma cannot receive text messages on her landline that she's had since the 1960s.

   ✔ You can use either keyboard — onscreen or sliding — to compose your text missive. See Chapter 4.

   ✔ You can press and hold the :-) button on the onscreen keyboard to see a whole range of smiles and other symbols (*emoticons*) that you can instantly insert into your messages.

   ✔ Yes, using Swype to type is much faster than using the standard onscreen keyboard. See Chapter 4.

   ✔ You can also dictate text messages by clicking the Microphone button on the onscreen keyboard. See Chapter 4 for more information on voice input.

- Add a subject to your message by touching the Menu soft button and choosing Add Subject.

- Phone numbers and email addresses sent in text messages become links. You can touch a link to call that number or visit the Web page.

- You cannot put the Enter (new line) key in the middle of a text message. In other words, a text message cannot appear with a break between two lines. To break a line between two messages, send two messages.

- Press the Back soft button to dismiss the onscreen keyboard, which can be useful when the keyboard obscures all or part of a message.

- Continue a conversation at any time: Open the Text Messaging application, peruse the list of existing conversations, and touch one to review what has been said or to pick up the conversation.

- Do not text and drive. Do not text and drive. Do not text and drive.

Common text-message abbreviations

Texting isn't about proper English. Indeed, many of the abbreviations and shortcuts used in texting are slowly becoming part of the English language, such as LOL and BRB.

The weird news is that these acronyms weren't invented by teenagers. Sure, the kids use them, but the acronyms find their roots in the Internet chat rooms of yesteryear. Regardless of a shortcut's source, you might find them handy for typing messages quickly. Or, maybe you can use this reference for deciphering an acronym's meaning. You can type acronyms in either upper- or lowercase.

2	To, also		IC	I see
411	Information		IDK	I don't know
BRB	Be right back		IMO	In my opinion
BTW	By the way		JK	Just kidding
CYA	See you		K	Okay
FWIW	For what it's worth		L8R	Later
FYI	For your information		LMAO	Laughing my [rear] off
GB	Goodbye		LMK	Let me know
GJ	Good job		LOL	Laugh out loud
GR8	Great		NC	No comment
GTG	Got to go		NP	No problem
HOAS	Hold on a second		OMG	Oh my goodness!

PIR	People in room (watching)	TTYL	Talk to you later
POS	Person over shoulder (watching)	TY	Thank you
QT	Cutie	U2	You too
ROFL	Rolling on the floor, laughing	UR	Your, you are
SOS	Someone over shoulder (watching)	VM	Voicemail
TC	Take care	W8	Wait
THX	Thanks	XOXO	Hugs and kisses
TIA	Thanks in advance	Y	Why?
TMI	Too much information	YW	You're welcome
TTFN	Ta-ta for now (goodbye)	ZZZ	Sleeping

Sending a text message when you know only the phone number

I recommend that you create a contact for anyone you plan to message. It just saves time to have the contact there, with — at minimum — a name and phone number. When you don't want to first create a contact, send any cell phone a text message by following these steps:

1. **Open the Text Messaging app.**

   You see a list of current conversations (if any), organized by contact name or phone number. If not, press the Back soft button.

2. **Choose New Text Message, found at the top of the touchscreen.**

3. **Input a cell phone number in the To field.**

   The onscreen keyboard automatically appears, though you have to touch the ?123 key to see the number keys.

   When the number you type matches one or more existing contacts, you see those contacts displayed. Choose one to send a message to that person; otherwise, continue typing the phone number.

4. **Touch the Enter Message Here text box.**

5. **Type your text message.**

6. **Touch the Send button to send the message.**

The message is sent instantly. You can wait for a reply or do something else with the phone, such as snooze it or choose to talk with a real person, face to face. Or, you can always get back to work.

Whether to send a text message or an email?

The concept of sending a text message is similar to sending an email message. Both methods of communication have advantages and disadvantages.

Text messages are short and to the point. They're informal, more like quick chats. Indeed, the speed of reply is often what makes text messaging useful. But, like email, sending a text message doesn't guarantee a reply.

An email message can be longer than a text message. You can receive email on any computer or device that accesses the Internet. Email message attachments are handled better, and more consistently, than text message (MMS) media. Though email isn't considered formal communication, not like a paper letter or a phone call, it ranks a bit higher in importance than text messaging.

You can send a single text message to multiple recipients: Just type additional phone numbers or contact names in the To field when you're composing a new message. You can use the icon that appears on the right side of the To field to browse the Contacts list.

Receiving a text message

Whenever a new text message comes in, you see a message appear at the top of the Droid 2 touchscreen. The message goes away quickly, and then you see the New Text Message notification, shown in the margin.

To view the message, pull down the notifications, as described in Chapter 3. Touch the messaging notification and that conversation window immediately opens.

Multimedia Messages

When a text message contains a bit of audio or video or a picture, it ceases becoming a mere text message and transforms into — *ta-da!* — a multimedia message. This type of message even has its own acronym, MMS, which supposedly stands for Multimedia Messaging Service.

✔ You can send pictures, video, and audio using multimedia messaging.

✔ There's no need to run a separate program or do anything fancy to send media in a text message; the same Text Messaging app is used on the Droid 2 for sending both text and media messages. Just follow the advice in this section.

✔ Not every mobile phone can receive MMS messages. Rather than receive the media item, the recipient is directed to a Web page where it can be viewed on the Internet.

Composing a multimedia message

One of the easiest ways to send a multimedia message is to start with the source, such as a picture or video stored on your phone. You can then choose to use MMS to share that media item, by heeding these directions:

1. **Locate in the Gallery the image or video you want to share.**

   You have to be viewing the image or video, so if it appears in a folder or an album, open the album and then touch the image to view it.

   See Chapter 17 for more information on how the Gallery works.

2. **Press the Menu soft button.**

3. **Choose Share.**

4. **Choose Text Messaging from the pop-up menu.**

   When the image or video is too large to send as a text message, you see a warning message. Dismiss the warning and try again with a smaller image or video.

5. **Type a contact name or phone number into the To text field.**

   Type only the first part of a contact name, and then choose the proper contact from the list that appears.

6. **Type a message in the Enter Message Here text box.**

7. **Touch the Send button to send the multimedia message.**

Unlike sending a text message, sending the multimedia message takes some time.

After the message is sent, you see a copy of the image or video in the message history.

Attaching media to a message

You don't need to go hunting for already created multimedia to send in a message; you can attach media directly to any message or ongoing conversation. It works like this:

1. **Compose a text message as you normally do.**

   Refer to the directions earlier in this chapter, in the section "Composing a new text message to a contact."

2. **Press the Menu soft button.**

3. **Choose Insert.**

   A pop-up menu appears, listing various media items you can attach to a text message. Here's a summary:

Take Picture: Take a picture right now and send it in a text message.

Picture: Choose an image stored in the phone's Gallery.

Audio: Attach a song from the music library.

Record Audio: Record an audio clip, such as your voice, and then send it.

Video: Choose a video you've taken with the phone and stored in the Gallery.

Record Video: Record a video and then send it as media in a text message.

Slideshow: Create a collection of photos to send together.

Name card: Attach contact information in the form of a vCard.

More options may appear on the menu, depending on which apps you have installed on your Droid 2.

4. Choose a media attachment from the pop-up menu.

What happens next depends on the attachment you've selected.

For the Pictures and Video attachments, you choose from among media stored on your phone.

For Capture Picture, Capture Video, and Record Audio, you create the media and then send it.

The Slideshow option presents a second screen, where you collect pictures from the Gallery. Use the icons on top of that screen to add pictures from the Gallery. Use the Preview button to examine the slideshow.

The Name Card option displays the phone's address book. Choose a contact and that contact's information is then translated into a vCard file and attached to your text message.

5. Optionally, compose a message to accompany the media attachment.

6. Touch the Send button to send your media text message.

In just a few, short, cellular moments, the receiving party will enjoy your multimedia text message.

✔ Not every phone is capable of receiving multimedia messages.

✔ Be aware of the size limit on the amount of media you can send; try to keep your video and audio attachments brief.

✔ A *vCard* is a contact-information file format, commonly used by email programs and contact management software. Whether the recipient can do anything with a vCard in a multimedia text message is up to the recipient's phone software.

Text messaging alternatives

Life doesn't turn totally dismal when you find yourself unduly bound by text message limitations on your cell phone contract. Just because you have a 250-message limit doesn't mean that you and your friends must stay horribly out of touch or that your thumbs will grow weak from lack of typing. A smattering of free alternatives to text messaging are available, all of which use the Internet and two of which come preinstalled on the Droid 2.

Talk: The Talk app connects you with the Google Talk service on the Internet. It's not really a texting app, but, rather, a chat app. You can summon a list of friends, all configured from your Google account, and chat it up — as long as they're available. My advice is to configure Google Talk on your computer first and then

you can find the same friends available on your Droid 2.

Skype mobile: The Skype mobile app can be used to chat as well, if you've set up a slew of friends and they also have Skype mobile or the full-fledged Skype on their desktop computers. Chatting on Skype is easy and free. Also see Chapter 21 for additional information on Skype mobile.

Of course, these apps use the Internet, so if your phone has a data restriction, you face, theoretically, a surcharge for using more Internet than your cell phone plan allows. Even so, text applications such as Google Talk and Skype mobile (chat) tend not to eat up much in terms of Internet usage. So type away!

Receiving a multimedia message

Multimedia attachments come into your Droid 2 just like any other text message does, but you see a thumbnail preview of whichever media was sent, such as an image, a still from a video, or a Play button to listen to audio. To preview the attachment, touch it. To do more with the multimedia attachment, long-press it. Choose how to deal with the attachment by selecting an option from the menu that's displayed.

For example, to save an image attachment, long-press the image thumbnail and choose the Save Picture command.

Some types of attachments, such as audio, cannot be saved.

Message Management

Even though I'm a stickler for deleting email after I read it, I don't bother deleting my text message threads. That might be because I receive far more email than text messages. Anyway, were I to delete a text message conversation, I would follow these exact steps:

1. **Open the conversation you want to remove.**

   Choose the conversation from the main Messaging screen.

2. **Touch the Menu soft button.**

3. **Choose Delete.**

4. **Touch the Yes button to confirm.**

   The conversation is gone.

If I wanted to delete every dang doodle conversation shown on the main Messaging screen, I'd follow these steps:

1. **Touch the Menu soft button.**

2. **Choose Select Multiple.**

3. **Touch the box next to each conversation you want to zap.**

   Obviously, if you want to keep one, don't touch its box.

   A green check mark appears by conversations slated for execution.

4. **Touch the Delete button.**

The selected messages are gone.

It's an emergency alert!

Another type of message you can receive on your Droid 2 is the emergency alert. To peruse your options, open the Applications Tray and open the EMERGENCY app. On the main screen, you see any pending alerts, such as evacuation alerts for your area or even AMBER Alerts. Of course, considering that the notification settings for the EMERGENCY app are preset to be active, you would have already seen such alerts on the Droid 2 home page.

To configure emergency alerts, press the Menu soft button when viewing the main Emergency Alert screen. Choose the command Emergency Alert Settings. You can review the types of available alerts by choosing the Receive Alerts menu command.

Press the Home soft button to exit the EMERGENCY app.

10

Mail of the Electronic Kind

*1*t has been said that the number-one reason for most people to use the Internet is email. That was probably before Facebook became popular. Even so, email is now the preferred form of written communications, eclipsing the personal, hand-written note years ago. Though some nostalgia over the change may linger, I have to confess that I can read none of my relatives' handwriting anyway, so perhaps the whole personal letter thing was over-blown to begin with. Anyway.

As a communications device, your Droid 2 is more than capable of sending and receiving email. In fact, because it's a Google phone, you instantly receive updates of your Gmail on the Droid 2. You can also configure the phone to access your non-Gmail email, making your electronic missives conveniently available wherever you go.

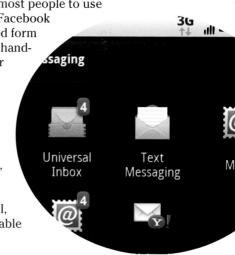

Mail Call!

Electronic mail is handled on the Droid 2 by two apps: Gmail and Email.

The Gmail app hooks directly into the Gmail account associated with your Google account. In fact, they're exact echoes of each other: The Gmail you receive on your computer is also received on your phone.

You can also use the Email app on your phone to connect to non-Gmail electronic mail, such as the standard mail service provided by your ISP.

Regardless of the app, electronic mail on your phone works just like it does on your computer: You can receive mail, create new messages, forward email, send messages to a group of contacts, and work with attachments, for example. As long as your phone has a data connection, email works just peachy.

- You can run the Gmail and Email apps by touching the Launcher on the Home screen and then locating the apps on the Applications Tray.

- Adding the Gmail or Email app icon to the Home screen is easy: See Chapter 22.

- A Gmail account was created for you when you signed up for a Google account. See Chapter 2 for more information about setting up a Google account.

- Both Gmail and Email programs can be configured to handle multiple email accounts, as discussed later in this chapter.

- Though you can use your phone's Web browser to visit the Gmail Web site, you should use the Gmail app to pick up your Gmail. I believe that you'll find the Gmail app's interface more usable on your phone than the Gmail Web site interface.

- If you forget your Gmail password, visit this Web address:

  www.google.com/accounts/ForgotPasswd

- Refer to Chapter 14 for information on the Droid 2 data connection.

You've Got Email

The Droid 2 works flawlessly with Gmail. In fact, if Gmail is already set up to be your main email address, you'll enjoy having access to your messages all the time by using your phone.

Regular email, handled by the Email program, must be set up before it can be used. See the later section "Email Configuration" for details. After completing that quick and occasionally painless setup, you can receive email on your phone just as you can on a computer.

Getting a new message

You're alerted to the arrival of a new email message in your phone by a notification icon. The icon differs between a new Gmail message and an Email message.

 For a new Gmail message, you see the New Gmail notification, shown in the margin, appear at the top of the touchscreen.

 For a new email message, you see the New Email notification.

To deal with the new-message notification, drag down the notifications and choose the appropriate one. You're taken right to your inbox to read the new message.

  ✔ See the later section "Setting email options" to set up how the phone reacts when you get a new email message.

  ✔ Refer to Chapter 3 for information on notifications and how to peruse them.

Checking the inbox

To peruse the mail you have, start your email program — Gmail for your Google mail or Email for other mail you have configured to work with the Droid 2 — and open your electronic inbox.

To check your Gmail inbox, start the Gmail app. It can be found on the Applications Tray, or it might dwell on the Home screen just to the left of the main Home screen. The Gmail inbox is shown in Figure 10-1.

 To open the inbox screen when you're reading a message, press the Back soft button.

To check your Email inbox, open the Email app. You're taken to the inbox for your primary email account, though when you have multiple email accounts on your Droid 2, you should use the Messaging app, covered in the next section.

Message subject

Unread missives   Sender

Message with attachment

Starred messages

Messages that have been read

Figure 10-1: The Gmail inbox.

✔ Gmail is organized using *labels*, not folders. To see your Gmail labels from the inbox, touch the Menu soft button and choose Go to Labels.

✔ Email messages that appear on your Droid 2 aren't deleted from the mail server. That way, you can read the same email messages later, using a computer. Most computer email programs, however, are configured to delete messages from the mail server. When they do, those messages may no longer show up on the Droid 2.

Visiting your universal inbox

The Messaging app is your home plate for every account on your Droid 2 that receives messages. It includes your email accounts, both Gmail and Email, as well as social networking sites and even text messaging, as shown in Figure 10-2.

Compose new message

All your messages

New message

Various email accounts

Figure 10-2: All your messages in one place.

New messages for an account are noted by a number shown in a red rect-angle (refer to Figure 10-2).

To view all messages — from email to Facebook updates — touch the Universal Inbox icon.

You compose a new message by touching the green Plus button (refer to Figure 10-2). From the menu that appears, choose an account or a method for creating the new message. You then see the appropriate program (Email, Facebook, Text Messaging) to craft the new message.

Notice that your Gmail inbox is missing from the Messaging window. Gmail is its own program on the Droid 2; your Gmail messages don't show up in the universal inbox. This situation may change in future Droid 2 software updates.

Reading an email message

As mail comes in, you can read it by choosing the New Email notification, described earlier in this chapter. You can also choose new email by viewing the inbox. The message appears on the screen, as shown in Figure 10-3. Reading and working with the message operate much the same as in any email program you've used.

Browse messages by touching the arrow buttons at the bottom of the message screen. In Figure 10-3, they point left and right, but in the Email program, shown in Figure 10-4, they point up and down. That difference was created merely to confuse you.

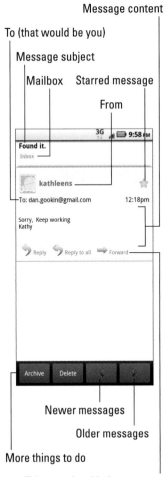

Message content

To (that would be you)

Message subject

Mailbox   Starred message

From

Figure 10-3: Reading a Gmail message on your phone.

Display boring information

Message content

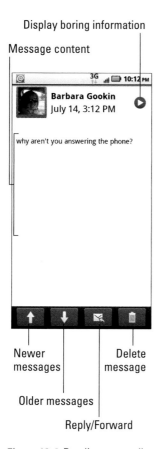

Newer messages

Delete message

Older messages

Reply/Forward

Figure 10-4: Reading an email message.

 The Email message window lacks as many buttons as the Gmail message window. To access additional commands, touch the Menu soft button.

Here are some things you can do with an email message you read on your Droid 2:

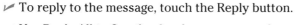

- ✔ To reply to the message, touch the Reply button.

- ✔ Use Reply All in Gmail only when everyone else *must* get a copy of your reply. Because most people find endless Reply All email threads annoying, use the Reply All option judiciously.

- ✔ Type or dictate your message reply; refer to Chapter 4 for information on typing and talking, if you're unfamiliar with either.

- Touch the Send button to send the reply message.

- Touch Cancel to cancel your reply, and then touch the Yes button to confirm.

- To forward a Gmail message, touch the Forward button. In the Email program, the Forward command appears on the same menu as the Reply command.

- Refer to the later section "Make Your Own Mail" for information on (surprisingly) composing a new electronic message, which also applies when you forward or reply to an email.

- When you touch the Star icon in a Gmail message, you're flagging the message. Those starred messages can be viewed or searched separately, making them easier to locate later.

- To delete a message, touch the Delete button. I see no reason to delete messages in the Email program, because they're deleted when your computer's email program picks them up later.

- I find it easier to delete (and manage) Gmail using a computer.

Searching Gmail

You can use the Search soft button to search Gmail on your phone, just as you can search for anything else. The key is to use the Search soft button while you're in the Gmail program. Here's how:

1. **Open the Gmail inbox.**

2. **Touch the Search soft button.**

3. **Type the text to find.**

   You can also dictate the text by first pressing the Microphone button on the keyboard and then speaking what you're trying to find.

4. **Touch the Search button to begin the search.**

   Peruse the results.

The search results are limited to text in those programs' messages. To perform a wider search throughout the entire phone, touch the Search soft button when viewing the Home screen.

Make Your Own Mail

Every so often, someone comes up to me and says, "Dan, you're a computer freak. You probably get a lot of email." I generally nod and smile. Then they say, "How can I get more email?" The answer is simple: To get mail, you have to send mail. Or, you can just be a jerk on a blog and leave your email address there. That works too, though I don't recommend it.

Composing a new Gmail message

Crafting a Gmail epistle on your Droid 2 works similarly to creating email on your computer. Figure 10-5 shows the basic setup. Here's how to compose a Gmail message:

Here's how to get there:

1. **Start the Gmail app.**

2. **Ensure that you're viewing the inbox.**

   If not, press the Back soft button.

 3. **Press the Menu soft button.**

4. **Choose Compose.**

   A new message screen appears, looking similar to Figure 10-5 but with none of the fields filled in.

Fun buttons

To (recipient)

Message subject

Message content

Onscreen keyboard

Figure 10-5: Writing a new Gmail message.

5. **Type the first few letters of a contact name, and then choose a matching contact from the list that's displayed.**

   You can also send to any valid email address not found in your Contacts list, by typing that address.

   To summon the CC field, press the Menu soft button and choose the command Add Cc/Bcc.

6. **Type a subject.**

7. **Type or dictate the message.**

8. **Touch the Send button to whisk your missive to the Internet for immediate delivery.**

Copies of the messages you send are saved in your Gmail account, which is accessed from your phone or from any computer connected to the Internet.

Composing a non-Gmail message

Sending an email message from any of your online email accounts other than Gmail is handled by the Messaging app. You can use the Email app as well, which works the same way, but I believe that you'll find using the Messaging app far more flexible. It works like this:

1. **Open the Messaging app.**

2. **Touch the green Plus button found in the upper right part of the screen.**

   If you have any draft messages pending, you see a list displayed. To start a new message, choose the New Message option.

3. **If prompted, choose the email account you want to use to send the message.**

   Or, you can choose to compose a text message, though that topic is covered specifically in Chapter 9.

4. **Craft the message.**

   Figure 10-6 illustrates the New Message window. Fill in the blanks just as you would when composing an email message on your computer.

5. **Touch the Send button to send the message.**

Copies of the messages you send in the Email program are stored in the Sent mailbox. To see that mailbox, open an individual email account from the main Messaging window. Press the Menu soft button and choose Folders to see the mailbox folders associated with that account.

The Font menu, shown in Figure 10-6, contains options for setting the text font (typeface), text size, and text foreground and background colors.

Text formatting   Insert smiley graphic

To (recipient)   Format bulleted list

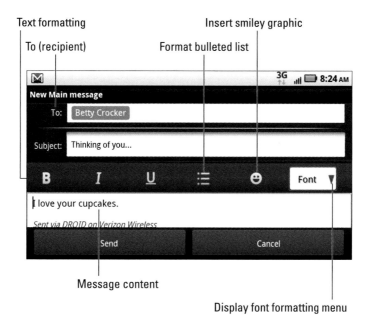

Message content

Display font formatting menu

Figure 10-6: Composing an email message.

To display the CC and BCC fields, press the Menu soft button and choose the Add CC and Add BCC commands.

Starting a new message from a contact

A quick and easy way to compose a new message is to find a contact and then create a message using that contact's information. Heed these steps:

1. **Open the Contacts list.**

   Touch the Contacts button to the right of the Launcher on the Home screen.

2. **Locate the contact to whom you want to send an electronic message.**

   Review Chapter 8 for ways to hunt down contacts in a long list.

3. **Touch the email icon next to the contact's email address.**

   The icon looks like a wee postage stamp with an at-symbol (@) in the middle.

4. **Choose the Compose command to use Gmail to send the message or choose Email to send an email message using your main email account.**

   At this point, creating the message works as described in the preceding sections; refer to them for additional information.

Message Attachments

You can send and receive email attachments by using your Droid 2. Though this feature is nice, an email attachment is more of a computer thing, not something that's wholly useful on a cell phone.

For receiving attachments, the Droid 2 lets you view the attachment, to see its contents. Not every attachment is viewable, however. It all depends on the type of file attached to the message.

Email messages with attachments are flagged in the inbox with the Paper Clip icon, which seems to be the standard I-have-an-attachment icon for most email programs. When you open one of those messages, you may see the attachment name appear, as shown in Figure 10-7. Touch the Preview button to witness the attachment on your phone.

Figure 10-7: An email attachment.

What happens after you touch the Preview button depends on the type of attachment. Sometimes, you see a list of apps from which you can choose one to open the attachment. Many Microsoft Office documents are opened by the QuickOffice app.

Some attachments cannot be opened. In those cases, use a computer to fetch the message and attempt to open the attachment. Or, you can reply to the message and inform the sender that you cannot open the attachment on your phone.

- ✔ Sometimes, pictures included in an email message aren't displayed. You find a Show Pictures button in the message, which you can choose to display the pictures.

- ✔ You cannot save certain email attachments on your phone. Wait until you retrieve these messages on your computer to save their attachments.

- ✔ You can add an attachment to an email message you create: Touch the Menu soft button and choose either the Attach or Attach Files command. You can then choose what to attach.

- ✔ You can browse the Gallery and choose a photo or video to email: Long-press the photo and choose the Share command from the bottom of the screen. Choose Email or Gmail from the pop-up menu to begin a new message with that photo or video attached.

- ✔ See Chapter 17 for more information on the Gallery.

Email Configuration

There are a few things you can do to customize the email experience on your Droid 2. You can add one or more of your Internet email accounts so that you can receive email on your phone at any time. You can customize an email signature, plus set other options, some of which are boring, so I don't discuss them in this section.

Setting up an email account

When you have and use non–Gmail email accounts, you can configure the phone's Email program to work with each of them. Here's how it's done:

1. **Start the My Accounts app.**

   The My Accounts app is found in the Applications Tray, which you access by touching the Launcher button at the bottom of the Home screen.

2. **Touch the Add Account button.**

3. **Choose the Email icon to add your Internet email account.**

   If prompted, agree to the Motorola Service agreement; touch the Next button.

   The Droid 2 needs to know information about your email account — those techy tidbits typically supplied by your ISP or whatever outfit provides your email service.

4. **Input the email address you use for the account.**

5. **Input the password for that account.**

6. **Remove the check mark by the option Automatically Configure Account.**

   Though the Droid 2 is good, it's not good enough to guess how to configure a standard Internet email account without some additional information.

   If you're configuring a Web-based email account, such as Windows Live or MobileMe, you can keep the check mark and touch the Next button. In many cases, the Droid 2 can automatically configure those accounts. If so, you see a Success message; touch the Done button and you're ready to use the account on the Droid 2.

7. **Touch the Next button.**

8. **Choose General Settings.**

9. **Fill in the information for account name, real name, and email address.**

For the Account Name field, type a name to recognize the account, such as Comcast Email or AOL Email or whatever name helps you recognize the account.

In the Real Name field, type your name or screen name or whatever name you want to appear in the From field of your outgoing email messages.

The Email Address field is the address your recipients use when replying to your messages.

10. **Touch the OK button.**

11. **Choose Incoming Server.**

12. **Fill in the fields per the information provided by your Internet service provider (ISP).**

For most ISP email, the server type is POP3 (shown as the POP mail server).

The Server field contains the name of the ISP's POP3 server.

The Port is 110 for a POP3 server, so you can leave that field as is.

The *username* is the name you use to log in to your ISP to retrieve email.

The password is your ISP email password.

13. **Touch the OK button.**

14. **Choose Outgoing Server.**

15. **Fill in the fields.**

Fill in the SMTP Server name as provided by your ISP.

The Port is 25 for SMTP servers.

As you did in Step 12, fill in your username and password for your ISP's email. If the information is already there, confirm that it's correct.

16. **Touch the OK button.**

17. **Choose Other Settings.**

18. **Ensure that Never Delete Messages is chosen from the list.**

By selecting Never Delete Messages, you ensure that email you receive on your Droid 2 can be picked up later when you use your computer.

19. **Touch OK.**

20. **Touch OK again to create the email account.**

The account is now listed in the My Accounts screen, along with Google and Facebook and whatever other accounts you're accessing from your Droid 2.

You can set up a ton of email accounts on the Droid 2, one for each email account you have. They all appear in a list in the Messaging program, as shown earlier, in Figure 10-2.

Not every Web-based email account can be automatically configured by the Droid 2. When doubt exists, you see an appropriate warning message. In most cases, the warning message also explains how to properly configure the Web-based email account to work with your phone.

You can add a Yahoo! Mail account directly: In Step 3 of the preceding list, choose the Yahoo! Mail icon.

Creating a signature

I highly recommend that you create a custom email signature for sending messages from your phone. Here's my signature:

```
DAN

This was sent from my Droid 2.
Please forgive the typos.
```

To create a signature for Gmail, obey these directions:

1. **Start Gmail.**

2. **Press the Menu soft button.**

3. **Choose More and then Settings.**

   If you see no settings, choose Back to Inbox and repeat Steps 2 and 3.

4. **Choose Signature.**

5. **Type or dictate your signature.**

6. **Touch OK.**

You can obey these same steps to change your signature; the existing signature shows up after Step 4.

To set a signature for the Email program, heed these steps:

1. **In the Email program, start a new message.**

2. **Press the Menu soft button.**

3. **Choose More and then choose Email Settings.**

4. **Choose Compose Options.**

5. **Edit the Email Signature area to reflect your new signature.**

   The preset signature is *Sent via DROID on Verizon Wireless.* Feel free to edit it at your whim.

6. **Touch the Done button.**

7. **Press the Back button to return to the message, where you can touch Cancel to stop composing a new message.**

The signature you set appears in all outgoing messages.

Setting email options

A smattering of interesting email settings are worth looking into. To reach the Settings screen in Gmail, follow Steps 1 through 3 in the first set of steps in the preceding section; for Email, follow Steps 1 through 4 in the second set of steps.

Here are some items worthy of note:

- ✔ Specify a default email account in the Email program by choosing Default Email Account. Then choose the account name you want to use for sending messages.

- ✔ To specify how frequently the Email program checks for new messages, choose Email Delivery on the Email Settings screen. Put a check mark by Data Push and then set the check frequency by choosing the Fetch Schedule item.

- ✔ Choose Email Notifications in Gmail, or Notifications in Email, to have the phone alert you to new messages.

- ✔ Choose a specific ringtone for the account by touching Select Ringtone, beneath Notifications for Gmail. In the Email program, choose Email Notifications and then Select Ringtone.

- ✔ Specify whether the phone vibrates upon the receipt of new email by choosing Vibrate.

- ✔ The ringtone and vibration options are available only when Email Notifications is selected.

Fun on the Web

In This Chapter

▶ Looking at a Web page on your phone

▶ Browsing around the Web

▶ Bookmarking pages

▶ Working with multiple browser windows

▶ Searching the Web

▶ Sending a link to a friend

▶ Downloading stuff from the Web

▶ Changing the home page

*A*s a Web designer myself, I confess that no one truly sets out to craft Web pages for easy viewing on a doinky cell phone screen. Sure, special *mobile* versions of Web pages are available; my Wambooli Web site has such a feature. But Web designers secretly desire you to view their work on a lovely, roomy, pixel-laden desktop monitor.

Despite the yearning of Web page designers, it's entirely possible to venture out on the Web using your Droid 2. Though the screen may not be large enough to show you everything, the browsing experience you enjoy on your computer carries over quite well to your phone. This chapter shows you how everything works and offers some tips to make your mobile Web browsing adventures more enjoyable.

✔ If possible, activate the Droid 2 Wi-Fi connection before you venture out on the Web. Though you can use the phone's cellular data connection, the Wi-Fi connection can be *far* faster. See Chapter 14 for more information.

- ✔ Depending on your cell plan, you may be charged extra for data sent and received by your Droid 2.

- ✔ The Droid 2 has apps for Gmail, Facebook, Twitter, and YouTube and, potentially, other popular locations or activities on the Web. I highly recommend using these applications on the phone over visiting the Web sites using the phone's browser.

Behold the Web Page

The World Wide Web should be familiar to you. Using the World Wide Web on a cell phone, however, may not be. Don't worry: Consider this section your quick orientation.

Viewing the Web

Begin your venture out on the Internet by starting the Browser app. You might find it on the main Home screen, or you can locate it on the Applications Tray. The Browser app is your phone's Web browser. Figure 11-1 shows how it looks.

Because the Droid 2 screen isn't a full desktop screen, not every Web page looks good on it. Here are a few tricks you can use:

- ✔ Pan the Web page by dragging your finger across the touchscreen. You can pan up, down, left, and right.

- ✔ Double-tap the screen to zoom in or zoom out.

- ✔ Pinch the screen to zoom out, or spread two fingers to zoom in.

- ✔ Tilt the phone to its side to read a Web page in Landscape mode. Then you can spread or double-tap the touchscreen to make teensy text more readable.

Visiting a Web page

To visit a Web page, type its address in the Address box (refer to Figure 11-1) and then type the Web page address. You can also type a search word, if you don't know the exact address of a Web page. You can touch the Enter or Return button on the sliding keyboard or the Go button on the onscreen keyboard to search the Web or visit a specific Web page.

If you don't see the Address box, swipe your finger so that you can see the top of the window, where the Address box lurks.

Bookmark page

Address box

Web page

Use the phone's location services

Figure 11-1: The Browser.

You click links on a page by using your finger on the touchscreen. A better way is to use the arrow keys on the sliding keyboard: Press an arrow key to highlight various links on the page. Press the OK key to select a link.

✔ To reload a Web page, press the Menu soft button and choose the Refresh command. Refreshing updates a Web site that changes often, and the command can also be used to reload a Web page that may not have completely loaded the first time.

✔ To stop a Web page from loading, touch the X button that appears to the left of the Address box. (The X button replaces the Bookmarks button — refer to Figure 11-1.)

Browsing back and forth

To return to a previous Web page, press the Back soft button. It works just like clicking the Back button on a computer's Web browser.

The Forward button also exists in the Browser program: Press the Menu soft button and choose the Forward command.

To review the long-term history of your Web browsing adventures, follow these steps:

1. **Press the Menu soft button.**

2. **Choose Bookmarks.**

3. **At the top of the Bookmarks page, choose History.**

To view a page you visited weeks or months ago, you can choose a Web page from the History list.

To clear the History list, press the Menu soft button while viewing the list and choose the Clear History command.

Using bookmarks

Bookmarks are those electronic breadcrumbs you can drop as you wander the Web. Need to revisit a Web site? Just look up its bookmark. This advice assumes, of course, that you bother to create (I prefer *drop*) a bookmark when you first visit the site. Here's how it works:

1. **Visit the Web page you want to bookmark.**

2. **Touch the Bookmark button, found at the top of the Browser window.**

   Refer to Figure 11-1 to see the location of the Bookmark button. After pressing the button, you see the Bookmarks screen, shown in Figure 11-2. The screen lists your bookmarks, showing Web site thumbnail previews.

3. **Touch the Add button.**

   The Add button appears in the upper left square on the Bookmarks screen (refer to Figure 11-2). It has the name of the site or page you're bookmarking just below the square.

4. **If necessary, edit the bookmark name.**

   The bookmark is given the Web page name, which might be kind of long. I usually edit the name to make it shorter so that it fits beneath the thumbnail square.

5. **Touch OK.**

After the bookmark is set, it appears in the list of bookmarks. You can swipe the list downward to see the bookmarks and all their fun thumbnails.

Another way to add a bookmark is to touch the Most Visited tab at the top of the Bookmarks screen (refer to Figure 11-2). That screen lists the Web pages you visit most often. To add one of those pages, long-press the thumbnail and choose the command Add Bookmark.

Add bookmark   Browsing history

Display bookmarks

Frequently visited
Web pages

Bookmark thumbnails

Figure 11-2: Adding a bookmark.

🖙 To visit a bookmark, press the Menu soft button and choose the
Bookmarks command. Touch a bookmark thumbnail to visit that site.

🖙 Remove a bookmark by long-pressing its thumbnail on the Bookmarks
screen. Choose the command Delete Bookmark. Touch the OK button
to confirm.

🖙 Bookmarked Web sites can also be placed on the Home screen: Long-
press the bookmark thumbnail and choose the command Add Shortcut
to Home.

🖙 You can switch between Thumbnail and List views for your bookmarks:
When viewing the Bookmarks screen, press the Menu soft button and
choose the List View command to switch to List view. To return to
Thumbnail view, press the Menu soft button and choose Thumbnail View.

✔ You can obtain the MyBookmarks app at the Android Market. The app can import your Internet Explorer, Firefox, and Chrome bookmarks from your Windows computer into the Droid 2. See Chapter 20 for more information on the Android Market.

 ✔ Refer to Chapter 4 for information on editing text on the Droid 2.

Managing multiple Web page windows

Because the Browser app sports more than one window, you can have multiple Web pages open at a time on your Droid 2. You can summon another browser window in one of several ways:

 ✔ *To open a link in another window,* press and hold that link by using your finger or holding down the OK key on the sliding keyboard. Choose the command Open in New Window from the menu that appears.

 ✔ *To open a bookmark in a new window,* long-press the bookmark and choose the command Open in New Window.

 ✔ *To open a blank browser window,* press the Menu soft button and choose New Window.

You switch between windows by pressing the Menu soft button and choosing the Windows command. All open Browser windows are displayed on the screen; switch to a window by choosing it from the list. Or, you can close a window by touching the Minus button to the right of the window's name.

New windows open using the home page that's set for the Browser application. See the section "Setting a home page," later in this chapter, for information.

Searching the Web

The handiest way to find things on the Web is to use the Google widget, often found floating on the first Home screen to the left of the main Home screen, and shown in Figure 11-3. Use the Google widget to type something to search for or touch the Microphone button to dictate what you want to find on the Internet.

Figure 11-3: The Google widget.

To search for something anytime you're viewing a Web page in the Browser app, press the Search soft button. Type the search term into the box. You can choose from a suggestions list, shown in Figure 11-4, or touch the Go button to complete the search using the Google search engine.

Figure 11-4: Searching for things on the Internet.

To find text on the Web page you're looking at, rather than search the entire Internet, follow these steps:

1. **Visit the Web page where you want to find a specific tidbit o' text.**

2. **Press the Menu soft button.**

3. **Choose the More command.**

4. **Choose Find on Page.**

5. **Type the text you're searching for.**

6. **Use the left- or right-arrow button to locate that text on the page — backward or forward, respectively.**

   The found text appears highlighted in green.

7. **Touch the X button when you're done searching.**

See Chapter 22 for more information on widgets, such as the Google widget.

Sharing a page

The Android operating system lets you easily share information you find on your phone. With regard to the Web pages you visit, you can easily share links and bookmarks. Follow these steps:

1. **Long-press the link or bookmark you want to share.**

2. **Choose the command Share Link.**

   A pop-up menu of places to share appears, looking similar to Figure 11-5. The variety and number of items on the Share Via menu depends on the applications installed on your phone. For example, you might see Twitter or Facebook appear, if you've set up those social networking sites on your Droid 2 (see Chapter 12).

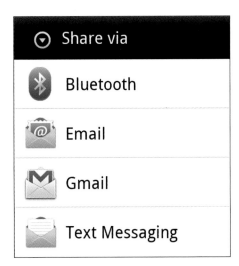

Figure 11-5: Options for sharing a Web page.

3. **Choose a method to share the link.**

   For example, choose Email to send the link by mail or Text Messaging to share via a text message.

4. **Do whatever happens next.**

   Whatever happens next depends on how you're sharing the link.

Most likely, whatever happens next opens another application, where you can complete the process. Refer to various parts of this book for specific information.

The Perils and Joys of Downloading

One of the most abused words in all computerdom is *download*. People don't understand what it means. It's definitely not a synonym for *transfer* or *copy*, though that's how I hear it used most often.

For the sake of the Droid 2, a *download* is a transfer of information from another location to your phone. When you send something from the phone, you *upload* it. There. Now the nerd in me feels much better.

You can download information from a Web page into your phone. It doesn't work exactly like downloading does for a computer, which is why I wrote this section.

- There's no need to download program files to your Droid 2. If you want new software, you can obtain it from the Android Market, covered in Chapter 20.
- When the phone is downloading information, you see the Downloading notification.

Grabbing an image from a Web page

The simplest thing to download is an image from a Web page. It's cinchy: Long-press the image. You see a pop-up menu appear, from which you choose the command Save Image.

- The image is copied and stored on your Droid 2 — specifically, in the Gallery in a special folder named Download.
- Refer to Chapter 17 for information on the Gallery.
- Technically, an image is stored on the phone's MicroSD card. You can read about storage on the MicroSD card in Chapter 13.

Downloading a file

When a link opens a document on a Web page, such as a Microsoft Word document or a PDF (Adobe Acrobat) file, you can download that information to your phone. Simply long-press the download link and choose the command Save Link from the menu that appears.

You can view the link by referring to the Download History screen. This screen appears after the download is complete. See the next section.

Reviewing your downloads

You can view downloaded information by perusing the Download History screen, shown in Figure 11-6. That screen normally appears right after you download anything, or you can summon it at any time while using the Browser app, by pressing the Menu soft button, choosing the More command, and then choosing Downloads.

Figure 11-6: The Download History screen.

The stuff you download is viewed by using special apps on your phone, such as the QuickOffice app, which can view Microsoft Office files, or QuickPDF, which displays PDF documents. Don't fret the process: Simply choose from the Download History screen the item you downloaded and you can then see it on your phone.

✔ Well, of course, some of the things you can download you cannot view. When that happens, you see an appropriately rude error message.

✔ You can quickly review any download by choosing the Download notification.

Web Controls and Settings

More options and settings and controls exist for the Browser program than just about every other program I've used on the Droid 2. It's complex. Rather than bore you with every dang doodle detail, I thought I'd present just a few of the options worthy of your attention.

Setting a home page

The *home page* is the first page you see when you start the Browser application, and it's the first page that's loaded when you fire up a blank window. To
set your home page, heed these directions:

1. **Browse to the page you want to set as the home page.**

2. **Press the Menu soft button.**

3. **Choose More.**

4. **Choose Settings.**

   A massive list of options and settings appears.

5. **Choose Set Home Page.**

   It's way down the list, so swipe the list downward as necessary.

   After choosing the Set Home Page command, you see a Set Home Page
   box, where you can type the home page address. Because you obeyed
   Step 1, you don't need to type that address now.

6. **Touch OK.**

   The home page is set.

Unless you've already set a new home page, the Droid 2 comes configured
with the Google Mobile search page as your home page.

If you want your home page to be blank (not set to any particular Web page),
set the name of the home page (refer to Step 5) to `about:blank`. That's the
word *about,* a colon, and then the word *blank,* with no period at the end and
no spaces in the middle. I prefer a blank home page because it's the fastest
Web page to load. It's also the Web page with the most accurate information.

Changing the way the Web looks

You can do a few things to improve the way the Web looks on your phone.
First and foremost, don't forget that you can orient the phone horizontally to
see a wide view on any Web page.

From the Settings screen, you can also adjust the text size used to display a
Web page. Heed these steps:

1. **Press the Menu soft button.**

2. **Choose More.**

3. **Choose Settings.**

4. **Choose Text Size.**

5. **Select a better size from the menu.**

   For example, try Large or Huge.

6. **Press the Back soft button to return to the Web page screen.**

I don't make any age-related comments about text size at this time, and especially at this point in my life.

Setting privacy and security options

With regard to security, my advice is always to be smart and think before doing anything questionable on the Web. Use common sense. One of the most effective ways that the Bad Guys win is by using *human engineering* to try to trick you into doing something you normally wouldn't do, such as click a link to see a cute animation or a racy picture of a celebrity or politician. As long as you use your noggin, you should be safe.

As far as the phone's settings go, most of the security options are already enabled for you, including the blocking of pop-up windows (which normally spew ads).

If Web page cookies concern you, you can clear them from the Settings window. Follow Steps 1 through 3 in the preceding section and choose the option Clear All Cookie Data.

You can also choose the command Clear Form Data and remove the check mark from Remember Form Data. These two settings prevent any characters you've input into a text field from being summoned automatically by someone who may steal your phone.

You might be concerned about various warnings regarding location data. What they mean is that the phone can take advantage of your location on Planet Earth (using the Droid 2 GPS or global satellite positioning system) to help locate businesses and people near you. I see no security problem in leaving that feature on, though you can disable location services from the Browser's Settings screen: Remove the check mark by Enable Location. You can also choose the item Clear Location Access to wipe out any information saved in the phone and used by certain Web pages.

See the earlier section "Browsing back and forth" for steps on clearing your Web browsing history.

The Social Networking Thing

In This Chapter

▶ Accessing Facebook on your phone

▶ Updating your Facebook status

▶ Sharing photos on Facebook

▶ Configuring Twitter for the Droid 2

▶ Sending a tweet

▶ Accessing other social networking sites

*I*t's entirely possible to be quite a social person, to have hundreds (if not thousands) of friends, and to have people cling to your every movement yet never leave your house. That's the miracle of social networking on the Internet. Web sites such as Facebook and Twitter have thrust even the most mundane human life into a 24-hour digital ogle-fest. Thanks to the Droid 2 and its social networking abilities, you can do more to become a digital social networking butterfly. Now you can fete the world with your life broadcast digitally on the Internet *and* leave your house.

Your Life on Facebook

The most popular of all social networking sites is Facebook. At this Internet destination, you can offer your thoughts, say what you're doing, share photos and videos, play games, and enjoy other diversions. To get started, you need a Facebook account, if you don't have one already. Then you can use the Facebook or social networking apps on your Droid 2 to keep up with your busy online social life.

✔ Though you can access Facebook on the Web by using the Browser app, I highly recommend that you use the Facebook app on the Droid 2.

✔ You can also use the Social Networking app to view or set Facebook status updates, though it's not as useful as the Facebook app.

✔ Facebook is one of the most popular sites on the Internet at the time this book goes to press. On some days, it sees more Internet traffic than Google.

Creating a Facebook account

To use Facebook on your Droid 2, you must have a Facebook account. The easiest way to do that is to visit www.facebook.com on your computer and register for a new account. Remember your login name and password.

You confirm your Facebook account by replying to an email message. After you do that, Facebook is ready for your thoughts and photos and other personal details. Also, after confirming your Facebook account, you can set it up on your phone by following these steps:

1. **From the Home screen, touch the Launcher button to display the Applications Tray.**

2. **Open the My Accounts icon.**

    If you see a Facebook account listed, you're done. Otherwise:

3. **Touch the Add Account button.**

4. **Choose Facebook.**

5. **Touch the Email text box.**

6. **Type the email address you used to sign up for Facebook.**

7. **Touch the Password text box.**

8. **Type your Facebook password.**

    The characters you type turn into big dots so that no one looking at the phone can see your password.

9. **Touch the Next button.**

    The Droid 2 signs you in to your Facebook account.

10. **If you see an alert about Facebook now being the source for your contact pictures, touch the OK button.**

    The Droid 2 synchronizes information between your phone's Contacts list and your Facebook Friends list. Part of that process includes the pictures, some of which may be missing for your contacts but available on Facebook.

11. **Touch the Done button.**

    You're done.

Adding your Facebook account by following these steps doesn't install the Facebook app on your phone. To do that, see the later section "Visiting Facebook."

If you opt not to install the Facebook app, you can use the Social Networking app that comes with the Droid 2 to manage your Facebook account, though I believe that you'll find the Facebook app a better resource.

Checking your social networking status

The Social Networking app keeps track of your status updates and news feeds on Facebook (as well as on other social networking sites). Start the app from the Launcher to review current status updates.

You also see Facebook status updates whenever you receive a phone call from a Facebook friend. The friend's status appears below their contact information during the incoming call.

The Social Networking app is continuously updated; keep it visible on the Droid 2 touchscreen to instantly monitor status updates as they flow in.

You can find new messages and notifications from Facebook by using the Messaging app.

Visiting Facebook

The true interface to Facebook on your Droid 2 is the Facebook app. You can download the app from the Android Market, as described in Chapter 20, or you can use the barcode that appears in the margin to quickly obtain an app link, as described in this book's Introduction.

Start the Facebook app after it's downloaded. You may need to accept an end user license agreement. Then you have to log in to your Facebook account using the Facebook app. (The Facebook app is different from the Social Networking app; both require you to log in.)

The main Facebook screen is shown in Figure 12-1. It's a rather simplistic interface, yet it's the spot where you can check most of the things you do on Facebook, including uploading a photo or keeping your status up-to-date wherever you go with your Droid 2.

Figure 12-1: Facebook on your phone.

When you choose an item from the main Facebook screen, another screen opens, with more information. Here are the items on the main Facebook screen:

News Feed: View status updates newly added photos, and other information about your Facebook friends.

Profile: Review your personal Facebook page, your status updates, and whatever else you're wasting your time doing on Facebook.

Friends: See a list of all your Facebook friends, search for friends, or touch a friend's icon to see their status and other information.

Photos: Review your Facebook photo albums or use the Droid to take a digital picture and then send it to Facebook. See the later section "Sending a picture to Facebook."

Events: Check for upcoming birthdays, anniversaries, parties, or events you plan to attend.

Messages: See any private messages sent to you on Facebook.

Requests: Review any requests made by friends for you to participate in many interesting and tedious diversions.

 To return to the main Facebook screen from another area, press the Back soft button.

- ✔ You can also check the status for your Facebook friends by reviewing the Social Networking widgets on the Home screen. The widgets are preinstalled on the leftmost Home screen.

- ✔ When things related to you happen on Facebook, you see the Facebook notification icon. When you receive lots of Facebook notices or updates, a number in a red circle appears on the icon, indicating the number of new Facebook updates.

- ✔ Sometimes, choosing a Facebook notification opens the Facebook app, and sometimes it opens the Browser app to visit Facebook on the Web.

- ✔ Review Chapter 3 to see how to deal with notifications.

- ✔ See Chapter 22 for information on placing the Facebook app icon on the Home screen.

- ✔ To sign out of Facebook on your phone, touch the Menu soft button when viewing the main Facebook screen and then choose the Logout command. Touch the Yes button to confirm.

Setting your Facebook status

With Facebook on your phone, you can add a new status, such as "Taking a shower now and it's getting extremely difficult to type on the touchscreen," while you're standing there naked in the shower and typing on a cell phone (which I don't recommend). Still, your Facebook friends may live for these moments.

To update your Facebook status on the Droid 2, follow these steps:

1. From the main Facebook screen, choose either News Feed or Profile.

2. Type or dictate your status in the What's On Your Mind text box.

Your Facebook friends see your status update instantly, plus they see the tiny Mobile icon appear next to your status update, as shown in Figure 12-2.

Dan Gookin Once my cat figures out how to open the door, he will no longer need me

28 seconds ago via Facebook for Android · Comment · Like

Figure 12-2: A mobile Facebook update.

The Mobile icon tells your pals that the update was made by using your cell phone.

Sending a picture to Facebook

One of the handiest reasons to use Facebook on a cell phone is that you can take a picture and instantly upload it. This feature lets you easily capture and share various intimate and private moments of your life with drooling throngs of humanity.

The key to sharing a picture on Facebook is to locate the wee Camera icon, found to the left of the What's On Your Mind text box. After touching that icon, you see a pop-up appear, with these two options:

Choose from Gallery: After choosing this option, you're switched to the Gallery app, from which you can choose any photo already stored on your phone.

Capture a Photo: After you choose this option, the Droid 2 switches into Camera mode, where you can snap a picture of whatever is around you. After taking the picture, you see a quick prompt, from which you can choose Done to accept the picture, Retake to try to take the picture again, or Cancel to give up and go back to playing horseshoes.

Whether you choose a picture from the Gallery or take a picture using the Droid 2 camera, you end up at a screen similar to the one shown in Figure 12-3. Use this screen to add a caption to the image and publish it on Facebook.

After a spell, the image is uploaded to your Facebook Mobile Uploads album.

You can use the Facebook app to view the image in Facebook, or you can use Facebook on any computer connected to the Internet.

> ✔ Images are uploaded into the Mobile album, unless you choose another album, as shown in Figure 12-3.

> ✔ Refer to Chapter 16 to see how the Droid 2 camera works.

> ✔ See Chapter 17 for more information on using the Gallery app.

Search Facebook

Choose an album to upload into

Photo

Chicken out

Send image to Facebook

Optional image caption

Figure 12-3: Uploading an image to Facebook.

Changing various Facebook settings

The commands that control Facebook are stored on the Settings screen, which you access by touching the Menu soft button while viewing the main Facebook screen (shown in Figure 12-1) and choosing the Settings command.

Most settings are self explanatory: You simply choose which Facebook events you want the Droid 2 to monitor. Two items you might want to set are the refresh interval and the way the phone alerts you to new Facebook activities.

Choose Refresh Interval to specify how often the Droid 2 checks for new Facebook activities. You might find the one-hour value to be too long for your active Facebook social life, so choose something quicker. Or, to disable Facebook notifications, choose Never.

Three options determine how the Droid 2 reacts to Facebook updates:

Vibrate: Vibrates the phone

Phone LED: Flashes the notification light on the front of the Droid 2

Notification Ringtone: Plays a specific ringtone

For the notification ringtone, choose the Silent option when you want the phone not to make noise upon encountering a Facebook update.

Become Famous with Twitter

The Twitter social networking site proves the hypothesis that everyone will be famous on the Internet for 140 words or fewer.

Like Facebook, Twitter is used to share your existence with others or simply to follow what others are up to or thinking. It sates some people's craving for attention and provides the bricks that pave the road to fame — or so I believe. I'm not a big Twitter fan, but your phone is capable of letting you *tweet* from wherever you are.

- They say that of all the people who have accounts on Twitter, only a small portion of them actively use the service.

- A message posted on Twitter is a *tweet*.

- You can post messages on Twitter or follow other people or organizations who post messages.

Setting up Twitter on the Droid 2

My advice is to set up an account on Twitter using a computer, not your phone. Visit `http://twitter.com` on a computer and follow the directions there for creating a new account.

After creating a Twitter account, you use the Social Networking app on your phone to log in to Twitter and then view Twitter updates or make tweets. To set up Twitter using the Social Networking app, follow these steps:

1. **Start the My Accounts app.**

   You can also use the Social Networking app to set up your Twitter account, but doing so just takes you back to the My Accounts app. So I'm saving you two steps.

2. **Touch the Add Account button.**

3. **Choose Twitter.**

4. **Type your Twitter username into the Username field.**

5. **Type your Twitter password.**

6. **Touch the Next button.**

   You're prompted to use Twitter as the source for your contact pictures. My advice: If you're already using Facebook as the source, touch No.

7. **Touch the Done button.**

   Your Twitter account is set up for social networking on the Droid 2.

You can now use the Social Networking app to review messages, or tweets, sent by those whom you're following on Twitter.

You can also review tweets by opening the Messaging app.

Getting the Twitter app

Perhaps the best way to use Twitter on your Droid 2 is to obtain the Twitter app. It provides a better interface into Twitter than the Social Networking and Messaging apps do on your phone. And, it looks more "Twittery," like the Twitter Web site.

The Twitter app can be obtained from the Android Market. Use the barcode in the margin to see a quick link to the app. Refer to Chapter 20 for additional information on installing the app on your phone.

Tweeting to other twits

The Twitter app (see the preceding section) provides an excellent interface to many Twitter tasks, as shown in Figure 12-4. The two most basic tasks, however, are reading and writing tweets.

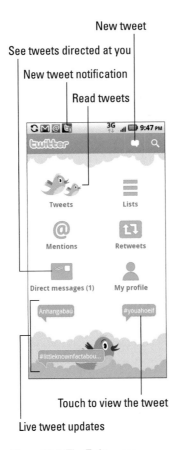

New tweet

See tweets directed at you

New tweet notification

Read tweets

Tweets   Lists

Mentions   Retweets

Direct messages (1)   My profile

Touch to view the tweet

Live tweet updates

Figure 12-4: The Twitter app.

To read tweets, choose the Tweets item (refer to Figure 12-4). Recent tweets are displayed in a list, with the most recent information at the top. Scroll the list by swiping it with your finger.

To tweet, touch the Create Tweet icon found in the upper right corner of the screen (refer to Figure 12-4). Use the Create Tweet screen to send text, upload an image from the Gallery, or take a new picture.

You can also compose a new tweet by using the Social Networking or Messaging apps, though the techniques are rather laborious compared with using the Twitter app.

Other Social Networking Opportunities

The Web seems to see a new social networking phenomenon just about every week. The field isn't limited to Facebook and Twitter, though both capture a lot of media attention and are extremely popular.

Other common social networking sites include

- Google Buzz
- LinkedIn
- Meebo
- MySpace

 These sites may have special Android apps you can install on your Droid 2, such as the MySpace Mobile app.

As with Facebook and Twitter, you should always configure an account using a computer and then set up options on your phone.

After adding some social networking apps, you may see them appear on various Share menus on the Droid 2. Use the Share menus to help you share media files with your online social networking pals.

Share and Synchronize

In This Chapter

▷ Getting the phone and the computer to talk

▷ Mounting the phone as computer storage

▷ Replacing the MicroSD card

▷ Synchronizing media with doubleTwist

▷ Working with the V CAST Media Manager

*N*o man is an island. Neither should a technological gizmo be an island. Not only is water bad for a gizmo's electronics, but it would also be lonely. The Droid 2 is anything but lonely, thanks to its wireless networking abilities. I believe that the Droid 2, beyond those abilities, also yearns for a physical form of communications; it dreams of being able to touch something. . . .

To fulfill your phone's desires, I offer you this chapter. Its topic is the exchange of information between your phone and your computer. It's called *sharing*, which you learned about in kindergarten. The things to share are your phone's contacts, photos, music, and videos and other types of digital information that flows easily and quickly between the Droid 2 and your computer — as long as you heed the advice in this chapter.

Mode

Windows Media Sync

USB Mass Storage

Make the Connection

ge Only

The Droid 2 does a super job of sharing your stuff on the Internet. You can upload images to the Picasa Web site or buy music from the Amazon MP3 store, for example, and the phone always synchronizes information between itself and various online Google applications, such as Calendar and Gmail.

You can also share digital information between your Droid 2 and your computer. Before that happens, you need to properly connect the two gizmos, both physically and mentally. This section covers both aspects.

Connecting the phone to the computer

Communication between your computer and the Droid 2 works fastest when both devices are physically connected. That connection happens by using the USB cable that came with the phone. Like nearly every computer cable in the Third Dimension, the USB cable has two ends:

✔ The A end of the USB cable plugs into the computer.

✔ The micro–USB end of the cable plugs into the left flank of the Droid 2.

Follow these steps to connect the phone to the computer and put the two devices on speaking terms:

1. **Plug the USB cable into one of the computer's USB ports.**

2. **Plug the USB cable into the phone.**

    If the phone is turned on, an alert may sound. If you can see the screen, you see an alert notification: USB Connection. The USB notification icon (shown in the margin) appears.

    At this point, you can choose to do nothing; to make the phone and the computer start talking, however, you have to deal with the USB notification.

3. **Pull down the notifications.**

    Refer to Chapter 3 for specific instructions on pulling down notifications.

4. **Choose USB Connection.**

    You see four methods for using the USB connection to your computer, as shown in Figure 13-1.

    You can use any of the first three options — PC Mode, Windows Media Sync, or USB Mass Storage — for sharing and synchronizing between the Droid 2 and your computer. Each one is subtly different. For example, Windows Media Sync simply tells the computer that the Droid 2 is a media device, which lets you more easily share music, photos, and videos.

    The fourth option, Charge Only, uses the USB cable to recharge the battery; the phone isn't recognized by the computer as a storage device.

5. **Select an option and touch the OK button.**

    The phone's main storage device, the MicroSD card, is mounted on your computer's storage system.

Figure 13-1: USB connection options.

The first time you connect the Droid 2 to a PC, you see the AutoPlay dialog box appear in Windows. Choose the option Install Motorola Driver and follow the directions on the screen to proceed with installation. The Motorola driver is required by Windows so that your computer and the phone can communicate in a happy manner.

After the phone is connected, you use your computer to access the phone's MicroSD card. The card appears as a storage device mounted to your computer, just like a media card or thumb drive. In Windows, the MicroSD card can be accessed from the Computer window. On a Macintosh, the phone's MicroSD card appears as an icon on the desktop. See the later section "Accessing information on the MicroSD card."

 ✔ When in doubt about which USB connection mode to choose, I recommend selecting the USB Mass Storage option.

 ✔ On a Macintosh, use either the Charge Only or USB Mass Storage option for connecting the phone. The Mac may not recognize the Droid 2 when you set the PC Mode or Windows Media Sync options.

 ✔ When you're done accessing information on the Droid 2, you should properly unmount the phone from your computer system. See the next section.

✓ The Droid 2 remains connected to the computer even when the touchscreen turns off (the phone "sleeps").

✓ Even after choosing Charge Only mode, you may still see the MotoConnect feature become activated and a Web page appear on the computer screen after you connect the Droid 2. See the later sidebar "The joys and perils of MotoConnect" for information on halting this rude behavior.

✓ If you don't have a USB cable for your phone, you can buy one at any computer- or office-supply store. Get a USB-A-male-to-micro-B-USB cable. Tell them Murray the Squid sent you.

✓ Another advantage of connecting your phone to your computer is that the phone charges itself as long as it's plugged in. It charges even when it's turned off, but the computer must be on for the phone to charge.

✓ The phone charges even when you choose a USB option other than Charge Only.

✓ The Droid 2 cannot access its MicroSD card while the phone is mounted into a computer storage system. Items such as your music and photos are unavailable until you disconnect the phone from the computer; you see a message saying that the SD card is busy, unmounted, or unavailable. See the next section.

Disconnecting the phone from the computer

After transferring information between the computer and phone, you should properly unmount the MicroSD card from the computer's storage system. Heed these steps:

1. **Pull down the notifications.**

   Refer to Chapter 3 if you need more help accessing your phone's notifications.

2. **Choose USB Connection.**

3. **Choose Charge Only.**

4. **Touch the OK button to confirm.**

   The MicroSD card is unmounted and can no longer be accessed from your computer. The phone's icon disappears from the Computer window or desktop.

5. **If you're using a Macintosh, drag the Droid 2 storage icon into the Trash.**

   You must properly unmount the phone from the Mac's storage system before you disconnect the cable.

6. **If necessary, unplug the USB cable.**

The joys and perils of MotoConnect

When you connect the Droid 2 to a Windows computer, you may experience the effects of the MotoConnect program. Specifically, after connecting the Droid 2, you may see a Web page open and urge you to download the V CAST Media Manager program, which is covered elsewhere in this chapter.

To manage MotoConnect, you use its icon in the notification area, usually found on the far right end of the taskbar, at the bottom of the computer screen. Disable MotoConnect by right-clicking the Motorola icon and choosing When Phone Connects, Launch⇨Nothing.

If you choose to keep the phone connected to the computer, the phone continues to charge. (Only when the computer is off does the phone not charge.) Otherwise, the computer and phone have ended their little *tête-à-tête* and you and the phone are free again to wander the earth.

✔ Do not unplug the Droid 2 when the USB cable is connected and the MicroSD card is mounted. Doing so may damage the MicroSD card and render invalid *all* information stored on your phone. It's A Bad Thing.

✔ You can leave the A end of the USB cable plugged into the computer, if you find it convenient. I do. That makes it easier to reconnect the phone later.

Your Phone's Storage

Information stored on your phone (pictures, videos, music) is kept on the *MicroSD card.* The card works like a storage device in your computer, keeping your phone's information stored in files and organized using folders. It's all complex computer stuff, and you're free to merrily skip it all — unless you're curious about how things are stored on the phone or you need to exchange information between the phone and your computer.

Accessing information on the MicroSD card

To view the information on your phone, stored on the MicroSD card, follow these steps:

1. **Connect the phone to the computer.**

2. **Mount the phone's MicroSD card on the computer's storage system.**

   See specific directions in the section "Connecting the phone to the computer," earlier in this chapter. My recommendation is to choose the USB connection option USB Mass Storage.

3a. In Windows, open the Computer window.

You can choose Computer from the Start menu or press the Win+E key combination to see the Computer window. The icon representing the phone looks like a typical Windows hard drive icon. The only puzzle is figuring out which drive letter icon represents the phone.

To know for certain which icon represents the Droid 2 MicroSD card, unmount the phone (follow the directions in the earlier section "Disconnecting the phone from the computer") and then remount it. The icon that disappears and then reappears in the Computer window represents your phone. Generally, it should be assigned the same drive letter every time you mount it.

3b. On a Macintosh, open the new drive icon that appears on the desktop.

Macs line up storage icons on the right edge of their screens, from top to bottom. The Droid 2 MicroSD card appears as a generic drive icon and has the name NO NAME, unless you were clever and named the MicroSD card something else.

After you mount the Droid 2 MicroSD card to your computer, you can access the information stored there. The information is made available as though your phone were a thumb drive or another form of external computer storage, which in fact is what it is when the Droid 2 is connected to your computer.

- ✔ To transfer a file to your phone, such as a ringtone or contact, simply drag the file's icon from wherever it dwells on your computer to the MicroSD icon. This action copies the file, creating a duplicate file on the phone.

- ✔ I wouldn't bother trying to organize files and folders on the MicroSD card. Sure, you can try, but the Droid 2 manages those folders. Anything you do is pointless, unless you're one of those obsessive people who feels compelled to organize everything.

- ✔ The best way to transfer music, photos, and videos between the phone and your PC is to use the doubleTwist program, covered in the next section.

- ✔ There's no need to synchronize information such as dates, contacts, and email messages between the Droid 2 and your computer. All that information is synchronized automatically and wirelessly between the phone and your Google account.

- ✔ When you're done accessing the MicroSD card from your computer, unmount it by following the directions in the earlier section "Disconnecting the phone from the computer."

✔ You don't need to use a computer to access files on your Droid 2. The Files app, found in the Applications Tray, can be used to browse files and folders found on the phone. Apps are also available at the Android Market for managing the files and folders on your Droid 2. One that I can recommend is Linda Manager. It's free from the Android Market. See Chapter 20.

Unmounting, removing, and replacing the MicroSD card

Most of the time, the MicroSD card dwells contently inside your Droid 2. Rarely, if ever, do you need to remove it. If you decide to remove it, you must unmount it first. This type of unmounting is different from unmounting the phone when it's connected to the computer. (Well, it's similar, but not the same.)

The good news is that you don't need to formally unmount the MicroSD card. That's because in order to remove the card, you have to remove the phone's battery. Therefore, the phone is turned off when you remove the MicroSD card and, by the laws of physics and sanity, is already unmounted.

To remount the MicroSD card, simply turn your phone on again.

The manual steps for unmounting the MicroSD card are listed here:

1. **Ensure that the phone isn't connected to a computer by a USB cable.**

   Free the phone from the computer, as described earlier in this chapter.

2. **From the Applications Tray, choose Settings.**

3. **Choose SD Card & Phone Storage.**

4. **Choose Unmount SD Card.**

   You should hear an alert, after which you can turn off the phone and remove its MicroSD card.

After the MicroSD card has been unmounted by following these steps, you have no access to the information stored there: The Droid 2 doesn't show your photos or music or other types of information.

✔ To reaccess the MicroSD card after unmounting it, turn on the phone again.

✔ You can get a second, larger-capacity MicroSD card for use with your phone at any computer- or office-supply store. You have to format the MicroSD card when you insert it into the Droid 2.

✔ To format a new MicroSD card, follow the steps in this section. After (or in place of) Step 4, choose the command Format SD Card.

✔ See Chapter 1 for information on removing the MicroSD card from the phone.

The DLNA thing

The Droid 2 is compliant with the Digital Living Networking Alliance, known as DLNA. Compliant devices are configured so that they can easily share information — specifically, media files such as pictures, videos, and music. When two DLNA gizmos are connected, either directly or wirelessly, the warmth from their sharing fills the room.

Seriously, on the Droid 2, DLNA makes it easier for your phone to share information with DLNA-compliant computers, game consoles, televisions, and other gizmos. You must first connect the devices, directly or wirelessly, and then run either the DLNA or Media Share app, both of which can be found on the Applications Tray.

That Syncing Feeling

The physical part of connecting your Droid 2 to a computer involves the cables and communicating with the MicroSD card. The mental part is *synchronization,* or the process of exchanging your stuff between the phone and the computer. The result is that you end up with the information you want where you want it.

Synchronizing with doubleTwist

One of the most popular ways to move information from an Android phone into a computer — and vice versa — is to use the third-party utility *doubleTwist.* This amazing program is free, and it's available at www.doubletwist.com.

The doubleTwist app isn't an Android app. You use it on your computer. It lets you easily synchronize pictures, music, videos, and Web page subscriptions between your computer and its various media libraries and any portable device, such as the Droid 2. Additionally, doubleTwist gives you the ability to search the Android Market and obtain new apps for your phone.

To use doubleTwist, connect your phone to your computer as described elsewhere in this chapter. Ensure that USB sharing is on; mount the MicroSD card as a USB mass storage device. The doubleTwist program often starts automatically as soon as you connect the Droid 2. If it doesn't, start it manually. The simple doubleTwist interface is illustrated in Figure 13-2.

To best use doubleTwist, first ensure that the Motorola Droid 2 (recognized for some reason as *Motorola A955* in Figure 13-2) is chosen from the list of media storage locations on the left side of the window. Then select all items on the General tab (refer to Figure 13-2). Click the Sync button and the categories that you've selected are then synchronized between the phone and your computer.

Items stored on your computer

Choose what to sync   Be more specific

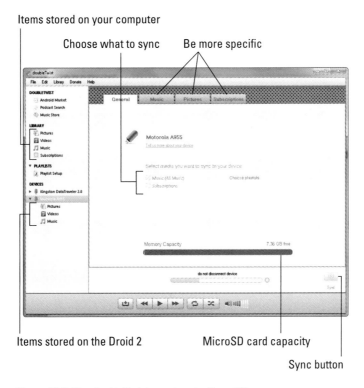

Items stored on the Droid 2   MicroSD card capacity

Sync button

Figure 13-2: The doubleTwist synchronization utility.

Of course, if you have a lot of photos or videos or music on the computer, you may want to be more selective: The phone's MicroSD card can hold only so much stuff. In that case, click each tab (refer to Figure 13-2) and choose the music, pictures, videos, and subscriptions you want to synchronize between the phone and the computer. Then click the Sync button to transfer the information.

✔ Versions of doubleTwist are available for both the PC and the Mac.

✔ Refer to a handy computer book for information on installing new software, such as doubleTwist.

✔ doubleTwist doesn't synchronize contact information. The Droid 2 automatically synchronizes your phone's Contacts list with Google.

✔ You can use many programs on your desktop computer to store photos, videos, and music. On the PC, all three types of media are stored using Windows Media Player. On the Mac, photos can be stored using iPhoto, and iTunes is the main music program. You have to use those programs, or similar ones, to move the media to your computer before you can use doubleTwist to synchronize that media to your phone.

- ✔ Even though you can use other programs to organize media on your computer, doubleTwist still searches everywhere on the computer to look for photos, video, and music.

- ✔ A doubleTwist app available from the Android Market is a media-playing program, not one used for synchronizing files between your Droid 2 and a computer.

- ✔ *Subscriptions* are podcasts or RSS feeds or other types of updated Internet content that can be delivered automatically to your computer.

Using the V CAST Media Manager

One thing that the MotoConnect software does is display a Web page where you can download the V CAST Media Manager. Do so. The V CAST Media Manager, shown in Figure 13-3, is a program for coordinating media — music, videos, pictures — between your PC and the Droid 2.

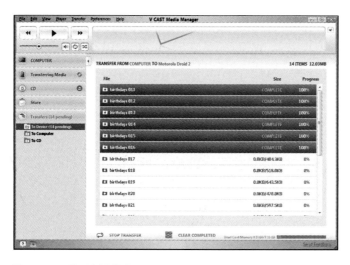

Figure 13-3: The V CAST Media Manager, copying files.

After downloading and installing the V CAST Media Manager, connect the Droid 2 to your Windows computer and activate the USB connection as described earlier in this chapter. You can then use the V CAST Media Manager to view and synchronize media between the phone and the PC.

Network Your Droid 2

*T*he Droid 2 packs more power than a typical computer from 20 years ago. The graphics are better. Arguably, even the Droid 2 munchkin keyboard is better than the cheesy membrane keyboards that were popular on early PCs. But you know what the best thing is — what makes the Droid 2 far superior to those ancient computers? No wires. That means no wires to power the Droid 2, but also no wires for basic communications and networking.

Your Droid 2 can access wireless networks with ease, the same wireless networks you may have used with a laptop computer or have seen other people at Starbucks use with their laptop computers. You can also access Bluetooth devices with Droid 2 wireless networking. This chapter covers all the basic wireless networking stuff.

...en an open network ...

...i networks

Imperial Wambooli
Secured with WPA/WPA2 PSK

macaskill
Secured with WPA/WPA2 PSK

...d Wi-Fi network

Wireless Network Access

Though you can't see it, wireless communications is going on all around. No need to duck — the wireless signals are intercepted only by items such as cell phones and laptop computers. The Droid 2 uses those signals to let you talk on the phone and communicate over the Internet and other networks.

Using the digital network

The Droid 2 uses the cellular network to not only send and receive phone calls but also communicate with the Internet. The phone can access several types of cellular digital network:

3G: The *third generation* of wide-area data networks is several times faster than the previous generation of data networks. 3G networks also provide for talking and sending data at the same time.

EDGE: The best of the second generation of cellular technologies allows for wide-area communications with the Internet, but not at the same time as when using voice communications.

GPRS: This second-generation (2G) network is for sending data, thought it isn't as fast as EDGE.

Your phone always uses the best network available. So, if the 3G network is within reach, it's the network the Droid 2 uses for Internet communications. Otherwise, the 2G (GPRS or EDGE) network is chosen.

A notification icon for the network used by the phone appears in the status area, right next to the Signal Strength icon. When digital information is being transmitted, the arrows in the network icon become animated, indicating that data is being sent or received or both.

As the time this book goes to press, 4G networks are starting to appear. These new networks sport speeds as much as ten times faster than 3G networks. Hopefully, soon the Droid 2 hardware and cellular service will be updated to handle the new 4G networks.

Creating a 3G mobile hotspot

You can configure the Droid 2 to share its cellular data network connection with as many as eight other devices. Those devices connect wirelessly with your phone, accessing a shared 3G network just like a laptop computer or another type of mobile device accesses a Wi-Fi network. In this process, a mobile wireless *hotspot* is created. The Droid 2 is one of the few smartphones that's up to the task.

To set up a 3G mobile hotspot with your Droid 2, heed these steps:

1. From the Applications Tray, open the 3G Mobile Hotspot icon.

You may see text describing the process. If so, dismiss the text.

2. **Touch the box to place a green check mark by the 3G Mobile Hotspot option.**

   A warning message appears, recommending that you plug your Droid 2 into a power source because the 3G mobile hotspot feature sucks down a lot of battery juice.

3. **Touch the OK button to dismiss the warning.**

   If you've not yet set up a 3G mobile hotspot, you need to supply some information.

4. **Input a name for your Droid 2 hotspot.**

   A name is already generated and appears on the touchscreen. You can type a new name, if you like.

5. **Input a password.**

   The password must be applied, and it must be at least eight characters long.

 I recommend placing a check mark by the Show Password option; you don't get a second chance to confirm the password, and if you mistype something using the onscreen keyboard, you'll never know what you did wrong.

6. **Touch the Save button to save your settings and set up the hotspot.**

   You're done, though one more warning message may appear: Click the OK button to dismiss the final warning.

 When the 3G hotspot is active, you see the Mobile Hotspot Service status icon appear, as shown in the margin. You can then access the hotspot using any computer or mobile device that has Wi-Fi capabilities.

To turn off the 3G hotspot, pull down the Mobile Hotspot Service notification and remove the green check mark.

 ✔ You cannot activate 3G network sharing and use a Wi-Fi connection at the same time on the Droid 2. (See the next section, about the Wi-Fi connection on your Droid 2.)

 ✔ The range for the Droid 2 Wi-Fi hotspot is about 30 feet.

 ✔ Whether your Droid 2 allows for 3G data sharing depends on your cellular carrier. Some carriers may limit that ability, and others may charge extra.

 ✔ To change hotspot settings, press the Menu soft button when using the 3G Mobile Hotspot app. (You have to stop the service first.) Choose Advanced and then choose Wifi AP Mode. You can change the device name, security level, password, and channel. Touch the Save button to confirm the new settings.

Turning on Wi-Fi

The cellular network's data connection is handy, mostly because it's available (almost) all over. For faster network communications, you can set up your Droid 2 to communicate with a wireless computer network, or *Wi-Fi*. It's the same method used by desktop computers and laptops for hooking up to the Internet.

To turn on the Droid 2 Wi-Fi network, follow these steps:

1. **On the Home screen, press the Menu soft button.**
2. **Choose Settings.**
3. **Choose Wireless & Networks.**
4. **Choose Wi-Fi.**

    A green check mark appears by the Wi-Fi option, indicating that the phone's Wi-Fi capabilities are now activated. If you've configured the phone to automatically connect to a nearby wireless network, the network name appears on the screen.

A helpful shortcut for turning on Wi-Fi is to use the Power Control widget, shown in Figure 14-1. This widget is preinstalled on the second Home screen, to the left of the main Home screen. Touch the Wi-Fi button and the Droid 2 turns on its Wi-Fi capabilities.

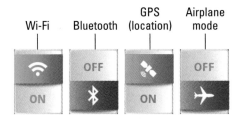

Figure 14-1: The Power Control widget.

To turn off Wi-Fi, repeat the steps in this section. Doing so turns off the phone's Wi-Fi access, disconnecting you from any networks.

See the next section for information on accessing a Wi-Fi network.

 ✔ Turning on Wi-Fi places an extra drain on the battery. So:

 ✔ Don't forget to turn off Wi-Fi when you're out of range or just out and about. That way, you save battery power (not a lot, but some).

 ✔ The Power Control widget (refer to Figure 14-1) is a collection of four individual Motorola widgets. A second Power Control widget, available under the Android Widgets category, also features a button for adjusting screen brightness.

 ✔ Also see Chapter 23 for information on prolonging battery life.

Accessing a Wi-Fi network

Turning on the phone's Wi-Fi access is only the first part of connecting to a wireless network. The next step is joining the network. Just as you would do on a computer, you need to hunt down the wireless network by name and, optionally, input a password. Here's how it works:

1. **Press the Menu soft button while viewing the Home screen.**

2. **Choose Settings.**

3. **Choose Wireless & Networks.**

4. **Ensure that Wi-Fi is on.**

   A green check mark must appear next to the Wi-Fi option.

5. **Choose Wi-Fi Settings.**

   You see a list of Wi-Fi networks displayed, as shown in Figure 14-2.
   If no wireless network is displayed, you're sort of out of luck regarding wireless access from your current location.

6. **Choose a wireless network from the list.**

   In Figure 14-2, I chose the Imperial Wambooli network, which is my office network.

7. **Optionally, type the network password.**

   Touch the Password text box to see the onscreen keyboard.

   Touch the Show Password check box so that you can see what you're typing; some of those network passwords can be *long*.

8. Touch the Connect button.

You should be immediately connected to the network. If not, try the password again.

Available networks

The phone's Wi-Fi is on

You're alerted to nearby Wi-Fi networks

Manually add a Wi-Fi network

The network's signal strength

Network is password protected

Figure 14-2: Hunting down a wireless network.

 After your phone is connected, you see the Wi-Fi status icon appear atop the touchscreen. It indicates that the phone's Wi-Fi is on and that it's connected and communicating with a Wi-Fi network.

The VPN connection

Honestly, if you don't know what a VPN is, you don't need to bother with the VPN connection. But when you're at an organization that uses a virtual private network, you can use the Droid 2 to access information on that network from your phone.

After opening the Settings icon, choose Wireless & Networks, VPN Settings, and then Add VPN. Type the name of your VPN and then fill in the complex instructions provided to you by the VPN manager at your organization. Or, just feign frustration and have someone else configure the phone. When you're done, press the Menu soft button and choose the Save command.

To connect with a VPN, choose Wireless & Networks from the Settings screen and then choose VPN Settings. Choose the VPN you've already set up and then touch the Connect button.

Some wireless networks don't broadcast their names, which adds security but also makes accessing them more difficult. In those cases, choose the Add Wi-Fi Network command (refer to Figure 14-2) to manually add the network. You need to input the network name, or *SSID,* and the type of security. You also need the password, if one is used. You can obtain this information from the guy with the pierced nose who sold you coffee, or from whoever is in charge of the wireless network at your location.

✔ Not every network has a password.

✔ Some public networks are open to anyone, but you have to use the Browser app to find a login page that lets you access the network: Simply browse to any page on the Internet and the login page shows up.

✔ The phone automatically remembers any Wi-Fi network it's connected to as well as that network password.

✔ If the network password has changed you need to update the Droid 2: Long-press the Wi-Fi network name (refer to Figure 14-2) and choose the Modify Network command from the pop-up menu. You can input the new password on the next screen.

✔ To disconnect from a Wi-Fi network, simply turn off Wi-Fi on the phone. See the preceding section.

✔ A Wi-Fi network is faster than a cellular data network, so it makes sense to connect with Wi-Fi whenever you can.

✔ Unlike a cellular data network, a Wi-Fi network's broadcast signal goes only so far. My advice is to use Wi-Fi whenever you plan to remain in one location for a while. If you wander too far away, your phone loses the signal and is disconnected.

Bluetooth Gizmos

One type of computer network you can confuse yourself with is Bluetooth. It has nothing to do with the color blue or any dental problems. *Bluetooth* is simply a wireless protocol for communication between two or more gizmos.

The primary way Bluetooth is used on a cell phone is by using a pair of those wireless earphones you see stuck on people's heads. Those people must think they're being all high-tech and cool, but they look like they have tiny staplers stuck to their earlobes. They also look like they're talking with invisible people, so stay clear!

Activating Bluetooth

You must turn on the phone's Bluetooth networking before you can use one of those Borg-earpiece implants and join the ranks of walking nerds. Here's how to turn on Bluetooth for the Droid 2:

1. **From the Applications Tray, choose Settings.**

2. **Choose Wireless & Networks.**

3. **Choose Bluetooth.**

   Or, if a little green check mark already appears by the Bluetooth option, Bluetooth is already on.

You can also turn on Bluetooth by using the Power Control widget (refer to Figure 14-1). Just touch the Bluetooth button to turn it on.

To turn off Bluetooth, repeat the steps in this section.

✔ When Bluetooth is on, the Bluetooth status icon appears, as shown in the margin.

> ✔ Activating Bluetooth on the Droid 2 can quickly drain the battery. Be mindful to use Bluetooth only when necessary, and remember to turn it off when you're done.

Using a Bluetooth device

To make the Bluetooth connection between the Droid 2 and a set of those "I'm so cool" earphones, you need to *pair* the devices. That way, the Droid 2 picks up only your earphone and not anyone else's.

To pair the phone with a headset, or any other Bluetooth gizmo, follow these steps:

1. **Ensure that Bluetooth is on.**
2. **Turn on the Bluetooth headset.**
3. **Choose Settings from the Applications Tray.**
4. **Choose Wireless & Networks.**
5. **Choose Bluetooth Settings.**
6. **Ensure that a check mark appears by the Discoverable option.**
7. **Choose Scan for Devices.**
8. **If necessary, press the main button on the Bluetooth gizmo.**

   The main button is the one you use to answer the phone. You may have to press and hold the button.

   Eventually, the device should appear on the screen,

9. **Choose the device.**
10. **If necessary, input the device's passcode.**

    It's usually a four-digit number, and quite often it's simply 1234.

And now, the device is connected. You can stick it in your ear and press its main Answer button when the phone rings.

By the way, when a Bluetooth device is on and paired with the phone, the notification light (on the front of the Droid 2) flashes blue for an incoming call.

After you've answered the call (by pressing the main Answer button on the earphone), you can chat away. The Call in Progress notification icon is blue for a Bluetooth call, as shown in the margin.

If you tire of using the Bluetooth headset, you can touch the Bluetooth button on the touchscreen to use the Droid 2 speaker and microphone. (Refer to Figure 5-2, in Chapter 5, for the location of the Bluetooth button.)

✔ You can turn the Bluetooth earphone on or off after it has been paired. As long as Bluetooth is on, the Droid 2 instantly recognizes the earphone when you turn it on.

✔ The Bluetooth status icon changes when a device is paired. The new icon is shown in the margin.

✔ You can unpair a device by long-pressing the icon for the Bluetooth headset on the main Bluetooth screen. Choose the Unpair command.

✔ Turning on Discovery (refer to Step 6 in the preceding step list) isn't necessary when pairing your Droid 2 with a Bluetooth headset.

✔ Don't forget to turn off the earpiece when you're done with it. The earpiece has a battery, and it continues to drain when you forget to turn the thing off.

Part IV
More than a Mere Mortal Cell Phone

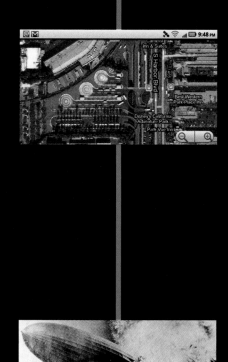

In this part . . .

1s the Droid 2 merely a cell phone? I think not! The closest gizmo it resembles is the *tricorder* from *Star Trek*. It's the gadget Mr. Spock toted around, wearing it like a party purse. When the science officer needed to gather information, he whipped out his tricorder and instantly knew every teensy scientific fact about everything around him, including where the bad guys were and where Captain Kirk could find booze and space women.

The Droid 2 may not help you score with green aliens, but it does more than other mortal cell phones can do. Though it can't find where the Klingons are hiding, it can help you find a gas station or sushi bar or your friend Brad's house. The Droid 2 can take pictures, record videos, play music, set your schedule, wake you in the morning, and more. All that stuff is covered in this part of the book.

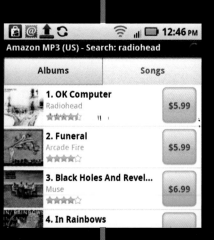

Never Get Lost Again

*T*he air smelled great. After six weeks beneath the Earth, inside the cramped Mole Machine, our party was happy to be aboveground, outside, and in the warm sun.

As Dr. Praetorius tended to the Mole Machine, I overheard Benjamin inquire about the location of the nearest Italian restaurant. Before Susan could berate him for his one-track, stomach-fueled mind, I whipped out my Droid 2.

"Why," I exclaimed, "the nearest Italian restaurant is just three blocks from our present location. Indeed, the good people who frequent Google Maps have given it five stars. Let's eat." And the crew beamed with approval.

Basic Map

I would guess that the biggest blessing from using the amazing Droid 2 Maps app is that you no longer have to hang your head in shame over not being able to refold a map. Yep — the Maps app involves no folding whatsoever. Instead, it charts the entire country, including freeways, highways, roads, streets, avenues, drives, bike paths, addresses, businesses, and points of interest. The Maps app is incredible.

Using the Maps app

You start the Maps app by choosing Maps from the Applications Tray. If you're starting the app for the first time, you can read its What's New screen; touch the OK button to continue.

The Droid 2 communicates with global positioning system (GPS) satellites, cell towers, Wi-Fi hotspots, and various pagan gods to hone in on your current location. It's shown on the map, similar to the one in Figure 15-1. The position is accurate to within a given range, as indicated by the blue circle.

Address

GPS is on

Street view

Zoom in

Zoom out

Your approximate
location and direction

Figure 15-1: An address and
your location on a map.

Here are some fun things you can do when viewing the basic street map:

Zoom in: To make the map larger (to move it closer), touch the Zoom In button, double-tap the screen, or spread your fingers on the touchscreen.

Zoom out: To make the map smaller (to see more), touch the Zoom Out button or pinch your fingers on the touchscreen.

Pan and scroll: To see what's to the left or right or at the top or bottom of the map, drag your finger on the touchscreen; the map scrolls in the direction you drag your finger.

The closer you zoom in to the map, the more detail you see, such as street names, address block numbers, and businesses and other sites — but no tiny people.

To see a satellite overlay on the map, press the Menu soft button, choose Layers, and then choose Satellite. The map image reloads, showing the satellite image on the map background, similar to what you see in Figure 15-2.

Street overlay

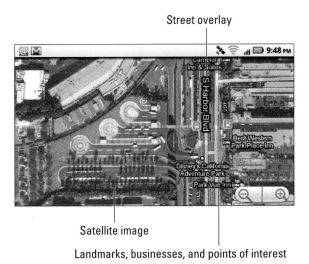

Satellite image

Landmarks, businesses, and points of interest

Figure 15-2: The satellite layer.

To remove the satellite image, press the Menu soft button and choose Layers and then Satellite.

✔ The Droid 2 uses GPS, the global positioning system. It's the same technology used by car navigation toys as well as by handheld GPS gizmos.

✔ When the Droid 2 is using GPS, you see the GPS Is On status icon appear.

✔ The compass arrow (refer to Figure 15-1) shows in which direction the phone is pointing.

✔ You can always go back to showing your current location on the map by pressing the Menu soft button and choosing the My Location command.

✔ You can add a Traffic layer by pressing the Menu soft button and choosing Layers and then Traffic. The Traffic information isn't available everywhere, however.

✔ Also see the later section "Locating your address," for details about the Street View feature.

✔ The Droid 2 warns you when various applications access the phone's Location feature. The warning is nothing serious — the phone is just letting you know that software will access the phone's physical location. Some folks may view that action as an invasion of privacy; hence the warnings. I see no issue with letting the phone know where you are, but I understand that not everyone feels that way. If you'd rather not share location information, simply decline access when prompted.

Useless trivia about the Traffic layer

The Traffic layer generated by the Maps app on the Droid 2 doesn't rely on the same traffic information you get from your local radio station. No, the app uses a much more clever method: Basically, Google uses information from your phone to determine where you are, which direction you're heading, and how fast you're moving. This information is compared with other Android phone users near you. Based on that data, the Google computers create a respectable picture of how traffic is flowing around you. That information is then used to generate the Traffic layer for the Maps app.

Spiffing up the map with Labs

The Maps app becomes more interesting and conveys more information when you employ the Labs feature. You might find handy the additions that Labs makes to the map, or you might find them annoying. Follow these steps to figure out whether you enjoy the Labs additions:

1. **Open the Maps app.**

2. **Press the Menu soft button.**

3. **Choose More.**

4. **Choose Labs.**

    You see a list of options you can add to the Map display. The app has quite a few of them, and descriptions are provided in the list.

5. **Choose a Labs item to add to the map.**

    The item is added right away, and you can play with it or see it in action.

The number and type of options available on the Labs menu changes as Google modifies and updates available features. Eventually, some Labs options, such as Traffic, make it to the big-time. Other options disappear altogether. My advice is to check the Labs list often to see what's up.

The Android Market app Compass also serves as a virtual compass for the Droid 2. See Chapter 20 for more information on the Android Market.

The Droid 2 Is Your Copilot

The best way to put the Maps app to work is when you're lost or looking for something. You can use Maps to locate people, places, and things. After they've been found, your phone tells you how to get there, turn by turn. So, even when you don't know where you are or where you're going, the Droid 2 can help.

Locating your address

The Maps app shows your location as a compass arrow on the screen. But *where* is that? I mean, if you need to phone a tow truck, you can't just say, "I'm the blue triangle on the orange slab by the green thing."

Well, you *can* say that, but it probably won't do any good.

To find your current street address, or any street address, long-press a location on the Maps screen. Up pops a bubble, similar to the one shown in Figure 15-3, that gives your approximate address.

Figure 15-3: Finding an address.

If you touch the address bubble (refer to Figure 15-3), you see a screen full of interesting things you can do, as shown in Figure 15-4.

The What's Nearby command displays a list of nearby businesses or points of interest, some of them shown on the screen (refer to Figure 15-4) and others available by touching the What's Nearby command.

Choose the Search Nearby item to use the Search command to locate businesses, people, or points of interest near the given location.

The Report a Problem command doesn't connect you with the police; instead, it's used to send information back to Google regarding an improper address or another map malfunction.

What's *really* fun to play with is the Street View command. Choosing this option displays the location from a 360-degree perspective. In Street View, you can browse a locale, pan and tilt, or zoom in on details to familiarize yourself with an area, for example — whether you're familiarizing yourself with a location or planning a burglary.

 Press the Back button to return to regular Map view from Street view.

Phone a business or location

Return to the map

Your location

Mark the location
as a favorite

Get directions

Street view

Street view preview

Figure 15-4: Things to do with a location.

Finding locations on the map

The Maps app can help you find places in the real world, just like the
Browser app helps you find places on the Internet. Both operations work
basically the same:

 Open the Maps app and press the Search soft button. You can type a variety
of terms into the Search box, as explained next.

Look for a specific addresses

To locate an address, type it into the Search box; for example:

```
1600 Pennsylvania Ave., Washington, D.C. 20006
```

Touch the Search button on either the onscreen or sliding keyboard and that location is then shown on the map. The next step is getting directions, which you can read about in the later section "Getting directions."

- ✔ You don't need to type the entire address. Often times, all you need is the street number and street name and then either the city name or zip code.

- ✔ If you omit the city name or zip code, the Droid 2 looks for the closest matching address near your current location.

Look for a type of business or restaurant or point of interest

You may not know an address, but you know when you crave sushi or Tex-Mex or perhaps Ethiopian food. Maybe you need a hotel or gas station. To find a business entity or a point of interest, type its name in the Search box; for example:

```
Movie theater
```

This command flags movie theaters on the current Maps screen or nearby.

Specify your current location, as described earlier in this chapter, to find locations near you. Otherwise, the Maps app looks for places near the area you see on the screen.

Or, you can be specific and look for businesses near a certain location by specifying the city name, district, or zip code, such as

```
Italian 92123
```

After typing this command and touching the Search button, you see a smattering of Italian restaurants found in my old neighborhood in San Diego and similar to the one shown in Figure 15-5.

To see more information about a result, touch its cartoon bubble, such as the one for Filippi's Pizza Grotto, shown in Figure 15-5. The screen that appears offers details, plus perhaps even a Web site address and phone number. You can press the Get Directions button (refer to Figure 15-4) to get driving directions; see the later section "Getting directions."

✏ Each letter or dot on the screen represents a search result (refer to Figure 15-5).

✏ Use the Zoom controls or spread your fingers to zoom in to the map.

✏ You can create a contact for the location, keeping it as a part of your Contacts list: After touching the location balloon, choose the command Add As a Contact. (Scroll down to find the command.) The contact is created using data known about the business, including its location and phone number and even a Web page address — if that information is available.

Search results and locations

First result found

Zoom controls

Display results as a list

Figure 15-5: Search results for *Italian* in Kearny Mesa.

Look for a contact's location

You can hone in on where your contacts are located by using the map. This trick works when you've specified an address for the contact — either home or work or another location. If so, the Droid 2 can easily help you find that location or even give you directions.

 The key to finding a contact's location is the little pushpin icon, shown in the margin. Anytime you see that icon in a contact's information, you can touch it to view the location by using the Maps app.

Getting directions

One command associated with locations on the map is Get Directions. Here's how to use it:

1. **Touch a location's cartoon bubble displayed by an address, a contact, or a business, or from the result of a map search.**

 2. **From the list of options, choose the Get Directions command or touch the Get Directions button.**

   You may be asked whether you want to navigate or get directions. If you choose Navigate, the Droid 2 goes into Navigation mode; refer to the next section.

   When you choose Get Directions, you see an input screen, similar to the one shown in Figure 15-6. The Droid 2 already has chosen your current location (shown as My Location in the figure) as the starting point, and the location you searched for, or are viewing on the map, as the destination.

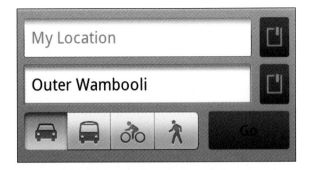

Figure 15-6: Going from here to there.

3. **To change the start point, touch the button to the right of the Start Point text box (refer to Figure 15-6).**

   Or, you can type a starting point.

4. **To change the destination, touch the button to the right of the Destination text box (refer to Figure 15-6).**

5. **Choose your method of transportation: car, public transportation, bicycle, or walking.**

   Not all transportation options are available for all locations.

6. **Touch the Go button.**

   A list of directions appears on the phone's screen.

7. **Follow the directions to get where you want to go.**

The directions appear as a list, which you can follow line by line.

You can choose the Show on Map command to view your trail on the map. Zoom in to see more detail.

To remove the navigation route from the screen, press the Menu soft button and choose More and then Clear Map. The sliding keyboard shortcut for the Clear Map command is Menu+C.

You can also choose the Navigate option, which lets your phone dictate the list of directions to you as you travel. See the next section.

Navigating to your destination

When you'd rather not see a list of directions to reach a destination, you can activate the Droid 2 Navigation mode. In that mode, the phone displays an interactive map that shows your current location and turn-by-turn directions for reaching your final location. Navigation mode also dictates verbally how far you should go and when to turn, for example, and gives you other nagging advice — just like a backseat driver, albeit an accurate one.

 To use Navigation, choose the Navigation option from any list of directions. Or, touch the Navigation icon, shown in the margin.

You can also start the Droid 2 Navigation mode directly by choosing the Navigation app from the Applications Tray. Opening the Navigation app displays a list of options for choosing a destination: You can speak or type a destination, choose a destination from your Contacts list, or navigate to a starred location. A list of locations you've recently looked up also appears, for your convenience.

After choosing Navigation, sit back and have the phone dictate your directions. You can simply listen, or just glance at the phone for an update of where you're heading.

✔ To stop Navigation, press the Menu soft button and choose the Exit Navigation command.

✔ When you're using the Droid 2 in the car dock, the command to access the Maps app's navigation feature is My Location.

✔ When you tire of hearing the Navigation voice, press the Menu soft button and choose the Mute command.

✔ I refer to the navigation voice as *Gertrude*.

✔ The neat thing about Navigation is that whenever you screw up, a new course is immediately calculated.

✔ A direct link to the Navigation app is on the Car Dock screen — handy for when you're using the Droid 2 in a car dock in your automobile.

✔ The Navigation app is beta software. It may change, and many of its features may not be available. I recommend, therefore, that you use the Maps app for navigating to your destination.

✔ In Navigation mode, the phone uses a lot of battery power. The phone doesn't dim when you travel long distances; the touchscreen remains active. Voice commands also put a drain on battery life. See Chapter 23 for more information on maintaining the phone's battery.

Adding a navigation shortcut to the Home screen

When you visit certain places often — such as home — you can save yourself the time you would spend repeatedly inputting navigation information, by creating a navigation shortcut on the Home screen. Here's how:

1. **Long-press a blank part of the Home screen.**

2. **From the pop-up menu, choose Shortcuts.**

3. **Choose Directions & Navigation.**

4. **Type a contact name, address, destination, or business in the text box.**

   As you type, suggestions appear in a list. You can choose a suggestion to save yourself some typing.

5. **Choose a traveling method.**

   Your options are car, public transportation, bicycle, and on foot.

6. **Scroll down a bit to type a shortcut name.**

7. **Choose an icon for the shortcut.**

8. **Touch the Save button.**

    The Navigation shortcut is placed on the Home screen.

To use the shortcut, simply touch it on the Home screen. Instantly, the Maps app starts and enters Navigation mode, steering you from wherever you are to the location referenced by the shortcut.

⋗ See Chapter 22 for additional information on creating Home screen shortcuts.

⋗ I keep all navigation shortcuts in one place, on the first Home screen to the right.

Where are your friends?

One Google Maps feature is *Latitude,* a social network program that lets you share your physical location with your friends, also assumed to be using Latitude. Being able to more easily know where your friends are makes it possible to meet up with them — or, I suppose, to avoid them. It's all up to you.

To join Latitude, you press the Menu soft button when viewing a map and then choose the Join Latitude command. If you have the Latitude app, you can use it to directly access Latitude. (The app is just a shortcut to the Maps app.)

After opening Latitude, read the information and then touch the Allow & Share button to continue. If you don't see the Join Latitude command, you've already joined; start Latitude by choosing the Latitude command.

To make Latitude work, you need to add friends to it, and those friends need to use it. After adding Latitude friends, you can share your location with them as well as view their locations on a map. You can also chat with Google Talk, send them email, get directions to their location, and do other interesting things.

To disable Latitude, press the Menu soft button when Latitude is active and choose the Privacy command. Choose the option Turn Off Latitude.

A Thousand Words

In This Chapter

▶ Using the phone's camera

▶ Taking a still picture

▶ Adding picture effects

▶ Looking at the picture you just shot

▶ Shooting video with the phone

▶ Previewing your video

The old adage goes that a picture is worth a thousand words. That is, unless you're working for a magazine, in which case the rates they pay authors and photographers are not correlated.

Among your phone's many abilities worthy of boasting about is its capacity as both a still camera and video recorder. No longer do you need to fret about not having a camera with you. As long as you're carrying your Droid 2, you can capture the moment or record the event. This chapter explains how it all works.

The Droid 2 Has a Camera

As a resident of the Digital Century, you most likely always have your cell phone with you. Consider it a bonus that the cell phone, your Droid 2, can double as a camera. It may not be perfect, but it's handy — especially when you see leprechauns dancing with elephants and need a picture as proof or else no one will ever believe you.

Taking a picture

To use your Droid 2 phone as a camera, you need to know that the back of the phone holds the lens. To take a picture, you need to hold the phone away from your face, which I hear is hell to do when you wear bifocals. Before doing that, start the Camera app.

Summon the Camera app from the Applications Tray. After starting the Camera app, you see the main Camera screen, as illustrated in Figure 16-1.

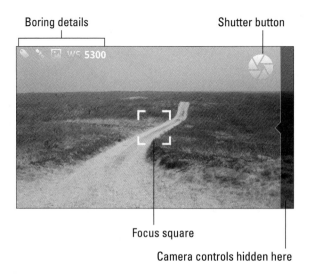

Figure 16-1: Your phone as a camera.

To take a picture, point the camera at the subject and touch the Shutter button, found on the right or top side of the Droid 2, depending on whether you're taking a portrait or landscape photograph. (Refer to Figure 1-2, in Chapter 1, for the physical shutter button's location.)

Press the button lightly to adjust focus and ready the flash; press the shutter button firmly to snap the picture.

For a second, the picture you just snapped appears on the phone's touchscreen. You see a prompt that tells you to touch the screen for more options. Here are those options:

Share: A menu of sharing options is presented. See Chapter 17 for specific information on what (and how) you can share the image you just took.

Set As: You can choose to make the image your Droid 2 wallpaper (its Home screen background) or assign the image to a contact.

Quick Upload: Choose this item to instantly send the image to your online photo-sharing album at the Picasa Web site (if you've configured the Droid 2 to share images with Picasa).

Delete: The image gets tossed into the digital dustbin and you can try again.

If you don't touch the screen to see the options, the phone returns to Camera mode and you can take more pictures.

- As on other digital cameras, the shutter doesn't snap instantly when you shoot the picture: The camera takes a moment to focus, the flash may go off, and then you hear the shutter sound effect.

- The camera doesn't take a moment to focus if you first press the shutter button lightly to focus the image and then press the button firmly to snap the picture.

- You can zoom in or out by pressing the Volume Down or Volume Up buttons, respectively. Because the zoom is a *digital zoom*, the image is magnified, as opposed to an optical zoom, which is done by adjusting the camera's lens.

- If you plan to take a lot of pictures, consider placing a shortcut to the Camera app on the Home screen. See Chapter 22 for details.

- The phone can be used as a camera in either landscape or portrait orientation, though the phone's controls and gizmos are always presented in landscape format (refer to Figure 16-1).

- The camera focuses automatically, though you can drag the focus square around the touchscreen to specifically adjust the focus (refer to Figure 16-1).

- You can take as many pictures with your Droid 2 as you like, as long as you don't run out of storage for them on the phone's MicroSD card.

- You can use the Gallery to manage images and delete the ones you don't want. See Chapter 17 for more information about the Gallery.

- The Droid 2 not only takes a picture but also keeps track of where you were located on Planet Earth when you took it. See Chapter 17 for information on reviewing a photograph's location.

- If your pictures appear blurry, ensure that the camera lens on the back of the Droid 2 isn't dirty.

- Refer to Figure 1-3, in Chapter 1, for the location of the camera on the back of the Droid 2.

- The Droid 2 stores pictures in the JPEG image file format. Images are stored in the DCIM/Camera folder on the MicroSD card; they have the JPG filename extension.

Adjusting the camera

Your Droid 2 is more phone than camera — still, it has various camera adjustments you can make. Some adjustment controls are found on the screen when the Camera app first starts, as shown in Figure 16-2. Others are found by pressing the Menu soft button when using the Camera app.

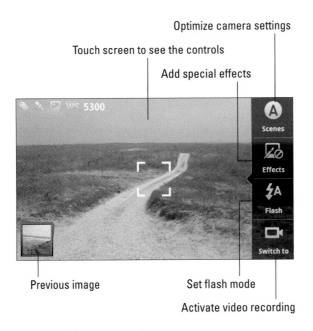

Optimize camera settings

Touch screen to see the controls

Add special effects

Previous image

Set flash mode

Activate video recording

Figure 16-2: Camera controls.

Though you have many camera settings to make, here are a few items worthy of note:

Scenes: Choosing this option lets you preconfigure the Droid 2 camera for taking certain types of pictures. After touching the Scenes button, swipe the options left or right. Choose one to configure the camera to, ideally, take that type of picture.

Effects: Add special color effects by touching the Effects button and then swiping left or right through the various effects. After choosing an effect, press the Back soft button to take the picture.

Flash Mode: Setting the camera's flash mode is done by choosing the Flash command, shown in Figure 16-2. The camera has three flash modes:

> *Auto Flash:* In this mode, the camera determines whether the flash goes off. Sometimes it does, such as when it's dark, and sometimes it doesn't, such as when you're taking a picture of the sun.

> *Flash On:* The flash always blinds your victims.

> *Flash Off:* The flash never goes off, even in the dark.

Picture Mode: Set options for how to use the camera by pressing the Menu soft button and choosing Picture Modes. You can choose from four ways to use the camera, as described in Figure 16-3.

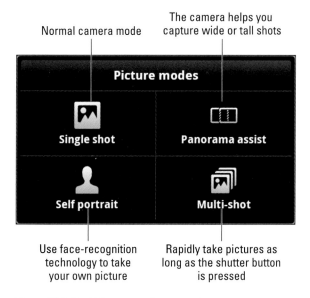

Figure 16-3: Droid 2 camera picture modes.

The Multi-shot option allows the camera to take pictures as long as you press the shutter button. This feature is useful for capturing action pictures, such as in sporting events or train wrecks.

The Panorama Assist option helps you take multiple images that can be laid out in a panorama, either vertically or horizontally. When that option is set, the camera helps you point the camera in the right direction and at the right position to line up the panoramic shots.

- ✔ The Droid 2 camera comes with a self-portrait feature. To activate it, press the Menu soft button while using the camera, and then choose Picture Modes and then Self Portrait. Turn the phone around so that the camera is pointing at your face, press firmly on the shutter button, and pray. You need to pray because the Droid 2 may or may not find your face and the light from the flash will blind you while it's doing so.

- ✔ To help the Droid 2 camera take better pictures of people (or yourself), activate the face detection feature: Press the Menu soft button when using the Camera. Choose Settings and then choose Face Detection to place a green check mark by that item.

- ✔ You can force a flash by choosing Flash On mode. That way, dark objects in the foreground show up against a light background, such as when taking a picture of someone in front of a nuclear explosion.

Reviewing the picture

All pictures you take with your camera can be accessed using the Gallery program, which is covered in Chapter 17. Even so, right after you take a picture, you're given a chance to review it and other, recent pictures.

To review the image you just took, touch the Previous Image button (refer to Figure 16-2). You see a "camera roll" of recent images. Touch your image to examine it more closely.

After the previous image is shown full-screen, you can examine it in detail: Double-tap or spread your fingers on the touchscreen to zoom in; double-tap or pinch the touchscreen to zoom out. Drag your finger to pan the image.

To do something with the image, press the Menu soft button. You see a screen similar to the one shown in Figure 16-4. (If you see a different menu appear, you aren't viewing the previous image; see Chapter 17 for more information on using the Gallery app.)

Image preview

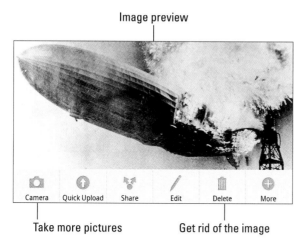

| Camera | Quick Upload | Share | Edit | Delete | More |

Take more pictures   Get rid of the image

Figure 16-4: Picture review.

When the image doesn't meet your liking, touch the Delete button. To remove the image, touch the OK button when prompted.

Touch the Camera button (refer to Figure 16-4) to return to the Camera app and take more pictures.

  ✔ Deleting an image frees up the space it used on the phone's MicroSD card.

  ✔ There's no easy or obvious way to undelete an image, so be careful! In fact:

  ✔ I recommend that you do your deleting and other photo management duties by using the Gallery app, discussed in Chapter 17.

  ✔ By pressing the Share button, you can instantly share the image with friends on the Internet. You can share by email or text message or by using social networking sites such as Facebook and Twitter, if you have the Droid 2 configured for use with those apps. Other options, such as sharing with the Picasa photo-sharing Web site, might also appear on the Share button's list.

✔ The Print to Retail option on the Share button allows you to send the image to a photo-processing location near you, where it can be printed.

✔ How you share a photo depends on where you want the image to end up. See Chapter 9 for information on sending multimedia text messages; Chapter 10 covers the Email and Gmail programs, and Chapter 12 delves into Facebook and Twitter.

✔ Use the More button to access additional menu items. One such item, Set As, lets you instantly assign the photo as the Home page *wallpaper* (background image) or to set the image for a contact.

✔ The next time you're face-to-face with a contact, remember to snap that person's photo. Use the picture-review window's Set As button to assign the image as the contact's photo — with the contact's permission, of course.

You Ought to Be on Video

When the action is hot, when you need to capture more than a moment (and maybe the sounds), you switch the Droid 2 camera into Video Capture mode. Doing so may not turn you into the next Martin Scorsese, because I hear he uses the Droid X to make his films.

Recording video

Video chores on the Droid 2 are handled by the Camcorder app, found on the Applications Tray. You can also get to Video mode by choosing the Switch To button when using the Droid 2 camera (refer to Figure 16-2).

The Camcorder app looks amazingly similar to the Camera app, with the addition of a time indicator, as illustrated in Figure 16-5.

Start shooting the video by pressing the phone's shutter button — the same button used to take a picture. You can use the button on the screen (shown in Figure 16-5) or the shutter button on the Droid 2.

When recording, you see the red dot in the upper left corner of the screen light up and the recording time is noted (refer to Figure 16-5).

To stop recording, press the Shutter button again (either button).

Recording time   Shutter button

Touch to reveal controls

Figure 16-5: Your phone is a video camera.

The video is stored on the phone's MicroSD card. You can watch the video immediately by touching the Previous Video button as covered in the next section. Otherwise, the phone is ready to shoot another video.

✔ While the phone is recording, a Mute button appears on the touchscreen. Use it to mute the sound.

✔ Unlike in Camera mode, you cannot use the Droid 2 volume controls to zoom in or out as you record video.

✔ To ensure that video is recorded in High Definition (HD) mode, press the Menu soft button while using the Camcorder app. Choose Video Modes and then select Fast Motion.

✔ See the next section for more information on previewing a recently shot video.

✔ Chapter 17 covers the Gallery app, used to view and manage videos stored on your phone.

✔ Hold the phone steady! The camera still works when you whip around the phone, but wild gyrations render the video unwatchable.

✔ The length of video you can record is limited by how much storage space is available on the MicroSD card.

✔ The video is stored on the Droid 2 MicroSD card using the Third Generation Partnership Project video file format. The video files stored on the phone, in the DCIM/Camera folder, have the 3GP filename extension.

Reviewing your movie

To review your video masterpiece, touch the screen in the Camera app and then touch the Previous Video button that appears in the lower left corner (similar to the picture shown earlier, in Figure 16-2). Choose your video from the list (it's the first one shown). Touch the big Play button (the triangle) to review the video.

You can use onscreen controls to pause or play the video as well as reverse and fast-forward the scene. The controls disappear as the video plays, but you can touch the screen to bring them back.

 When your video is done playing, you can press the Back soft button to return to the Camcorder app.

✔ The best way to review, manage, and delete the videos you've shot is by using the Gallery app. See Chapter 17.

✔ Also see Chapter 17 for information on publishing your video to YouTube.

 ✔ Though deleting a video frees up storage space on the phone's MicroSD card, undeleting or recovering a deleted video is neither easy nor obvious.

Your Digital Photo Album

To understand the need to carry around pictures, it helps to have children. If the need doesn't hit you then (and you're probably too overwhelmed), the onslaught of grandchildren will definitely turn you into one of those humans who constantly carries around pictures in their purse or wallet. Yeah, a load of pictures is something else to carry around — but not when you have a Droid 2. That's because your phone is also your photo album.

The Droid 2 stores a copy of the digital pictures you snap, and the videos you record, right there inside the phone. It can also store pictures you've synchronized from your computer or from the Internet. It even has a nifty slideshow program that you can show people, if you first trap them in an elevator and get it stuck between floors. All of that (except for the elevator part) is covered in this chapter.

puter, idaho, Simon Gookin, mmer, 2010, Dad's house

Location:

Lat: Long:

Modified on:

September 2, 2010 9:18 PM

olution:

Behold the Image Gallery

Pictures and videos you shoot with your Droid 2 aren't lost forever. Nope, they're stored on the phone's MicroSD card. After they're stored or created there, you can access them from the Gallery app, where you can view them or edit them or do a number of other interesting things.

Perusing the Gallery

To access images and videos stored on your Droid 2, you start the Gallery app. You can find it on the Applications Tray.

When the Gallery opens, you see images organized into categories, as shown in Figure 17-1. The number and variety of categories you see depends on how you synchronize your phone with your computer or photo-sharing services on the Internet, such as Picasa.

Figure 17-1: The Gallery's main screen.

Touch a category to open it and view the pictures or videos it contains. When the Droid 2 is held in portrait (vertical) orientation, the media is presented in a humongous grid. You can scroll up and down by flicking your finger on the touchscreen. In landscape (horizontal) orientation, the images appear in a list that you can scroll left or right with a flick of your finger.

To view an image or a video, touch it with your finger. The image appears in full size on the screen, and you can tilt the phone to the left to see the image in another orientation.

You can view more images in the album by swiping your finger left and right.

Videos appear with the Play Button icon, shown in the margin. Touching the icon plays the video.

To return to the main category in the Gallery, press the Back soft button.

- ✔ To keep the Gallery handy, consider placing its shortcut icon on the Home screen. Refer to Chapter 22.

- ✔ Refer to Chapter 11 for information on downloading photos from the Web.

- ✔ See Chapter 13 for more information about doubleTwist, which can be used to copy images and videos from your computer to the Droid 2.

- ✔ When previewing an image, you can double-tap the screen to zoom in and then double-tap again to zoom back out.

- ✔ To run a slideshow of the photos in an album, touch the Slideshow button, shown in the margin. The slideshow starts, displaying one image after another.

- ✔ Specify slideshow options by pressing the Menu soft button and choosing Settings. A screen full of options appears, which helps you set various aspects of the slideshow presentation.

Finding an image location on a map

In addition to snapping a picture, the Droid 2 also saves the location where you took the picture. That information is obtained from the phone's GPS, the same tool used to find your location on a map. In fact, you can use the information saved with a picture to see exactly where the picture was taken.

For example, Figure 17-2 shows the location where I took the image shown in Figure 16-1 (in Chapter 16). That location was saved by the phone's GPS technology and is available as part of the picture's data.

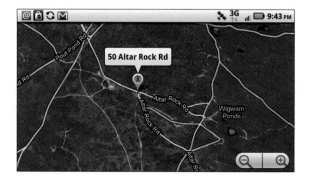

Figure 17-2: A picture's location.

To see where you've taken a picture, follow these steps:

1. **Summon the image in the Gallery.**

2. **Touch the Info button on the touchscreen.**

   The Info button is shown in the margin. After you touch the button, information about the picture appears on the screen.

3. **Choose Location.**

   The spot where you took the picture appears in the Maps app.

4. **Touch the Back button to return to the Gallery.**

Not every image has location information. In some cases, the Droid 2 cannot read the GPS to store the information. When that happens, location information is unavailable.

Working with pictures

The Gallery serves as a way to manage the pictures stored on your Droid 2. To individually manipulate an image, summon it in the Gallery by touching the image, as described earlier in this chapter. Press the Menu soft button to see a slate of commands you can use to manipulate the image. Here's what you can do:

Share an image: Send the image elsewhere using the Internet or a text message. See the later section "Sharing your pictures and videos" for details.

Delete an image: Touch the Delete button to remove the image you're viewing. You're prompted before the image is removed; touch the OK button to delete the image.

Use an image for a contact or as wallpaper: Touch the More button and choose the Set As command to apply the image you're viewing to a contact or to set that image as the Home screen wallpaper (background).

The Gallery offers three simple image-editing commands:

Crop: Choose the Edit command and then the Crop command to slice out portions of an image, such as when removing an unwanted relative or a former paramour from a family portrait. Figure 17-3 illustrates how to use the cropping tool that appears on the screen. Choose the Save command to keep the portion of the image that dwells within the orange rectangle. Choose the Discard command to abandon any cropping and return to the Gallery.

Figure 17-3: Working the crop thing.

Cropping an image doesn't alter the original picture in the Gallery. Instead, a new image is created with the crop settings you've chosen.

Rotate left, rotate right: Choose the Edit command and then choose Rotate. Use the circle control on the touchscreen to reorient the image. Touch the Save button when you're pleased with the results.

Additional editing commands are available. Find them by pressing the Menu soft button, choosing the Edit command, and then choosing Advanced Editing. I'm truly surprised at the variety and power of the available commands, some of which generally require the power of a full computer to accomplish.

Some images might not be available for editing, such as images imported into your phone from shared Picasa albums. Other, uneditable pictures may be stored in other albums on your Droid 2.

Tagging images

Because images contain visual information, searching and organizing images tend to be haphazard tasks. One method to help you keep your pictures and videos organized is to tag them.

A *tag* is simply a tidbit of text, short and punchy — for example, vacation, Grandma, 2009, Wisconsin, or exploding cupcake. By itself, a tag may seem useless, but the key to properly tagging an image is to apply more than one tag. An image tagged with all its descriptions — vacation, Grandma, 2009, Wisconsin, and exploding cupcake — is quite descriptive.

To apply a tag to an image in the Gallery, follow these steps:

1. **Touch an image to view it by itself on the Droid 2 touchscreen.**

2. **Touch the Info button.**

   If the Info button vanishes, just touch the screen again and it shows up.

   Lots of information about the image is displayed, similar to what's shown in Figure 17-4.

3. **Choose Tags.**

4. **Use either Droid 2 keyboard to type a tag.**

   Single word tags work best. If you need to be more descriptive, add more tags.

   You can use tags later to search for images. So think of a tag that you would use to find the image if you were doing a search.

   As you type, you may see contact names appear. If so, choose that contact name to tag the contact in the image.

5. **Touch the green plus-sign button to add another tag.**

6. **Touch the Done button when you're finished tagging the image.**

Touch to add tags

Touch to view location

Ugly picture filename

Current image tags

2010-09-02_21-18-05_834.jpg

Tags:
computer, idaho, Simon Gookin,
summer, 2010, Dad's house

Location:
Lat: Long:

Modified on:
September 2, 2010 9:18 PM

Resolution:
3.8MP

File size:
1.28MB

Image location information   Other trivia

Figure 17-4: Information about an image.

The tags you add appear on the image information screen, similar to the one shown in Figure 17-4. They're also used when you perform a search using the powerful Droid 2 Search command.

✔ By keeping tags succinct, you can easily sift and sort your images. For example, find all images from 2009 and then all birthday images from 2009.

✔ Many picture-viewing or media management programs on your computer allow for tagging. The tags are usually kept with the picture information so that when you copy or share the images, the tags come along for the ride.

✔ Tagging works only when you remember to do it!

Share Your Pics and Vids with the World

It's socially acceptable to share your phone's images and videos by queuing things up and then handing your phone to another human for their enjoyment. For those friends and relatives you'd rather not interact with personally, you can choose to share the media on your phone in a more digital fashion on the Internet.

Refer to Chapter 13 for information on synchronizing and sharing information between the Droid 2 and your computer.

Sharing your pictures and videos

Occasionally, you stumble across the Share command when working with photos and videos in the Gallery. This command is used to distribute images and videos from your Droid 2 to your pals on the Internet.

The menu that appears when you choose the Share command contains various options for sharing media, similar to the one shown in Figure 17-5. You may see more or fewer items on the Share menu, depending on which software you have installed on your Droid 2, which Internet services you belong to, and which type of media is being shared.

The following sections describe some of the items you can choose from the menu and how the media is shared.

Bluetooth

Bluetooth is perhaps the most difficult way to share files, but it's first alphabetically, so I'm forced to talk about it up front. Without boring you: Use a USB cable and directly connect the phone to a computer rather than use Bluetooth for sharing media. See Chapter 13.

The problem with file sharing using Bluetooth on the Droid 2 is that the devices can pair just fine. They don't, however, connect: Your laptop or a second mobile phone may claim that the Droid 2 is lacking a *service*. Because this is a software-related issue, it might be repaired in the future. If so, tune into my Web site for updated information:

```
www.wambooli.com/help/phone
```

Figure 17-5: Sharing options for media.

Email and Gmail

After selecting one or more image or video, choose Email or Gmail from the Share menu to send the media files from your Droid 2 as a message attachment. Fill in the To, Subject, and Message text boxes as necessary. Touch the Send button to send the media.

🖛 You may not be able to send video files as email attachments. That's probably because some video files are humongous. They would not only take too long to send but also might be too big for the recipient's inbox.

🖛 As an alternative to sending large video files, consider uploading them to YouTube instead. See the later section "Uploading a video to YouTube."

Facebook

To upload a mobile image to Facebook, choose the Facebook command from the Share menu. Optionally, type (or dictate) a caption. Touch the Upload button. Eventually, the media makes its way to Facebook, for all your friends to enjoy and make rude comments about.

- ✔ It helps to be signed into Facebook on your Droid 2 before you choose to share a picture or video.

- ✔ The Facebook option isn't available for sharing videos.

Online Album

This item puzzled me, until I chose it and figured out that it's another portal into the Picasa online photo-sharing Web site. Rather than use the Internet connection, however, the Online Album option sends the image to your Picasa account's Drop Box folder by using MMS, or media attached to a text message. That feature makes this option ideal for situations when you need to upload a photo but an Internet connection isn't available.

Photo Sharing

The Photo Sharing option is merely a shortcut to sending an image (not a video) to Facebook or your Picasa album. After choosing this option, you see a sharing screen from which you can choose Facebook or Picasa or add a sharing account, such as Photobucket or one of the other free online picture-sharing services.

I assume that at some point the Photo Sharing and Online Album options might be customizable. For example, they may allow you to send your Droid 2 images to online photo-sharing Web sites other than Picasa.

Picasa

Perhaps the most sane way to share photos is to upload them to Google's Picasa photo-sharing site. Heck, you probably already have a Picasa account synced with your phone, so this option is perhaps the easiest and most obvious to use. Here's how it works:

1. **View a picture in the Gallery.**

2. **Choose Picasa from the Share Picture Via menu (refer to Figure 17-5).**

3. **Type a caption.**

4. **Optionally, choose your Google account (if you have more than one).**

5. **Choose a Picasa album.**

    You may need to scroll up the top part of the screen a bit to see the Album item, which might be hidden behind the onscreen keyboard.

6. **Touch the Upload button to send the images.**

Because Picasa may automatically sync certain albums with your Droid 2, you can end up with two copies of the image on the phone. If so, you can delete the non-Picasa version of the image from its original gallery.

- Picasa is for sharing images only, not video.

- Your Google account automatically comes with access to Picasa. If you haven't yet set things up, visit `picasaweb.google.com` to get started.

- You can share images stored on the Picasa Web site by clicking the Share button found above each photo album.

- To make a Picasa album public, on the Internet (preferably using your computer) choose the Edit⇨Album Properties command, found just above the album. Choose Public from the pop-up menu, by the Visibility command in the Edit Album Information window.

Print to Retail

Here's a crazy idea: Connect your phone to a local photo developer, such as Costco, and have it send your images electronically so that they can be printed. After choosing the Print to Retail option, you can do exactly that: The Droid 2 uses its GPS powers to locate a printer near you. You can then fill in the various forms to have your pictures sent and printed.

Text Messaging

Media can be attached to a text message, which then becomes the famous MMS, or multimedia, message, that I write about in Chapter 9. After choosing the Messaging sharing option, input the contact name or phone number to which you want to send the media. Optionally, type a brief message. Touch the Send button to send the message.

- Some images and videos may be too large to send as multimedia text messages.

- The Droid 2 may prompt you to resize an image to properly send it as an MMS message.

- Not every cell phone has the ability to receive multimedia text messages.

Twitter

Images are shared on the popular Twitter social networking site by saving the image on a Twitter image-sharing Web site and then tweeting the link to that image. It helps to have the Twitter app installed on your Droid 2 and for you to be logged in to that account before you use Twitter to share an image.

The Twitter app on the Droid 2 uses the TwitPic Web site to share images. After choosing the Twitter option for sharing, you see the TwitPic link in your tweet message. Type additional text (whatever will fit) and then touch the Update button to tweet the pic's link.

YouTube

The YouTube sharing option appears when you've chosen to share a video from the Gallery. See the next section.

Uploading a video to YouTube

The best way to share a video is to upload it to YouTube. As a Google account holder, you also have a YouTube account. You can use the YouTube app on the Droid 2 along with your account to upload your phone's videos to the Internet, where everyone can see them and make rude comments upon them. Here's how:

1. **Activate the Wi-Fi connection for your Droid 2.**

   The best — the only — way to upload a video is to turn on the Wi-Fi connection, which is oodles faster than using the cell phone digital network. See Chapter 14 for information on how to turn on the Wi-Fi connection.

2. **From the Applications Tray, choose the Gallery app.**

3. **View the video you want to upload.**

   Or, simply have the video displayed on the screen.

4. **Press the Menu soft button**

5. **Choose the Share command.**

6. **Choose YouTube.**

7. **Type the video's title.**

8. **Touch the More Details button.**

9. **Optionally, type a description, specify whether to make the video public or private, add tags, or change other settings.**

10. **Touch the Upload button.**

    You return to the Gallery and the video is uploaded. It continues to upload, even if the phone falls asleep.

To view your video, open the YouTube app in the Applications Tray and choose the My Account command. If you don't see your recently uploaded video in the My Videos list, choose View All My Videos and find it there.

You can share your video by sending its YouTube Web page link to your pals. I confess that using a computer for this operation is easier than using your phone: Log in to YouTube on a computer to view your video. Use the Share button that appears near the video to share it via email, on Facebook, or elsewhere.

✔ YouTube often takes a while to process a video after it's uploaded. Allow a few minutes to pass (longer for larger videos) before the video becomes available for viewing.

✔ Wi-Fi access drains battery power, so don't forget to turn it off when you no longer need it after uploading your video.

✔ *Upload* is the official term to describe sending a file from your phone to the Internet.

✔ See Chapter 19 for more information on using YouTube on your Droid 2.

18

Music, Music, Music

*I*f you long to listen to your phone even when you're not making a phone call, you can employ the Droid 2 as your portable music player. Enjoying music is another way you can while away your time with your phone, especially when you tire of watching videos on YouTube, playing games you download from the Android Market, texting, taking pictures or videos, or doing any of the other boring little things your phone does.

The Hits Keep On Coming

Your Droid 2 is ready to entertain you with music whenever you want to hear it. Simply summon the Music app, and choose tunes to match your mood. It's truly blissful — well, until someone calls you and the Droid 2 ceases being a musical instrument and returns to being the ball-and-chain of the modern digital era.

Browsing your music library

Music Headquarters on your phone is the app named, oddly enough, Music. You can start the app by touching its icon found on the Applications Tray. Soon, you discover the main Music browsing screen, shown in Figure 18-1.

Albums

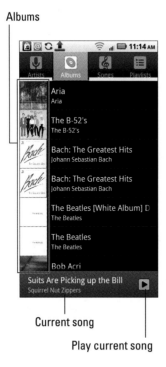

Current song

Play current song

Figure 18-1: The Music library.

All music stored on your phone can be viewed in four categories:

Artists: Songs are listed by recording artist or group. Choose Artist to see the list of artists. Then choose a specific artist to see their albums. Choosing an album displays the songs for that album. Some artists may have only one song, not in a particular album.

Albums: Songs are organized by album. Choose an album to list its songs.

Songs: All songs are listed alphabetically.

Playlists: Only songs you've organized into playlists are listed by their playlist names. Choose a playlist name to view songs organized in that playlist.

These categories are merely ways that the music is organized — ways to make the music easier to find when you may know an artist's name but not an album title or you may want to hear a song but not know who recorded it.

A *playlist* is a list you create to organize songs by favorite, theme, or mood or whatever characteristic you want. The section "Organize Your Music," later in this chapter, discusses playlists.

- ✔ Music is stored on the Droid 2 MicroSD card.

- ✔ The size of the MicroSD card limits the total amount of music that can be stored on your phone. Also, consider that storing pictures and videos on your phone horns in on some of the space that can be used to store music.

- ✔ See the later section "More Music" for information on putting music into your phone.

- ✔ Album artwork generally appears on imported music as well as on music you purchase online. If an album doesn't have artwork, it cannot be manually added or updated.

- ✔ When the Droid 2 can't recognize an artist, it uses the title Unknown Artist. It usually happens with music you copy manually to the Droid 2. Music that you purchase, or import or synchronize with a computer, generally retains the artist and album information. (Well, the information is retained as long as it was supplied on the computer or another original source.)

Playing a tune

To listen to music on the Droid 2, you first find a song in the library, as described in the preceding section, and then you touch the song title. The song plays in another window, as shown in Figure 18-2.

While the song is playing, you're free to do anything else with the phone. In fact, the song continues to play even if the phone goes to sleep. You can just continue listening, and look cool, wherever you go, because you're wearing ear buds and, obviously, you're a with-it person because you have a portable music player.

After the song is done playing, the next song in the list plays. Touch the Song List button (refer to Figure 18-2) to review the songs in the list; you can even rearrange songs by dragging them in the list.

The next song doesn't play if you have the Shuffle button activated (refer to Figure 18-2). In that case, the phone randomizes the songs in the list, so who knows which one is next?

Figure 18-2: A song is playing.

 The next song also might not play if you have the Repeat option on: The phone has two repeat settings: Repeat all songs in the list and repeat the current song endlessly. When the latter setting is active, the Repeat button appears as depicted in the margin.

To stop the song from playing, touch the Pause button (refer to Figure 18-2).

 When music plays on the phone, a notification icon appears, as shown in the margin. To quickly summon the Music app to see which song is playing, or to pause the song, pull down the notifications and choose the first item, which is the name of the song that's playing.

> ✐ Songs may play when you choose them from a list, which skips over the screen you see depicted in Figure 18-2. In that case, choose the song again from the list to see that screen.

> ✐ The volume is set by using the Volume buttons on the side of the phone: Up is louder, down is quieter.

 ✐ When you're browsing your music library, you may see a green Play icon, similar to the one shown in the margin. This icon flags any song that's playing or paused.

- Determining which song plays next depends on how you chose the song that's playing. If you choose a song by artist, all songs from that artist play, one after the other. When you choose a song by album, that album plays. Choosing a song from the entire song list causes all songs in the phone to play.

- To choose which songs play after each other, create a playlist. See the section "Organize Your Music," later in this chapter.

- After the last song in the list plays, the phone stops playing songs — unless you have Repeat on, in which case the list plays again.

- You can use the Droid 2 search abilities to help locate tunes in the phone's music library. You can search by artist name, song title, or album. The key is to press the Search soft button when you're using the Music app. Type all or part of the text you're searching for and touch the Search button on the onscreen keyboard. Choose the song you want to hear from the list that's displayed.

Turning your phone into a deejay

You need to do four things to make your Droid 2 the soul of your next shindig or soirée:

- Connect it to a stereo.
- Use the Shuffle command.
- Set the Repeat command.
- Provide plenty of drinks and snacks.

You can hook the Droid 2 to any stereo that has line inputs. You need, on one end, an audio cable that has a mini-headphone jack and, on the other end, an audio input that matches your stereo. Look for these cables at stores such as Radio Shack or any stereo store.

After your phone is connected, start the Music app and choose the party playlist you've created. If you want the songs to play in random order, choose the Shuffle command. The Shuffle button (refer to Figure 18-2) appears highlighted when that option is on.

You can also press the Menu soft button and choose the Party Shuffle command. After you activate Party Shuffle, all songs on your phone are played in random order. Depending on how eclectic your songs are, you might create an interesting party mood. When you're done partying, press the Menu soft button and choose Party Shuffle Off.

You might also consider choosing the Repeat command so that all songs repeat after they've played.

Enjoy your party, and please drink responsibly.

Organize Your Music

A *playlist* is a collection of tunes you create. You build the list by combining songs from one album or artist or another — whatever music you have on your phone. You can then listen to the playlist and hear the music you want to hear. That's how to organize music on your Droid 2.

Reviewing your playlists

Any playlists you've already created appear under the Playlists heading on the Music app's main screen. Touching the Playlists heading displays your playlists, similar to the ones shown in Figure 18-3.

To listen to a playlist, long-press the playlist name and choose the Play command from the menu that appears.

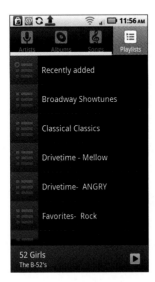

Figure 18-3: Playlists on the Droid 2.

You can also touch a playlist name to open the playlist and review the songs that are listed. Then you can choose any song from the list to start listening to that song.

A playlist is a helpful way to organize music when a song's information may not have been completely imported into the Droid 2. For example, if you're like me, you probably have a lot of songs by "Unknown Artist." The quick way to remedy that situation is to name a playlist after the artist and then add those unknown songs to the playlist. The next section describes how it's done.

Creating a playlist

To start a new playlist from scratch, you don't just create an empty playlist and then add songs. That might be how things work on your computer, but not on the Droid 2. Instead, you need to start by selecting the first tune you want to put on the playlist. Follow these steps:

1. **Play the song you want to use to start a new playlist.**

   You don't have to keep playing the song; feel free to pause the music after the song starts playing.

2. **Press the Menu soft button.**

3. **Choose Add to Playlist.**

4. **Choose New.**

5. **Type the playlist name.**

   Erase whatever silly text already appears in the input field. Type or dictate a new, better playlist name.

6. **Touch the Save button.**

   The new playlist is created and the song you were playing (refer to Step 1) is added to the playlist.

A new playlist has only one song. That's not much of a playlist, unless, of course, the song is by the Grateful Dead. To add more songs to a playlist, follow these steps:

1. **Play the song you want to add to the playlist.**

   You don't have to keep playing the song; feel free to pause the music after the song starts playing.

2. **Press the Menu soft button.**

3. **Choose the Add to Playlist command.**

4. **Choose an existing playlist.**

You may have to scroll down the list to see all your playlists.

You can continue adding songs to as many playlists as you like. Adding songs to a playlist doesn't noticeably affect the storage capacity of the MicroSD card.

✔ Songs in a playlist can be rearranged: Use the tab on the far left end of the song's title in the list to drag the song up or down.

✔ To remove a song from a playlist, long-press the song in the playlist and choose the command Remove from Playlist. Removing a song from a playlist doesn't delete the song from your phone. (See the next section for information on deleting songs from the Music library.)

✔ To delete a playlist, long-press its name in the list of playlists. Choose the Delete command. Though the playlist is removed, none of the songs in the playlist has been deleted.

Deleting music

To purge unwanted music from your Droid 2, follow these brief, painless steps:

1. **Locate the music that offends you.**

2. **Long-press the musical entry.**

If you don't want to hear the music, locate the music in a list: Artists, Albums, or Songs.

3. **Choose Delete.**

A warning message appears.

4. **Touch the OK button.**

The music is gone. *La, la, la, la: The music is gone.*

As the warning says (before Step 4), the music is deleted permanently from the MicroSD card. By deleting music, you free up storage space, and you cannot recover any music you delete. If you want the song back, you have to reinstall it, sync it, or buy it again, as described in the next section.

More Music

The Droid 2 may have come with a smattering of tunes preinstalled, or it might have come empty. I don't know which situation is worse: your tolerance of someone else's oddball musical tastes or your enjoyment of silence. Obviously, there's a need for more music, but where does this music come from? Well, there's no need to whip out a pen and notebook or take up the guitar: You can import music from your computer or buy new music from the Amazon MP3 store.

- ✒ Music, like pictures and video, is stored on the phone's MicroSD card. That card has only so much capacity. Though it would be nice to carry around all your music in the Droid 2, it's just not practical, so be judicious when adding music to your phone.

- ✒ See Chapter 13 for more information on managing the MicroSD card.

Synchronizing music with your computer

Your computer is the equivalent of the 20th century stereo system — a combination tuner, amplifier, and turntable, plus all your records and CDs. If you've already copied your music collection to your computer, or if you use your computer as your main music storage system, you can share that music with the Droid 2.

In Windows, you can use Windows Media Player to synchronize music between your phone and the PC. Here's how it works:

1. **Connect the Droid 2 to the PC.**

2. **Pull down the USB notification.**

3. **Choose the item Windows Media Sync.**

4. **Touch the OK button.**

5. **On your PC, start the Windows Media Player.**

   You can use most any media program, or "jukebox." These steps are specific to Version 12 of Windows Media Player, though they're similar to the steps you take in any media-playing program.

6. If necessary, click the Sync tab in Windows Media Player.

The Droid 2 appears in the Sync list on the right side of Windows Media Player, as shown in Figure 18-4.

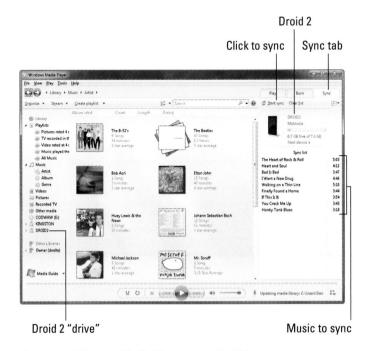

Figure 18-4: Windows Media Player meets Droid 2.

7. Drag to the Sync area the music you want to transfer to the Droid 2 (refer to Figure 18-4).

8. Click the Start Sync button to transfer the music to the Droid 2.

The Sync button may be located atop the list, as shown in Figure 18-4, or found on the bottom.

9. Close the Windows Media Player when you're done transferring music.

Or, you can keep the player open — whatever.

10. Unmount the Droid 2 from the PC's storage system.

Refer to Chapter 13 for specific unmounting instructions, also known as turning off USB storage.

When you have a Macintosh, or you detest Windows Media Player, you can use the doubleTwist program to synchronize music between your Droid 2 and your computer. Refer to the section about synchronizing with doubleTwist in Chapter 13 for more information.

- ✔ You must mount the Droid 2 — specifically, its MicroSD card — into your computer's storage system before you can synchronize music.

- ✔ The Droid 2 can store only so much music! Don't be overzealous when copying over your tunes. In Windows Media Player (refer to Figure 18-4), a capacity thermometer thing shows you how much storage space is used and how much is available on your phone. Pay heed to that indicator!

- ✔ Windows Media Player complains when you try to sync the Droid 2 to more than one PC. If so, you're warned after Step 6 in this section. It's not a big issue: Just inform Windows Media Player that you intend to sync with the computer for only this session.

- ✔ You cannot use iTunes to synchronize music with the Droid 2.

- ✔ Though the USB connection is on for your phone, and the phone's MicroSD card is mounted into the computer's storage system, the Droid 2 cannot access the MicroSD card. That means you cannot play music (or look at photos or access Contacts, for example) while the MicroSD card is mounted.

- ✔ It's also possible, though extremely unlikely, to manually add music to your phone. By *manually,* I mean mounting the Droid 2 into the computer's storage system and then copying and pasting music files from your computer to the phone's MicroSD card. The degree of insanity required to make this type of operation fun is so high that anyone attempting the procedure should immediately be sent to Congress.

Buying music at the Amazon MP3 store

You don't have the music on your computer. You don't even have the CD to *burn* into your computer! You can't jam an old CD into the Droid 2! At this point, a normal person would begin to panic, but because you have this book, you will instead visit the Amazon MP3 store to buy the music you need for your phone.

Before running through the steps, you must have an Amazon account. If you don't have one set up, use your computer to visit www.amazon.com and create one. You also need to keep a credit card on file for the account, which makes purchasing music with the Droid 2 work O so well.

Follow these steps to buy music for your phone:

1. **Ensure that you're using a Wi-Fi or high-speed digital network connection.**

   When in doubt about the cellular data network, activate the phone's Wi-Fi as described in Chapter 14. You can also refer to Chapter 14 for information on the various cellular data networks and their speeds.

2. **From the Applications Tray, choose the Amazon MP3 app.**

   The Amazon MP3 app connects you with the online Amazon music store, where you can search or browse for tunes to preview and purchase for your Droid 2.

3. **Touch the Search button to begin your music quest.**

   Or, you can browse the top-selling songs and albums or browse by category.

4. **Type some search words, such as an album name, a song title, or an artist name.**

   You can also dictate the search text. See Chapter 4 for more dictation information.

   Your search results appear, if any matches are found, as shown in Figure 18-5.

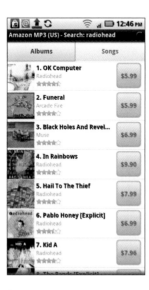

Figure 18-5: Albums found at the Amazon MP3 store.

5. **Touch a result.**

   If the result is an album, you see the contents of the album. Otherwise, a 30-second audio preview plays.

   When the result is an album, choose a song in the album to hear the preview.

   Touch the song again to stop the preview.

6. **To purchase the album or song, touch the big, orange button with the amount in it.**

   For example, the big, orange button at the top of the list (refer to Figure 18-5) specifies $5.99.

   Touching the button changes the price into the word *BUY*.

7. **Touch the word *BUY*.**

8. **If necessary, you may need to accept the license agreement.**

   This step happens the first time you buy something from the Amazon MP3 store.

9. **Log in to your Amazon.com account: Type your account name or email address and password.**

   Your purchase is registered, account authorized, and download started. If they aren't, touch the Retry button to try again.

10. **Wait while the music downloads.**

    Well, actually, you don't have to wait: The music continues to download while you do other things on the phone.

No notification icon appears when the song or album has finished downloading. Notice, however, that the MP3 Store downloading icon vanishes from the notification part of the screen. It's your clue that the new music is in the phone and ready for your ears.

✔ Amazon emails you a bill for your purchase. That's your purchase record, so I advise you to be a good accountant and print it and then input it into your bookkeeping program or personal finance program at once!

✔ You can review your Amazon MP3 store purchases by pressing the Menu soft button in the MP3 Store app and choosing the Downloads command.

✔ You can also buy music using the doubleTwist program. Refer to Chapter 13 for more information on doubleTwist.

Your Phone Is a Radio

Though they're not broadcast radio stations, some sources on the Internet — *Internet radio* — play music. You can listen to this Internet music if you put one of these two apps on your Droid 2:

- Pandora Radio
- StreamFurious

Pandora Radio lets you select music based on your mood and customizes what you listen to according to your feedback. The app works like the Internet site www.pandora.com, in case you're familiar with it.

StreamFurious streams music from various radio stations on the Internet. Though not as customizable as Pandora, it uses less bandwidth.

Both apps are available at the Android Market. They're free, though a paid, *Pro* version of StreamFurious exists.

- Various apps are also available at the Android Market that can turn your cell phone into an FM radio. I have nothing specific to recommend, mostly because the good apps aren't free. But keep your eyes peeled for FM radio apps for your Droid 2.
- See Chapter 20 for more information about the Android Market.

19

A Clutch of Apps

*Y*our phone is limited in its abilities only by the software — the *apps* — it has, and the Droid 2 comes with a lot of apps. Too many to write about all in one book, in fact. Too many to try all at once. Yet just enough to keep the task of scrolling the Applications Tray just a notch above tedious.

Though other chapters cover some of the major apps tied into the secondary (nonphone) duties of the Droid 2, a few apps are still worthy of a look. Some are useful, some are for diversion, and some can be dangerously fun. They're covered in this chapter.

An Appointment to Remember

Some people have date books. Others might write down appointments on business cards or on their palms. These methods might be effective, but they pale in comparison to the power of using your Droid 2 as your calendar and date keeper. Your phone can easily serve as a reminder of obligations due or delights to come. It all happens thanks to Google Calendar and the Calendar app on your phone.

Understanding the Calendar

The Droid 2 takes advantage of Google Calendar on the Internet. If you have a Google account (and I'm certain that you do), you already have Google Calendar. You can visit Google Calendar by using your computer to go to this Web page:

```
calendar.google.com
```

If necessary, log in using your Google account. You can use Google Calendar to keep track of dates or meetings or whatever else occupies your time. You can also use your phone to do the same thing, thanks to the Calendar app.

- ✔ I recommend that you use the Calendar app on your phone to access Google Calendar. It's a better way to access your schedule on the Droid 2 than using the Browser app to get to Google Calendar on the Web.

- ✔ Also see the later section "No Need to Alarm You" for information on using the Alarm & Timer app to set alarms on the phone.

- ✔ The Droid 2 comes with a Calendar widget. It should appear on the first Home page to the left of the main Home page. If not, you can add the widget to the Home page. (It's a Motorola widget.) The Calendar widget is useful for reminding you of upcoming appointments. See Chapter 22 for details on adding widgets to the Home screen.

Browsing dates

To see your schedule or upcoming important events, or just to know which day of the month it is, summon the Calendar app. Touch the Launcher button at the bottom of the Home screen to display a list of all apps on the phone; choose the one named Calendar.

The first screen you see is most likely the monthly calendar view, shown in Figure 19-1. The calendar looks like a typical monthly calendar, with the month and year at the top. Scheduled appointments appear as blue highlights on various days.

To view your appointments by week, press the Menu soft button and choose Week. Or, you can choose the Day command to see your daily schedule. Figure 19-2 shows both Week and Day views in the Calendar.

Event reminder

Selected day

Month   Today

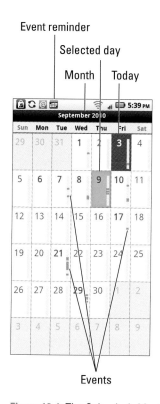

Events

Figure 19-1: The Calendar's Month view.

You can return to Month view at any time by pressing the Menu soft button and choosing the Month command.

> ✔ See the later section "Making a new event" for information on reviewing and creating events.

> ✔ Use Month view to see an overview of what's going on, but use Week or Day view to see your appointments.

> ✔ I check Week view at the start of the week to remind me of what's coming up.

> ✔ Different colors flag your events (refer to Figure 19-2) to represent different calendars to which the events are assigned. See the later section "Making a new event" for information on calendars.

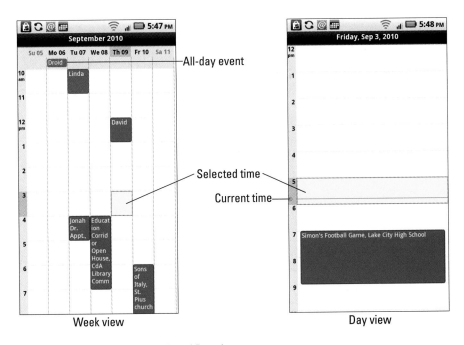

Week view   Day view

Figure 19-2: The Calendar's Week and Day views.

- ✏ Use your finger to flick the Week and Day views up or down to see your entire schedule, from midnight to midnight.

- ✏ Navigate the days, weeks, or months by flicking the screen with your finger. Months scroll up and down; weeks and days scroll from left to right.

- ✏ To see the current day highlighted or displayed, press the Menu soft button and choose the Today command.

Reviewing your schedule

To see more detail about an event, touch it. When you're using Month view, touch the date with the event on it and then choose the event from Day view. Details about the event appear similarly to the ones shown in Figure 19-3.

To see all upcoming events, you can switch to Agenda view: Press the Menu soft button and choose the Agenda command. Rather than list a traditional calendar, the Agenda screen shows only those dates with events and the events themselves. It's sort of a list.

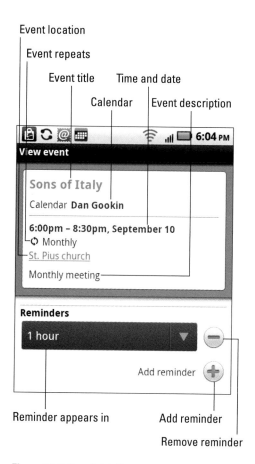

Event location
Event repeats
Event title   Time and date
Calendar   Event description

View event

Sons of Italy
Calendar **Dan Gookin**

6:00pm – 8:30pm, September 10
↻ Monthly
St. Pius church
Monthly meeting

Reminders
1 hour ▼ ⊖
Add reminder ⊕

Reminder appears in   Add reminder
Remove reminder

Figure 19-3: Event details.

As with events in the non-Agenda views, simply touch an event to see more details (refer to Figure 19-3).

✔ Not every event has the level of detail shown in Figure 19-3. The minimum amount of information necessary for an event is a name and the date and time.

✔ If you touch the event on the calendar too long — if you long-press — choose the item View Event from the menu.

✔ Use the sliding keyboard's arrow keys to move around the selected date or time. The selected date or time comes in handy when creating events.

✔ See the next section for information on event reminders.

Making a new event

The key to making your calendar work is to add events: appointments, things to do, meetings, or full-day events such as birthdays and vacations. To create a new event, follow these steps in the Calendar app:

1. **Select the day for the event.**

   Use Month or Week view and touch the day of the new event.

   To save time, use Day view and touch the hour at which the event starts.

2. **Press the Menu soft button.**

3. **Choose More and then New Event.**

   A screen appears, where you add details about the event.

4. **Type the event name.**

   For example, type `Picnic` or `Lunch with Mel` or `Colonoscopy`.

5. **Touch the Who field to add yourself.**

   Your account is named Me on the Droid 2.

   You can add other people to the event and they're sent email notifications about the event. If you don't want to bother those folks (or yourself), don't add them (or you) in the Who field.

6. **Use the buttons by Start to set the starting date and time.**

7. **Use the buttons by End to set the ending date and time.**

   When an event lasts all day, such as visiting your mother-in-law for an hour, simply touch the All Day button to put a check mark there. All-day events appear at the top of the day when the Calendar is shown in Week view (refer to Figure 19-2).

   At this point, you've entered the minimum amount of information for creating an event. Any details you add are okay but not necessary.

8. **Touch the Save button.**

   The Calendar app creates the event.

You can change an event at any time: Simply summon the event as described in the preceding section, press the Menu soft button while viewing the event, and choose the Edit Event command.

To remove an event, choose an event from the Calendar to view the event details. Press the Menu soft button and choose the Delete Event command. Touch the OK button to confirm.

✔ Adding an event location not only tells you where the event will be located but also hooks that information into the Maps app. My advice is to type information into an event's Where field just as though you're typing information to search for a map. When the event is displayed, the location is a clickable link (refer to Figure 19-3); touch the location link to see where it is on a map.

✔ Google Calendar lets you create multiple calendars, which help you categorize types of events. For example, I have a personal calendar, one for my kids' schedule, one for work, and a travel calendar. Different calendars' events show up in different colors (refer to Figure 19-2).

✔ Use the Repetition button to create repeating events, such as weekly or monthly meetings, anniversaries, and birthdays.

 ✔ Reminders can be set so that the phone alerts you before an event takes place. The alert can show up as a notification icon (shown in the margin), or it can be an audio alert or a vibrating alert.

✔ To deal with an event notification, pull down the notifications and choose the event. You can touch the Dismiss All button to remove event alerts.

✔ Alert types are set by pressing the Menu soft button in the Calendar app: Choose the More command and then Settings. Use the Select Ringtone option to choose an audio alert. Use the Vibrate option to control whether the phone vibrates to alert you of an impending event.

 ✔ You can also create events by using Google Calendar on the Internet. Those events are instantly synced with the calendar on your Droid 2 phone.

 ✔ I've noticed that event times can be affected by your travel. For example, I have set my East Coast appointments while on the West Coast, yet when I arrived on the East Coast, the Calendar app adjusted the appointment times by three hours. I don't know whether it's a bug, and I don't know how to fix the problem, given the current edition of the software.

Your Phone the Calculator

The Calculator is perhaps the oldest of all traditional cell phone apps. It's probably also the least confusing and frustrating app to use.

Start the Calculator app by choosing its icon from the Applications Tray. The Calculator appears, as shown in Figure 19-4.

42 CLEAR

7	8	9	(	)	×
4	5	6	.	÷	−
1	2	3	0	=	+

Figure 19-4: The Calculator.

- ✔ You can swipe the screen (refer to Figure 19-4) to the left to see a panel of strange, advanced mathematical operations you'll probably never use.

- ✔ Use the sliding keyboard's up- and down-arrow keys to scroll back through the previous calculations you've made.

- ✔ Long-press the calculator's text (or results) to cut or copy the results.

- ✔ I use the Calculator most often to determine my tip at a restaurant. It takes me almost as long to use the Calculator as it does for smarty-pants Barbara to do the 15 percent calculation in her head. That's when I tip 18 percent.

No Need to Alarm You

The Droid 2 keeps constant and accurate track of the time, which is displayed at the top of the Home screen and also when you first wake up the phone. When you'd rather have the phone wake you up, you can take advantage of the Alarm & Timer app.

Start the Alarm & Timer app by choosing its icon from the Applications Tray. The Alarm Clock is shown in Figure 19-5.

If you see an alarm you want to set, touch the gray square (refer to Figure 19-5) to set that alarm. A green check mark in a square indicates that an alarm is set.

Alarm set

Alarm created but not set

Alarm set

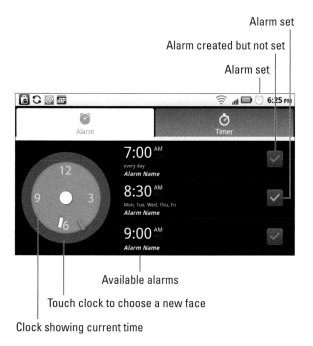

Available alarms

Touch clock to choose a new face

Clock showing current time

Figure 19-5: The clock.

To create your own alarm, follow these steps while using the Alarm Clock app:

1. **Press the Menu soft button.**

2. **Choose Add Alarm.**

3. **Choose Time to set the alarm time.**

   Use the gizmo to set the hour and minute and specify AM or PM. Touch the Set button when you're done setting the time.

4. **Touch the Sound button to choose a ringtone for the alarm — something suitably annoying.**

5. **Specify whether the phone vibrates by placing a check mark next to the Vibrate option.**

6. **Choose whether the alarm repeats.**

   Choose which days of the week you want the alarm to sound.

7. **Choose the Name item to type or dictate a label for the alarm.**

8. **Touch the Done button to create the alarm.**

   The alarm appears in a list on the main Alarm Clock screen, along with any other available alarms.

Alarms must be set or else they will not trigger. To set an alarm, touch it in the alarm list. Place a check mark in the gray box (refer to Figure 19-5).

- ✔ For a larger time display, you can add a Clock widget to the Home screen. Refer to Chapter 22 for more information about widgets on the Home screen.

- ✔ Turning off an alarm doesn't delete the alarm.

- ✔ To remove an alarm, long-press it from the list and choose the Delete Alarm command. Touch the OK button to confirm.

- ✔ The alarm doesn't work when you turn off the phone. The alarm does, however, go off when the phone is sleeping.

- ✔ A notification icon appears when an alarm has gone off but has been ignored.

- ✔ So tell me: Do alarms go *off* or do they go *on*?

There's No Tube Like YouTube

YouTube is the Internet phenomenon to prove Andy Warhol right: In the future, everyone will be famous for 15 minutes. Or, in the case of YouTube, they'll be famous on the Internet for the duration of a 10-minute video. That's because *YouTube* is *the* place on the Internet for anyone and everyone to share their video creations.

To view the mayhem on YouTube, or to contribute something yourself, start the YouTube app. Like all apps on the Droid 2, it can be found on the Applications Tray. The main YouTube screen is depicted in Figure 19-6.

To view a video, touch its name or icon in the list.

To search for a video, touch the Search button (refer to Figure 19-6). Type or dictate what you want to search for, and then peruse the results.

Get information

Search for videos

Record and upload a video

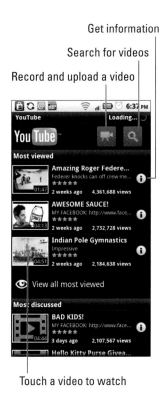

Touch a video to watch

Figure 19-6: YouTube.

Videos in the YouTube app play in Landscape mode, so tilt your phone to the left to see the videos in their proper orientation. The videos take up the entire screen; touch the screen to see the onscreen video controls.

 Press the Back soft button to return to the main YouTube app after watching a video or if you tire of a video and need to return to the main screen out of boredom.

   ✔ Use the YouTube app to view YouTube videos rather than use the Browser app to visit the YouTube Web site.

   ✔ Because you have a Google account, you also have a YouTube account. I recommend that you log in to your YouTube account when using YouTube on the Droid 2: Press the Menu soft button and choose the command My Account. Log in, if necessary. Otherwise, you see your account information, your videos, and any video subscriptions.

WARNING!

✔ Not all YouTube videos can be viewed on mobile devices.

✔ You can touch the Record & Upload button (refer to Figure 19-6) to shoot and then immediately send a video to YouTube. Refer to Chapter 16 for information on recording video with your Droid 2.

Movies in the Palm of Your Hand

Wouldn't it be fun to watch the latest Hollywood hits on your Droid 2? Would it be even more fun if the Droid 2 came with an app that did just that? Would it be "just the best" if watching those films were free?

Well, two out of three ain't bad.

The Droid 2 comes with the Blockbuster app, which can be used to rent or purchase mainstream movies that you can view right on your phone. The key is to have an account at Blockbuster. When you do, you can follow the directions on the screen after starting the Blockbuster app and get everything signed up and configured. All that's missing is the popcorn.

Even when you don't have a Blockbuster account, you can still use the app to see which films are available.

The Droid 2 Does Games

For all its seriousness and technology, one of the best uses of a smartphone is to play games. I'm not talking about the silly arcade games (though I admit that they're fun). No, I'm talking about some serious portable gaming.

To whet your appetite, the Droid 2 comes with a small taste of what the device can do in regard to gaming. It's the NFS Shift app, which is a car-racing game, shown in Figure 19-7.

NFS Shift uses the phone's accelerometer to steer a high-speed race car around various racing tracks from all over the globe. The game also plays stereotypical rock music, which either makes the action more exciting or merely irritates you.

Figure 19-7: Games on the Droid 2.

If you want to continue playing NFS Shift, you have to buy it. The program lets you know how much it costs after you complete your first free race.

Of course, gaming isn't limited to NFS Shift. Many games — arcade, action, and puzzle — can be found in the Android Market. See Chapter 20.

20

Shop at the Android Market

In This Chapter

▶ Using the Market app

▶ Searching for apps

▶ Downloading a free app

▶ Getting a paid app

▶ Reviewing apps you've downloaded

▶ Deleting apps

▶ Maintaining apps

Though the Droid 2 comes with a smattering of interesting and diverse apps, they are by no means all the apps the phone will ever have. That's because tens of thousands of Android apps are available for the Droid 2. You can add them to your phone's software repository at any time, and most of them are free. The place you need to visit to find those apps is the Android Market.

✔ Because the Droid 2 uses the Android operating system, it can run nearly all applications written for Android.

✔ You can be assured that all apps that appear in the Android Market on your phone can be used with the Droid 2. There's no way that you can download or buy something that's incompatible with your phone.

✔ App is short for *application*. It's another word for *software,* which is another word for a program that runs on a computer or on a mobile device, such as your Droid 2 phone.

Welcome to the Market

Shopping for new software for your Droid 2 can be done anywhere that you and your phone just happen to be. You don't even need to know what kind of software you want; like many a mindless ambling shopper, you can browse until the touchscreen is smudged and blurry with your fingerprints.

- You obtain software from the Market by *downloading* it into your phone. That file transfer works best at top speeds; therefore:

- I highly recommend that you connect to a Wi-Fi network if you plan to purchase software at the Android Market. See Chapter 14 for details on connecting the Droid 2 to a Wi-Fi network.

Visiting the Market

New apps await delivery into your phone, like animated vegetables shouting, "Pick me! Pick me!" To get to them, open the Market icon, which can be found on the main Home screen or accessed from the Applications Tray.

After opening the Market app, you see the main screen, similar to the one shown in Figure 20-1. You can browse for apps, games, or special apps from Verizon by touching the appropriate doodad, as shown in the figure.

Find apps by browsing the lists: Choose Apps (refer to Figure 20-1). Then choose a specific category to browse. You can sort apps by their popularity; separate categories exist for paid, free, and newer apps.

When you know an app's name or an app's category or even what the app does, searching for the app works fastest: Touch the Search button at the top of the Market screen (refer to Figure 20-1). Type all or part of the app's name or perhaps a description. Touch the keyboard's Search button to begin your search.

To see more information about an app, touch it. Touching the app doesn't buy it, but instead displays a more detailed description, screen shots, and comments, plus links to see additional apps or contact the developer.

- The first time you enter the Android Market, you have to accept the terms of service; touch the Accept button.

- Pay attention to an app's ratings. Ratings are added by people who use the apps, like you and me. Having more stars is better. You can see additional information, including individual user reviews, by choosing the app.

✔ In addition to getting apps, you can download widgets for the Home screen as well as wallpapers for the Droid 2. Just search the Android Market for *widget* or *live wallpaper.*

✔ See Chapter 22 for more information on widgets and live wallpapers.

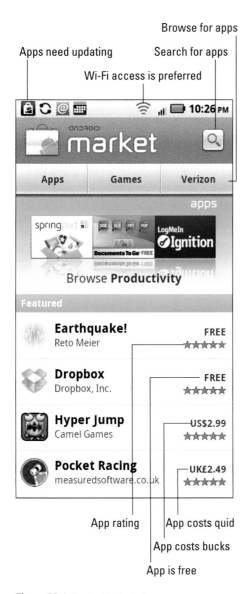

Figure 20-1: Android Market.

Getting a free app

After you locate an app you want, the next step is to download it. Follow these steps:

1. **If possible, activate the phone's Wi-Fi connection.**

    Downloads complete much faster over the Wi-Fi connection than over the digital cellular connection. See Chapter 14 for information on connecting your Droid 2 phone to a Wi-Fi network.

2. **Open the Market app.**

3. **Locate the app you want and open its description.**

    Refer to the preceding section for details. If you're just starting out, consider getting one of the V CAST apps in the Verizon category. (Most of them are free.)

4. **Touch the Install button.**

    The Install button is found at the bottom of the app's list o' details. Free apps feature an Install button. Paid apps have a Buy button. (See the next section for information on buying an app.)

    After touching the Install button, you're alerted to any services that the app uses. The alert isn't a warning, and it doesn't mean anything bad. It's just that your phone is telling you which of your phone's features the app uses.

5. **Touch the OK button to begin the download.**

    You return to the main Market screen as the app downloads. It continues to download while you do other things on your phone.

     After the download is successful, the phone's status bar shows a new icon, as shown in the margin. That's the Successful Install notification.

6. **Pull down the notifications.**

    See Chapter 3 for details, in case you've never pulled down notifications.

7. **Choose the app from the list of notifications.**

    The app is listed by its app name, with the text `Successfully Installed` beneath it.

At this point, what happens next depends on the app you've downloaded. For example, you may have to agree to a license agreement. If so, touch the I Agree button. Additional setup may involve signing in to an account or creating a profile, for example.

After the initial setup is complete, or if no setup is necessary, you can start using the app.

✔ Don't forget to turn off Wi-Fi after downloading your app; Wi-Fi is a drain on the phone's battery.

✔ The new app's icon is placed on the Applications Tray, along with all the other apps on the Droid 2.

✔ Yes, when you add an app, it shuffles all icons on the Applications Tray — no way around that.

✔ Peruse the list of services an app uses (in Step 4) to look for anything unusual or out of line with the app's purpose. For example, an alarm clock app that uses your contact list and the text messaging service would be a red flag, especially if it's your understanding that the app doesn't need to text message any of your contacts.

✔ You can also place a shortcut icon for the app on the Home screen. See Chapter 22.

✔ The Android market has many wonderful apps you can download. Chapter 26 lists some that I recommend, all of which are free.

Buying an app

Some great free apps are available, but many of the apps you dearly want probably cost money. It's not a lot of money, especially compared to the price of computer software. In fact, it seems odd to sit and stew over whether paying 99 cents for a game is "worth it."

I recommend that you download a free app first, to familiarize yourself with the process.

When you're ready to pay for an app, follow these steps:

1. **Activate the phone's Wi-Fi connection.**

2. **Open the Market app.**

3. **Browse or search for the app you want, and choose the app to display its description.**

   Review the app's price. It's priced in dollars, euros, pounds, or yen. You can buy an app priced in another currency; your credit card or cell phone bill is charged the proper amount.

4. **Touch the Buy button.**

5. **Touch OK.**

   If you don't have a Google Checkout account, you're prompted to set one up. Follow the directions on the screen.

6. **Choose the payment method.**

   You can choose to use an existing credit card, add a new card, or — most conveniently — add the purchase to your cellular bill.

   If you choose to add a new card, you're required to fill in all information about the card, including the billing address.

7. **Touch the Buy Now button.**

   The Buy Now button has the app's price listed.

   After you touch the Buy button, the app is downloaded. You can wait or do something else with the phone while the app is downloading.

The app may require additional setup steps, confirmation information, or other options.

The app can be accessed from the Applications Tray, just like all other apps available on your Droid 2.

Eventually, you receive an email message from Google Checkout, confirming your purchase. The message explains how you can get a refund from your purchase within 24 hours. The section "Removing installed software," later in this chapter, discusses how to do it.

  ✔ The option to add the purchase to your cell phone bill might not be available for all phone plans.

  ✔ Be sure to disable the phone's Wi-Fi after downloading the app, because Wi-Fi is an additional drain on the phone's battery.

Manage Your Applications

The Market is not only where you buy apps — it's also the place you return to for performing app management. That task includes reviewing apps you've downloaded, updating apps, and removing apps you no longer want or that you severely hate.

Reviewing your downloads

If you're like me, and if I'm like anyone (and my editor says that I'm not), you probably sport a whole host of apps on your Droid 2. It's kind of fun to download new software and give your phone new abilities. To review the apps you've acquired, follow these steps:

1. **Start the Market app.**

2. **Press the Menu soft button.**

3. **Choose Downloads.**

4. **Scroll your downloaded apps.**

The list of downloaded apps should look similar to the one shown in Figure 20-2.

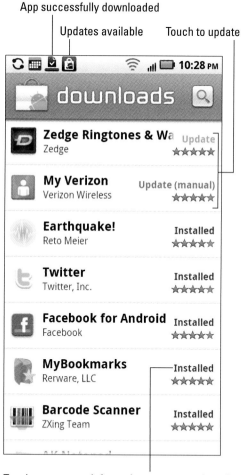

App successfully downloaded

Updates available   Touch to update

Touch to see more information, open, or uninstall

Figure 20-2: Apps downloaded for the Droid 2.

Besides reviewing the list, you can do two things with an installed app: Update it or remove it. The following two sections describe how each operation is done.

The Downloads list is accurate in that it represents apps you've downloaded. Some apps in the list, however, might not be installed on your Droid 2: They were downloaded, installed, and then removed. To review all apps installed on the phone, see the section "Controlling your apps," later in this chapter.

Updating an app

 One nice thing about using the Android Market to get new software is that the market also notifies you of new versions of the programs you download. Whenever a new version of any app is available, you see the Updates Available notification icon, shown in the margin.

Locate apps that need updating by pulling down the phone's notifications and choosing Updates Available. Or, you can visit the Downloads list, as described in the preceding section.

To update an app, obey these steps:

1. **Turn on the phone's Wi-Fi access, if it's available.**

   Updates are downloaded from the Internet, which means the faster your phone can connect, the more quickly the updates are made.

2. **Choose the updated app; touch it to open more details.**

   For example, touch an app with the Updates Available flag (refer to Figure 20-2).

3. **Touch the Update button.**

4. **Touch the OK button to heed the warning.**

   The update means that an entirely new version of the app is downloaded and installed, which replaces the installed version. That's okay.

5. **Optionally, read any services that the app uses on your phone and then touch the OK button.**

   The update is downloaded.

 As when you initially install the app, you're free to do other things with the phone while the update is downloading. When downloading is complete, the Successful Install notification appears, as shown in the margin. You can then start using your updated app or continue applying updates by repeating the steps in this section.

After the download is complete, pull down the notifications and select the downloaded app from the notifications list. When you first start the updated app, you may be asked to agree (again) to the licensing terms; touch the I Agree button. After that, you can start using the app.

✔ Some apps update themselves automatically. If so, the option to automatically update is found in the app itself: Press the Menu soft button and choose the Settings command. An automatic update option, if available, shows up on the app's Settings screen.

✔ When an app is flagged as a manual update (see Figure 20-2), you must select the app from the list and update it by following the directions in this section. The app cannot be updated automatically or as part of an "Update All" feature.

✔ Future releases of the Android operating system may feature an Update All button, which updates, all at one time, all apps that have pending updates. If so, in Step 3 touch the Update All button to make all your apps up-to-date.

✔ The Android operating system update might also apply an Update Automatically option for your apps. When selected, the apps automatically download their updates when available.

Removing installed software

There are a few reasons you'd want to remove installed software. The first, most odiously, is that you just don't like a program or it does something so hideously annoying that you find removal of the app to be emotionally satisfying. The second is that you have a better program that does the same thing. The third reason is to free up a modicum of storage on the phone's internal storage area or MicroSD card.

Whatever your reason, removing an app from your Droid 2 works like this:

1. **Start the Market app.**

2. **Press the Menu soft button.**

3. **Choose the Downloads heading to summon a list of all software you've downloaded into your phone.**

   Refer to Figure 20-2.

4. **Touch the app that offends you.**

5. **Touch the Uninstall button.**

6. **Touch the OK button to confirm.**

   The app is removed.

7. **Fill in the survey to specify why you removed the app.**

   Be honest, or be as honest as you can given the short list of reasons.

8. **Touch OK.**

   The app is gone!

The app continues to appear on the Downloads list even after it's been removed. After all, you downloaded it once. That doesn't mean that the app is installed. To review apps installed on the Droid 2, see the next section.

  ✔ In most cases, if you uninstall a paid app before 24 hours has passed, your credit card or account is fully refunded.

  ✔ You can always reinstall paid apps that you've uninstalled. You aren't charged twice for doing so.

Controlling your apps

The Droid 2 has a technical place where you can review and manage all apps you've installed on your phone. To visit that place, follow these steps:

1. **From the Home screen, touch the Menu soft button and choose Settings.**

2. **Choose Applications.**

3. **Choose Manage Applications.**

   A complete list of all applications installed on your phone is displayed. Unlike the Downloads list in the Market app, only installed applications appear in the list.

4. **Touch an application name.**

   Additional details and controls for the application are displayed, similar to the ones shown in Figure 20-3.

5. **Touch the Back button when you're done being baffled by the information.**

   You can also just touch the Home soft button to immediately escape to the Home screen.

You can use the Application Info screen (refer to Figure 20-3) to uninstall an app, similar to the steps described in the preceding section. This technique works for some older Android apps that don't appear on the Downloads list.

Refer to the information in the Storage section to determine how much space the app is using on the phone's internal storage or MicroSD card.

If the app is consuming a huge amount of space compared with other apps and you seldom use the app, consider it a candidate for deletion.

The Force Stop button is used to halt a program that runs amok. For example, I had to stop an older Android app that continually made noise and offered no option to exit. It was a relieving experience. See Chapter 23 for more details on shutting down apps run amok.

Figure 20-3: Detailed app information.

Part V
Hither and Thither

The 5th Wave — By Rich Tennant

Cell Phones

"This model comes with a particularly useful function — a simulated static button for breaking out of long winded conversations."

In this part . . .

1'm not certain about the exact difference between a cell phone and a mobile phone. I think they're both the same thing, though the term *cell phone* is more popular these days. I suppose that's because even an old, landline phone could be a "mobile phone" if you threw the thing out a window.

The chapters in this part of the book cover an assortment of topics here and there — stuff that just doesn't fit anywhere else. From taking your Droid 2 overseas to customizing your phone to performing basic maintenance and troubleshooting, it's all here. Or there. Then again, that's why I titled this part "Hither and Thither."

Release finger when done.

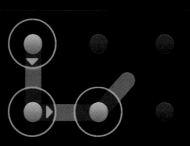

21

On the Road Again

In This Chapter

▷ Understanding roaming

▷ Disabling data-roaming features

▷ Entering Airplane mode

▷ Contacting friends abroad

▷ Using Skype mobile

▷ Using the Droid 2 overseas

*B*ack when life was simple, all I had to do was leave the house with my wallet. Then I had to carry around some keys: car keys, house keys, keys to work. As I grew older, glasses were added to the list of things I had to carry with me. Now I have my Droid 2, another must-have accessory that I must tote everywhere I go. I'm just glad that clothes come with pockets.

You can not only carry the Droid 2 with you but also take it wherever you go — across town, across the state, or across the country. You can even take the Droid 2 overseas. Talk about exotic: It's *all* possible. My gentle words of advice in this chapter help make your, and your phone's, travels fruitious and fortuitous.

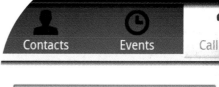

Where the Phone Roams

The word *roam* takes on an entirely new meaning when applied to a cell phone. It means that your phone receives a cell signal whenever you're outside your cell phone carrier's operating area. In that case, your phone is *roaming*.

Roaming sounds handy, but there's a catch: It almost always involves a surcharge for using another cellular service — an *unpleasant* surcharge.

The Droid 2 alerts you whenever you're roaming. You see a Roaming icon appear at the top of the screen, in the status area. The icon tells you that you're outside the regular signal area, possibly using another cellular provider's network.

There's little you can do to avoid incurring roaming surcharges when making or receiving phone calls. Well, yes: You can wait until you're back in an area serviced by your primary cellular provider. You can, however, altogether avoid using the other network's data services while roaming. Follow these steps:

1. **On the Home screen press the Menu soft button and choose Settings.**

2. **Choose Data Manager.**

3. **Choose Data Delivery.**

    You may see a warning when data roaming is activated on your phone: Dismiss the warning or choose the option that disables data roaming. Otherwise:

4. **Ensure that the Data Roaming option isn't selected.**

    Remove the green check mark by the Data Roaming option.

The phone can still access the Internet over the Wi-Fi connection when you're roaming. Setting up a Wi-Fi connection doesn't make you incur extra charges, unless you have to pay to get on the wireless network. See Chapter 14 for more information about Wi-Fi.

Another network service you might want to disable while roaming has to do with multimedia text messages, or *MMS*. To avoid surcharges from another cellular network for downloading an MMS message, follow these steps:

1. **Open the Text Messaging app.**

2. **If the screen shows a specific conversation, press the Back soft button to return to the main messaging screen.**

    (It's the screen that lists all your conversations.)

3. **Touch the Menu soft button.**

4. **Choose Messaging Settings.**

5. **Remove the green check mark by Auto-Retrieve.**

    Or, if the item isn't selected, you're good to go — literally.

For more information about multimedia text messages, refer to Chapter 9.

When the phone is roaming, you may see the text *Emergency Calls Only* displayed on the locked screen.

Airplane Mode

As anyone knows who has been flying recently, making a call from your cell phone while on an airborne plane is strictly forbidden. That's because, if you did, the navigation system would completely screw up, the plane would invert, and everyone onboard would die in a spectacular crash on the ground, in a massive fireball suitable for the 5 o'clock "Eyewitness News." It would be breathtaking.

Droid 2 air-travel tips

I don't consider myself a frequent flyer, but I travel several times a year. I do it often enough that I wish the airports had separate lines for security: one for seasoned travelers, one for families, and one, of course, for frickin' idiots. The last category would have to be disguised by placing a Bonus Coupons sign or Free Snacks banner over the metal detector. That would weed 'em out.

Here are some of my cell phone and airline travel tips:

✔ **Charge your phone before you leave home.** This tip probably goes without saying, but you'll be happier with a full cell phone charge to start your journey.

✔ **Take a cell phone charger with you.** Many airports feature USB chargers, so you might need just a USB-to-micro–USB cable. Still, why risk it? Bring the entire charger with you.

✔ **At the security checkpoint, place your phone in a bin.** Add to the bin all your other electronic devices, keys, and brass knuckles. I know from experience that keeping your cell phone in your pocket most definitely sets off airport metal detectors.

✔ **When the flight attendant asks you to *turn off* your cell phone for takeoff and landing, obey the command.** That's *turn off*, as in power off the phone or shut it down. It doesn't mean that you place the phone in Airplane mode. Turn it off.

✔ **Use the phone's Calendar app to keep track of flights.** The airline and flight number could serve as the event title. For the event time, I insert the take-off and landing schedules. For the location, I add the origin and destination airport codes. Referencing the phone from your airplane seat or in a busy terminal is much handier than fussing with travel papers. See Chapter 19 for more information on the Calendar.

✔ **Remember that some airlines may eventually feature Android apps you can use while traveling.** Rather than hang on to a boarding pass printed by your computer, for example, you just present your phone to the scanner. (At the time this book was published, a few airline-specific apps were available for the Droid 2, but none from major carriers. I predict that you'll soon see a lot of these apps. Refer to Chapter 20 for information on finding apps in the Android Market.)

✔ **Some apps you can use to organize your travel details are similar to, but more sophisticated than, using the Calendar app.** Visit the Android Market and search for *travel* or *airline* to find a host of apps.

Seriously, you're not supposed to use a cell phone when flying. Specifically, you're not allowed you make calls in the air. You can, however, use your Droid 2 to listen to music or play games or do anything else that doesn't require a cellular connection. The secret is to place the phone in *Airplane mode.*

The most convenient way to put the Droid 2 in Airplane mode is to press and hold the Power button. From the menu, choose Airplane Mode. You don't even need to unlock the phone to perform this operation.

The most inconvenient way to put the Droid 2 into Airplane mode is to follow these steps:

1. **From the Applications Tray, choose the Settings icon.**

2. **Choose Wireless & Networking.**

3. **Touch the square by Airplane Mode to set the green check mark.**

   When the green check mark is visible, Airplane mode is active.

 When the phone is in Airplane mode, a special icon appears in the status area, as shown in the margin. You might also see the text *No Service* appear on the phone's locked screen.

To exit Airplane mode, repeat the steps in this section but remove the green check mark by touching the square next to Airplane Mode.

 ✔ Officially, the Droid 2 should be powered *off* when the plane is taking off or landing. See Chapter 2 for information on turning off the phone.

✔ You can compose email while the phone is in Airplane mode. The messages aren't sent until you disable Airplane mode and connect again with a data network.

 ✔ Another quick way to activate or disable Airplane mode is to use the Power Control widget, which appears on the second Home screen to the left of the main Home screen.

✔ Bluetooth networking is disabled when you activate the Droid 2 Airplane mode, but it can be reenabled after Airplane mode is active. Even so, using Bluetooth during a flight isn't recommended on many airlines. See Chapter 14 for more information on Bluetooth.

 ✔ Many airlines now feature wireless networking onboard. You can turn on wireless networking for the Droid 2 and use a wireless network in the air. Simply activate the Droid 2 Wi-Fi feature, per the directions in Chapter 14, after placing the phone in Airplane mode — well, after the flight attendant tells you that it's okay to do so.

International Calling

You can use your cell phone to dial up folks who live in other countries. You can also take your cell phone overseas and use it in another country. Doing either task isn't as difficult as properly posing for a passport photo, but it can become frustrating and expensive when you don't know your way around.

Dialing an international number

A phone is a bell that anyone in the world can ring. To prove it, all you need is the phone number of anyone in the world. Dial that number using your Droid 2 and, as long as you both speak the same language, you're talking!

To make an international call with the Droid 2, you merely need to know the foreign phone number. That number includes the international country-code prefix, followed by the number.

Before dialing the international country-code prefix, you must dial a plus sign (+) on the Droid 2. The + symbol is the *country exit code,* which must be dialed in order to flee the national phone system and access the international phone system. For example, to dial Finland on your Droid 2, you dial +358 and then the number in Finland. The +358 is the exit code (+) plus the international code for Finland (358).

To produce the + code in an international phone number, press and hold the 0 key on the Droid 2 dialpad. Then input the country prefix and the phone number. Touch the Dial button (the green Phone icon) to complete the call.

- ✓ In most cases, dialing an international number involves a time zone difference. Before you dial, be aware of what time it is in the country or location you're calling.

- ✓ Dialing internationally also involves surcharges, unless your cell phone plan already provides for international dialing.

- ✓ The + character is used on the Droid 2 to represent the country exit code, which must be dialed before you can access an international number. In the United States, the exit code is 011. (In the United Kingdom, it's 00.) So, if you're using a landline to dial Russia from the United States, you dial 011 to escape from the United States and then 7, the country code for Russia. Then dial the rest of the number. You don't have to do that on the Droid 2, because + is always the country exit code and replaces the 011 for U.S. users.

✏ The + character isn't a number separator. When you see an international number listed as 011+20+xxxxxxx, do not insert the + character in the number. Instead, dial +20 and then the rest of the number.

✏ International calls fail for a number of reasons. One of the most common is that the recipient's phone company or service blocks incoming international calls.

✏ Another reason that international calls fail is the zero reason: Often times, you must leave out any zero in the phone number that follows the country code. So, if the country code is 254 for Kenya and the phone number starts with 012, you dial +254 for Kenya and then 12 and the rest of the number. Omit the leading zero.

✏ You can also send text messages to international cell phones. It works the same way as making a traditional phone call: Input the international number into the Messaging app. See Chapter 9 for more information on text messaging.

✏ Know which type of phone you're calling internationally — cell phone or landline. The reason is that an international call to a cell phone often involves a surcharge that doesn't apply to a landline.

Making international calls with Skype mobile

Your Droid 2 comes with the Skype mobile app, which can be used to make inexpensive international calls. It's an excellent option, especially when your cellular contract doesn't provide for international calling.

If you don't yet have a Skype account, use your computer to create one. You need that account to use Skype mobile. Set up the account by first obtaining the Skype program for your computer: Visit www.skype.com to get started. Further, you must have Skype Credit to make the international call. That credit can be purchased from within the Skype program on your computer.

The Skype mobile app is found in the Applications Tray. After starting the app, log in with your Skype ID and password.

You can't make an international call unless you've created a contact with an international number. The contact must be a Skype mobile contact, shown on the Contacts tab on the Skype mobile screen, illustrated in Figure 21-1.

To make an international call, touch the Call Phones tab at the top of the screen. Punch in the number, including the + symbol for international access, as described in this chapter and shown in Figure 21-1. Touch the Call button to make the call.

Touch to make the international call

Touch to make international calls

Touch to summon the dialpad

Skype contacts

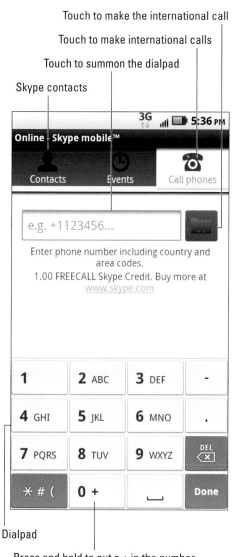

Dialpad

Press and hold to put a + in the number

Figure 21-1: Calling internationally with Skype mobile.

After the call is connected by Skype mobile, the Droid 2 touchscreen looks similar to the way it looks when you regularly place calls. You can use the phone's dialpad, if necessary, mute the call, or put it on speaker, for example.

When you're finished with the call, touch the End button.

- You're always signed into Skype mobile unless you sign out. Pressing the Home button to switch away from the app doesn't log you out of Skype.

- To log out of Skype mobile, press the Menu soft button, choose More, and then choose Sign Out.

- The first time you use the Skype mobile app, you're required to read various information and agree to the licensing terms. La-di-da.

- At the time this book went to press, Skype mobile required a digital cellular signal; it doesn't work over a Wi-Fi connection.

- Check with your cellular provider to see whether you're charged connection minutes for using Skype mobile. Even though the international call is free, you might still be dinged for the minutes you use on Skype to make the call.

Taking your Droid 2 abroad

The easiest way to use a cell phone abroad is to rent or buy one in the country where you plan to stay. I'm serious: Often, international roaming charges are so high that it's just cheaper to buy a throwaway cell phone wherever you go, especially if you plan to stay there for a while.

When you opt to use your Droid 2 rather than buy a local phone, phone calls and Internet access should run smoothly — *if* a compatible cellular service is in your location. (The Droid 2 uses the CDMA cellular network.) The foreign carrier accepts incoming and outgoing calls from your phone and cheerfully charges you the international roaming rate.

The key to determining whether your Droid 2 is usable in a foreign country is to turn it on. The name of that country's compatible cellular service should show up at the top of the phone, where Verizon Wireless (or whatever your carrier is) appears on the Droid 2 main screen. (Refer to Figure 2-1, in Chapter 2.)

- You receive calls on your cell phone internationally as long as the Droid 2 can access the network. Your friends need only dial your cell phone number as they normally do; the phone system automatically forwards your calls to wherever you are in the world.

- The person calling you doesn't pay extra when you're off romping the globe with your Droid 2. Nope — *you* pay extra for the call.

- You can also determine whether your Droid 2 can be used in a foreign country, by visiting this Web page:

```
http://b2b.vzw.com/international/technology/cdma.html
```

Customize Your Droid 2

In This Chapter

▶ Changing the Home screen background

▶ Working with icons and widgets on the Home screen

▶ Using folders for Home screen organization

▶ Adding security

▶ Silencing the phone's noise

▶ Enabling automatic answer and redial

▶ Modifying phone settings

▶ Setting accessibility options

*C*ustomization is one of those tasks that few people seem to try. Perhaps they don't know that just about everything about their Droid 2 can be changed, perfected to look or behave the way they want. Maybe those people are afraid that something will break. Maybe they don't realize how much better the phone can work by customizing it to the way they use it and setting the options they prefer. But that's them. For you, I present this chapter, which tells you how to customize the Droid 2 to make it your own.

It's Your Home Screen

The Droid 2 sports a roomy Home screen. It's really *seven* Home screens. Of course, the phone comes preconfigured with lots of icons and widgets festooning all seven of the Home screens. You can customize them by removing widgets and icons, especially those you seldom use, and replacing them with icons and widgets you do use. You can also add folders to organize things, and you can even put a new wallpaper on the Home screen. Truly, you can make the Home screen look just the way you want.

For the most part, the key to changing the Home screen is the *long-press:* Press and hold your finger on a blank part of the Home screen (not on an icon). You see a pop-up menu appear, as shown in Figure 22-1. From that menu, you can begin your Home screen customization adventure, as discussed in this section.

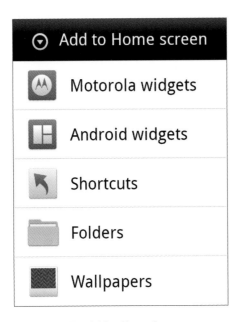

⊙ Add to Home screen

Ⓜ Motorola widgets

▦ Android widgets

↖ Shortcuts

🗀 Folders

▨ Wallpapers

Figure 22-1: The Add to Home Screen menu.

Changing wallpaper

The Home screen has two types of backgrounds, or wallpapers: traditional and live. *Live* wallpapers are animated. A not-so-live wallpaper can be any image, such as a picture from the Gallery.

To set a new wallpaper for the Home screen, obey these steps:

1. **Long-press the Home screen.**

   The Add to Home Screen menu appears, as shown in Figure 22-1.

2. **Choose Wallpapers.**

   Another menu appears, with three options (refer to Figure 22-2).

3. **Select an option based on the type of wallpaper.**

   Your choices are

Figure 22-2: Selecting wallpaper.

> ✐ *Live Wallpapers:* Choose an animated or interactive wallpaper from a list.

> ✐ *Media Gallery:* Choose a still image from those you've taken, stored in the Gallery app.

> ✐ *Wallpapers:* Choose a wallpaper from a range of stunning images (no nudity).

4. **Choose the wallpaper you want from the list.**

   For the Media Gallery option, you see a preview of the wallpaper where you can select and crop part of the image.

   For certain live wallpapers, a Settings button may appear. The settings let you customize certain aspects of the interactive wallpaper.

5. **Touch the Save or Set Wallpaper button to confirm your selection.**

   The new wallpaper takes over the Home screen.

Live wallpaper is interactive, usually featuring some form of animation. Otherwise, the wallpaper image scrolls slightly as you swipe from one Home screen to another.

> ✐ The Zedge app has some interesting wallpaper features. Check it out at the Android Market; see Chapter 20.

> ✐ You can also download wallpapers from the Android Market. Again, see Chapter 20.

> ✐ Be careful when using live wallpapers. The animation consumes processor power on the Droid 2, which sometimes affects the performance of other apps as well as your phone's battery life.

> ✐ See Chapter 17 for more information about the Gallery, including information on how cropping an image works.

Adding apps to the Home screen

You need not live with the unbearable proposition that you're stuck with only the apps supplied on the Home screen. Nope — you're free to add your own apps. Just follow these steps:

1. **Touch the Launcher button to hunt down the app you want to add to the Home screen.**

2. **Press — and keep pressing — an app's icon.**

   After a moment, you return to the Home screen with the app's icon still stuck under your finger.

3. **Slide your finger — still pressed down — left or right to go to a left or right part of the Home screen.**

   Seven Home screens are on the Droid 2.

4. **Position your finger — still pressed down — on the spot where you want the app's icon to be placed.**

5. **Release your finger.**

   A copy of the app's icon is placed on the Home screen. There's no need to clean your fingertip after completing these steps.

The app hasn't moved: What you see is a copy. You can still find the app on the Applications Tray, but now the app is — more conveniently — available on the Home screen.

- ✔ Keep your favorite apps, those you use most often, on the Home screen.

- ✔ You cannot drop an app in a spot where the Home screen is already full of apps or widgets. Try using a blank Home screen.

- ✔ When the Home screen gets too full, you can organize your apps into folders. See the later section "Organizing apps into folders."

Slapping down widgets

Just as you can add apps to the Home screen, you can add widgets. A *widget* works like a tiny, interactive or informative window, often providing a gateway into another app on the Droid 2.

The Droid 2 comes with a bazillion widgets, stuck to the Home screen like bugs on a windshield after a long car trip. You can place even more widgets on the Home screen by following these steps:

1. **Long-press the Home screen.**

2. **Choose Motorola Widgets or Android Widgets from the Add to Home Screen menu.**

3. From the list, choose the widget you want to add.

The widget is plopped on the Home screen.

The variety of available widgets depends on the applications you have installed. Some applications come with widgets, some don't.

✔ More widgets are available at the Android Market. See Chapter 20.

✔ The Motorola Widget category contains widgets customized for your Verizon Droid 2 phone. The Android Widget category contains widgets available to users of any Android phone. If you can't find the widget you want in one category, repeat Steps 1 and 2 to look in the other.

✔ You cannot install a widget when the Home screen has no room for it. Choose another Home screen, or remove icons or widgets from the current Home screen.

✔ To remove a widget, see the later section "Rearranging and removing icons and widgets."

Creating shortcuts

A shortcut is a doodad you can place on the Home screen that's neither an app nor a widget. Instead, a *shortcut* is a handy way to get at a feature or an informational tidbit stored in the phone without having to endure complex gyrations.

For example, I have a shortcut on my Home screen that uses the Maps app Navigation feature to help me return to my house. I don't use the app when I'm running from an irate mob, either.

To add a shortcut, long-press the Home screen and choose the Shortcuts command from the Add to Home Screen menu (refer to Figure 22-1). What happens next depends on which shortcut you choose.

For example, when you choose a bookmark, you add a Web page bookmark to the Home screen. Touch that shortcut to open the Browser app and visit that Web page.

Choose a Contact shortcut to display contact information for a specific person, The Droid 2 has shortcuts for Music and the Maps app (Direction & Navigation); plus, shortcuts for various apps are installed on your phone.

A nerdy shortcut to add is the Settings shortcut. After choosing this item, you can select from a number of on-off options that can appear on the Home screen as widgets.

The AnyCut app is useful for creating certain shortcuts that the Droid 2 cannot create by itself, such as a shortcut to direct-dial a contact. Check out AnyCut at the Android Market; see Chapter 20.

Rearranging and removing icons and widgets

Icons and widgets aren't fastened to the Home screen. If they are, it's day-old chewing gum that binds them, considering how easily you can rearrange and remove unwanted items from the Home screen.

Press and hold an icon on the Home screen to move it. Eventually, the icon seems to lift and break free, as shown in Figure 22-3.

You can drag a free icon to another position on the Home screen or to another Home screen, or you can drag it to the Trash icon that appears at the bottom of the Home screen, replacing the Launcher button (refer to Figure 22-3).

Widgets can also be moved around or removed in the same manner as icons.

- Dragging a Home screen icon or widget to the Trash removes the icon or widget from the Home screen. It doesn't remove the application, which is still found on the Applications Tray, or the widget, which you can add to the Home screen again, as described earlier in this chapter.

- When an icon hovers over the Trash, ready to be deleted, its color changes to red.

- See Chapter 20 for information on uninstalling applications.

- Your clue that an icon or widget is free and clear to navigate is that the Launcher button changes to the Trash icon (refer to Figure 22-3).

Organizing apps into folders

When you run out of room on the Home screen, or you feel like adding an extra level of Home screen organization, you can create a folder. The *folder* is used to store icons, similar to the way folders on your computer store files. The result is the same for both: organization.

Create a folder by following these steps:

1. **Long-press the Home screen.**

2. **Choose the Folders command.**

   A list appears, showing many different types of folders you can create on the Home screen. The number of items in the list depends on the various apps you have installed and whether the app allows you to create handy Home screen folders.

Icon being pressed
(appears larger)

Launcher button changes
to Trash

Figure 22-3: Moving an icon around.

3. **Select New Folder from the list.**

   The New Folder icon appears on the Home screen (titled Games in Figure 22-3). You probably want to rename it.

4. **Touch the folder icon to open it and show its contents.**

   New folders are empty, of course. Figure 22-4 shows a folder into which I've copied various game apps.

5. **Long-press the folder window's title.**

   Refer to Figure 22-4 for the location. When you press too briefly, the folder closes. Start over again in Step 4.

6. **Type or dictate a new folder name.**

   Touch the folder's Name field to summon the onscreen keyboard.

7. **Touch the OK button to lock in the new name.**

   Optionally, close the folder by touching its X button. Refer to Figure 22-4 for the location of the X button.

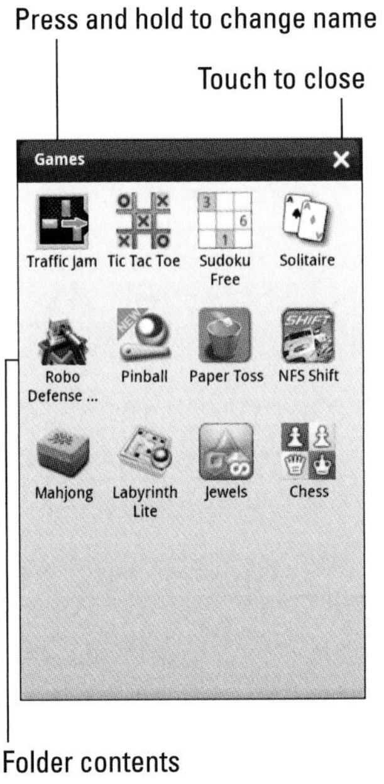

Press and hold to change name

Touch to close

Folder contents

Figure 22-4: A folder for games and fun.

Drag icons to move them into the folder, just as you drag icons around the Home screen. Or, you can drag icons from the Applications Tray into the folder. You simply need to "drop" the icon over the folder to copy it into the folder.

To move an icon out of a folder, long-press the icon. The folder closes, and then you can drag the icon to a new position on the Home screen or drag it to the Trash.

Delete folders by dragging them to the Trash.

Droid 2 Security

The Droid 2 comes with a lock, a simple touchscreen gizmo you slide to the right to unlock the phone and gain access to its information and features. It's the *keyguard*. For most folks, the keyguard is secure enough. For many others, the keyguard is about as effective as using wet tissue paper for armor.

You can add three additional types of security locks to your phone: a pattern lock, a PIN lock, or a password lock. The details are provided in this section.

Applying, or removing, a lock starts with these basic steps:

1. **From the Home screen, press the Menu soft button.**
2. **Choose Settings.**
3. **Choose Location & Security.**
4. **Choose Set Up Screen Lock.**

   The four types of screen lock are displayed:

   - *None:* No additional security lock is applied, or an existing security lock is removed.
   - *Pattern:* You must trace a pattern to unlock the phone.
   - *PIN:* You must input a personal identification number (PIN) to unlock the phone.
   - *Password:* You must type a password to unlock the phone.

5. **To set a lock, refer to the following sections; or, to remove an existing lock, choose None.**

   When you choose None, you're asked to unlock the phone one more time, tracing the pattern or typing the PIN or password to remove the existing lock.

When the Screen Lock item is deselected (you've chosen None for the phone's security level), the Droid 2 returns to its normal mode of operation: Pressing the Power button summons the keyguard screen.

Further, if the screen lock isn't in place, you cannot add the extra levels of security covered in the next two sections.

- ✔ The security you add affects the way you turn on and wake up your phone. See Chapter 2 for details.
- ✔ The security lock can be overridden when USB debugging is enabled. Unless you're writing software for the Droid 2, however, odds are good that you'll never have USB debugging turned on.

Creating an unlock pattern

One of the best ways to secure your phone and its information is to create an *unlock pattern,* a pattern that must be duplicated (or followed) to unlock the phone and make calls, though unlocking isn't required for answering the phone.

To set the unlock pattern, follow the steps in the preceding section to open the Screen Unlock Security screen. Then continue with these steps:

6. **Choose Pattern.**

   If you haven't yet set a pattern, you see some directions and the Next button. Keep touching the Next button, or let yourself be amused by the animation, and eventually you see the screen where you set the unlock pattern, as shown in Figure 22-5.

Keep dragging your finger

I started here

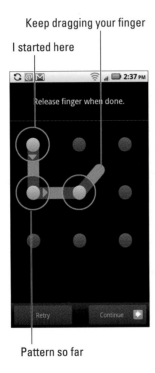

Pattern so far

Figure 22-5: Setting an unlock pattern.

7. **Draw the unlock pattern with one of your stubby fingers.**

   Or, use one of your elegant fingers. Honestly, I don't know how nice your fingers are. Use Figure 22-5 as your guide no matter what type of fingers you have.

   You can hit each dot only once in the pattern. The pattern must have a minimum of four dots.

8. **Touch the Continue button.**

9. **Draw the pattern again to confirm that you have more than a goldfish memory and can repeat yourself.**

   According to research paid for with your tax dollars, goldfish have a two-second memory. If you're a goldfish and can't remember your pattern, touch the Cancel button and start over again in Step 4.

10. **Touch the Confirm button.**

    You return to the main Location & Security Settings window.

11. **Ensure that a check mark appears by Use Visible Patten.**

    The check mark ensures that the pattern shows up. For even more security, you can disable this option, but you *really* have to remember how the pattern goes.

The pattern lock is required whenever you turn on the phone or awaken it from Snooze mode. Chapter 2 describes how to use the unlock pattern.

To remove the pattern, follow Steps 1 through 5 in the preceding section. Confirm the unlock pattern and it's disabled.

> ✔ The unlock pattern can be as simple or complex as you like. I'm a big fan of simple.

> ✔ Wash your hands! Smudge marks on the display can betray your pattern.

Setting a PIN

I suppose that using a *PIN,* or *p*ersonal *i*dentification *n*umber, is more left-brained than using a pattern lock. So, if you have no trouble remembering numbers or you do have trouble remembering patterns, and you want more security on your Droid 2, consider adding a passcode.

To add a passcode, follow Steps 1 through 5 in the earlier section "Droid 2 Security" and choose a PIN. You see an input screen, similar to Figure 22-6.

Punch in at least four numbers for the PIN. Touch the Continue button to confirm the PIN or the Cancel button to bail out (refer to Figure 22-6).

Do it again: After typing the PIN the first time, you're asked to repeat yourself. You need to assure the Droid 2 that you haven't just forgotten the number you chose. Touch the OK button to set the PIN lock.

The PIN is required when you turn on or wake up the Droid 2.

To disable the PIN, follow Steps 1 through 5 in the earlier section "Droid 2 Security." Type your PIN one last time and then choose None from the Screen Unlock Security window.

PIN goes here

Cancel   Back up and erase

Confirm/Accept

Figure 22-6: Entering a PIN.

Assigning your Droid 2 a password

The password lock works similarly to the PIN lock for your Droid 2. The main difference is that you can choose letters and symbols in addition to numbers for your secret code.

To slap down a password on your phone, follow the steps outlined in the earlier section "Droid 2 Security" and choose Password as your type of screen lock.

Type a password of at least four letters, numbers, or symbols. Basically, you can type any character that appears on the onscreen keyboard, though you can use either the onscreen or sliding keyboard to type the password.

Touch the Continue button to proceed, and then type your password a second time to confirm. Touch the OK button to lock the password in place.

As with other forms of Droid 2 security (pattern lock and PIN), you're prompted for your password every time you turn on or wake up the phone.

To remove the password lock, choose None after following the steps in the section "Droid 2 Security," earlier in this chapter.

Various Phone Adjustments

The Droid 2 has many options and settings for you to adjust. You can fix things that annoy you or make things better to please your tastes. The whole idea is to make the phone more usable for you.

Stopping the noise!

The Droid 2 features a bag of tricks designed to silence the phone. These techniques can come in quite handy, especially when a cell phone's digital noise can be outright annoying.

Vibration mode: You can make the phone vibrate for all incoming calls, which works in addition to any ringtone you've set (and still works when you've silenced the phone). To activate Vibration all-the-time mode, follow these steps:

1. **Press the Launcher button on the Home screen to display the Applications Tray.**
2. **Choose the Settings app.**
3. **Choose Sound.**
4. **Choose Vibrate.**
5. **Choose Always.**

Silent mode: Silent mode disables all sounds from the phone, except for music and YouTube and other types of media, as well as alarms that have been set by the Alarm & Timer and Calendar apps.

To enter Silent mode, follow Steps 1 through 4 in the previous set of steps, and for Step 5 place a check mark by the item Silent Mode.

Performing automatic phone tricks

Two phone settings on the Droid 2 might come in handy: Auto Answer and Auto Retry. Both options are found on the Call Settings screen: Start the Settings icon from the Applications tray and choose the Call Settings item.

By placing a check mark by Auto Answer, you direct the Droid 2 to automatically answer the phone whenever the headset is attached. The assumption is that you are using the phone — listening to music, for example — when a call comes in. When the Auto Answer item is on, the phone call is answered automatically.

By placing a check mark by Auto Retry, you direct the phone to automatically redial a number when the call doesn't go through. Obviously, this feature is ideal for radio show call-in contests.

Changing various settings

Here are a smattering of settings you can adjust on the phone — all made from, logically, the Settings screen. To get there from the Home screen, press the Menu soft button and choose the Settings command.

You can also view the Settings screen by choosing the Settings app on the Applications Tray.

Screen brightness: Choose Display and then choose Brightness. Move the slider on the screen to specify how bright the display appears.

Place a check mark by Automatic Brightness to have the Droid 2's internal eyeball examine the lighting situation and set the brightness accordingly.

Screen timeout: Choose Display and then choose Screen Timeout. Select a timeout value from the list. This duration specifies when the phone goes into Snooze mode.

Ringer volume: Choose Sound and then choose Volume. Use the sliders to set the volume for the various types of noises the Droid 2 makes. Touch OK when you're done.

Call Connect: Choose Sound and place a check mark by the option Call Connect. Whenever a new call comes in, you hear a sound, alerting you to the new call. This option is especially helpful when you use the Droid 2 to listen to music.

Network Lost Tone: Choose Sound and then place a check mark by the option Network Lost Tone. The Droid 2 plays a tone whenever a phone call is dropped because of a poor network connection.

Keep the phone awake when plugged in: Choose Applications and then choose Development. Place a check mark by the option Stay Awake.

Adjust the keyboards: Choose Language & Keyboard and then choose Multi-Touch Keyboard. A smattering of interesting options appears — options you can set when they please you or deactivate when they annoy you.

Settings for the sliding keyboard can be found on the Language & Keyboard screen: Choose the Device Keyboard menu item.

Disable automatic word correction and suggestions: To halt the keyboard's (often wrong) spell checking and suggestions, choose Language & Keyboard and then Multi-Touch Keyboard. There you find options for both the onscreen and sliding keyboards with regard to automatic word correction and suggestions:

Remove the check marks by Show Suggestions in both the On-Screen Keyboard and Device Keyboard areas. Also remove the check mark by the item Auto-Correct Errors in both areas, if that feature is vexing you.

Setting the double-tap Home soft button function

When you press the Home soft button twice, the Droid 2 opens the Voice Commands app. It doesn't have to. You can set which app or phone function launches when you press the Home soft button twice. Follow these steps:

1. **From the Home screen, press the Menu soft button.**
2. **Choose Settings.**
3. **Choose Applications.**
4. **Choose Double Tap Home Launch.**
5. **Choose a new function or app from the menu.**

Choose something you do often, such as the Dialer app to dial the phone, the Browser to cruise the Web, or the Camera to take a picture or video.

The options available are limited to only those items that show up on the menu (refer to Step 5). Perhaps a future release of the Android operating system will allow for more choices to be specified for the double-tap Home soft button feature.

Using accessibility settings

If you find the Droid 2 not meeting your needs or you notice that some features don't work well for you, consider taking advantage of some of the phone's accessibility features. Follow these steps:

1. **While at the Home screen, press the Menu soft button.**

2. **Choose Settings.**

3. **Choose Accessibility.**

4. **Place a check mark by the Accessibility option.**

   Two options become available when Accessibility is on:

   • *Voice Readouts:* Touching items on the screen directs the phone to read that text.

   • *Zoom Mode:* A magnification window appears on the touchscreen, allowing you to better see teensy information.

5. **Touch the OK button after reading the scary warning.**

   The accessibility feature is active.

6. **Repeat Steps 4 and 5 to activate other features.**

To disable any accessibility settings, repeat these steps and remove check marks in Step 4. Or, just uncheck the Accessibility setting to disable them all. Touch OK to confirm.

When you're using the Voice Readout option, use the sliding keyboard to choose menu items: Use the arrow keys to move through menu items. Press the OK key to choose an item.

23

Maintenance and Troubleshooting

In This Chapter

▶ Checking the phone's battery usage
▶ Making the battery last
▶ Cleaning the phone
▶ Keeping the system up-to-date
▶ Dealing with problems
▶ Finding support
▶ Getting answers to common questions

*P*ray tell, what kind of maintenance can a cell phone need? It isn't like you need to winterize your Droid 2. It has no regular tune-up schedule. And, thank goodness you never need to change its oil. For you, phone maintenance duties are rather light, and with the pleasant side effect of them being relatively painless. Because of that, I've had to toss in the topic of troubleshooting, just to make a full-length chapter.

Battery Care and Feeding

Perhaps the most important item you can monitor and maintain on your cell phone is its battery. The battery supplies the necessary electrical juice by which the phone operates. Without battery power, your Droid 2 is about as useful as a tin can and string for communications. Keep an eye on the battery.

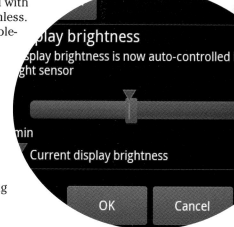

Monitoring the battery

The Droid 2 displays the current battery status at the top of the screen, in the status area, next to the time. The icons used to display battery status are shown in Figure 23-1.

Battery is fully charged and happy.

Battery is in use and starting to drain.

Battery running low. Charge it soon!

Battery frighteningly low. Stop using and charge at once!

Battery is being charged.

Figure 23-1: Battery status icons.

You might also see an icon for a dead or missing battery, but for some reason I can't get my phone to turn on and display that icon.

You can check the specific battery level by following these steps:

1. **From the Home screen, touch the Menu button.**

2. **Choose Settings.**

3. **Choose About Phone.**

4. **Choose Status.**

The top two items on the Status screen offer information about the battery:

Battery Status: This setting explains what's going on with the battery. It might say *Full* when the battery is full or *Charging* when the battery is being charged, or you might see other text, depending on how desperate the phone is for power.

Battery Level: This setting reveals a percentage value describing how much of the battery is charged. A value of 100 percent indicates a fully charged battery. A value of 110 percent means that someone can't do math.

Later sections in this chapter describe activities that consume battery power and how to deal with battery issues.

- Heed those low-battery warnings! The phone sounds a notification whenever the battery gets low. (See the orange battery icon shown earlier, in Figure 23-1). The phone sounds another notification when the battery gets *very* low. (See the red battery icon in Figure 23-1).

- When the battery is too low, the phone shuts itself off.

- In addition to the status icons, the Droid 2 notification light turns a scary shade of red when battery juice is dreadfully low.

- The best way to deal with a low battery is to connect the phone to a power source: Either plug the phone into a wall socket or connect the phone to a computer by using a USB cable. The phone charges itself immediately; plus, you can use the phone while it's charging.

- You don't have to fully charge the phone to use it. If you have only 20 minutes to charge and the phone goes back up to only a 70 percent battery level, that's great. Well, it's not great, but it's far better than a 20 percent battery level.

- When the battery gets very low, you see a pop-up message on the screen, urging you to plug it in *at once!*

- Battery percentage values are best-guess estimates. Just because you talked for two hours and the battery shows 50 percent doesn't mean that you're guaranteed two more hours of talking. Odds are good that you have much less than two hours. In fact, as the percentage value gets low, the battery appears to drain faster.

Determining what is sucking up power

A nifty screen on the Droid 2 reviews which activities have been consuming power when the phone is operating from its battery. The informative screen is shown in Figure 23-2.

To get to this screen, follow these steps:

1. **From the Home screen, touch the Menu button.**

2. **Choose Settings.**

3. **Choose Battery Manager.**

   You see a wonderfully big, graphic battery meter. It's pretty, but it's not your final destination.

4. **Touch the big battery icon.**

   You see a screen similar to the one shown in Figure 23-2.

Figure 23-2: Things that drain the battery.

The number and variety of items listed on the Battery Use screen depend on what you've been doing with your phone between charges and how many different programs you're using.

Carefully note which applications consume the most battery power. If possible, curb your use of those programs to conserve the juice. For example, I could have saved 11 percent by not playing that dratted, addicting Jewels game. Refer to Figure 23-2.

Managing battery performance

The Droid 2 features Battery Mode settings to help you manage the phone's power consumption. Similar to managing power on a computer, you can configure your phone to use one of four power modes:

Maximum Battery Saver: In this most restrictive mode, the phone may even turn off its digital cellular connection to save power. Just about anything that can be held back or have a timeout applied is restricted in Maximum Battery Saver mode.

Nighttime Saver: In this mode, the phone uses Performance mode (no battery savings) during daytime hours but switches to Maximum Battery Saver mode during the nighttime hours.

Performance: In this mode, nothing is held back, no timeouts are set, and the phone operates using all its capabilities. Performance mode has no power restrictions. It is, essentially, *no* power management.

Custom Battery Saver: In this mode, you get to customize your phone's battery-saving options. You can set timeout values and make other changes to customize the way the Droid 2 conserves power.

To set a battery profile on your Droid 2, follow these steps:

1. **From the Home screen, touch the Menu button.**
2. **Choose Settings.**
3. **Choose Battery Manager.**
4. **Choose Battery Mode.**
5. **Choose a battery profile from the list.**
6. **Optionally, read the warning message and touch the OK button.**

When you select Custom Battery Saver mode, you can touch the gear icon to the right of the Custom Battery Saver item to see another screen full of various battery options, timeouts, and additional settings that can be customized. Figure 23-3 describes what's up.

The Droid 2 ships with Nighttime Saver mode enabled.

Saving battery life

Here's a smattering of things you can do to help prolong battery life in your Droid 2:

Turn off vibration options: The phone's vibration is caused by a teensy motor. Though you don't see much battery savings by disabling the vibration options, it's better than no savings. To turn off vibration, follow these steps:

1. **From the Home screen, touch the Menu button.**
2. **Choose Settings.**
3. **Choose Sound.**
4. **Choose Vibrate.**
5. **Choose Never.**
6. **Also on the Sound Settings screen: Remove the check mark by Haptic Feedback.**

   The Haptic Feedback option is what causes the phone to vibrate when you touch the soft buttons.

Set time for off-peak hours

Timeout for
data connection

Data timeout for peak hours

Peak hours to start at this time

Display brightness settings

Figure 23-3: Battery settings for
Custom Battery Saver mode.

Additionally, consider lowering the volume of notifications by choosing the
Volume option. This option also saves a modicum of battery life, though in
my travels I've missed important notifications by setting the volume too low.

Dim the screen: If you look at Figure 23-2 (earlier in this chapter), you see
that the display sucks down quite a lot of battery power. Though a dim
screen can be more difficult to see, especially outdoors, it definitely saves on
battery life.

You set the screen brightness from the Settings app: Choose Display and
then choose Brightness.

Battery replacement

Unlike on some cell phones, you can easily replace the battery in the Droid 2. Chapter 1 discusses how to install and remove the battery. It's cinchy! But the real questions come when you need to replace the battery and have to decide what to replace it with.

Under normal usage, the battery in the Droid 2 should last at least as long as the typical two-year cellular contract. The battery is probably good for about four years if you treat it properly. Even so, at some point the battery will fail:

The battery charge decreases and, eventually, the battery doesn't even hold a charge.

Ensure that any replacement battery you buy is compatible with the Droid 2. A BP6X battery from Motorola (the phone's manufacturer) works best. Otherwise, ensure that the battery is a 3.7V battery designed for the Droid 2. Avoid buying batteries for your electronics at swap meets or from the back of trucks in grocery store parking lots.

Turn off Bluetooth: When you're not using Bluetooth, turn it off. Or, when you *really* need that cyborg Bluetooth ear thing, try to keep your phone plugged in. See Chapter 14 for information on turning off Bluetooth, though you can do it quickly from the Power Control widget.

Turn off Wi-Fi: Wi-Fi networking on the Droid 2 keeps you on the Internet at top speeds but drains the battery. Because I tend to use Wi-Fi when I'm in one place, I keep my phone plugged in. Otherwise, the battery drains like my bank account at Christmas. Refer to Chapter 14 for information on turning off the phone's Wi-Fi.

Disable automatic syncing: The Droid 2 syncs quite often. In fact, it surprises me when I update something on the Internet and find the phone updated almost instantly. When you need to save battery power and frequent updates aren't urgent (such as when you're spending a day traveling), disable automatic syncing by following these steps:

1. **From the Home screen, touch the Menu button.**
2. **Choose Settings.**
3. **Choose Accounts.**
4. **Choose your Google account.**
5. **Remove the green check mark by each item.**

When saving battery juice isn't important, remember to repeat these steps to reenable background and automatic synchronization.

Regular Phone Maintenance

The Droid 2 gives you only two tasks that you can do for regular maintenance on the phone: Keep it clean, which is probably something you're doing already, and keep important information backed up.

Keeping it clean

You probably already keep your phone clean. I must use my sleeve to wipe the touch screen at least a dozen times a day. Of course, better than your sleeve is something called a *microfiber cloth*. This item can be found at any computer- or office-supply store.

- ✔ Never use any liquid to clean the touch screen — especially ammonia or alcohol. Those substances damage the touch screen.

- ✔ If the screen keeps getting dirty, consider adding a *screen protector*. This specially designed cover prevents the screen from getting scratched or dirty but also lets you use your finger on the touchscreen. Be sure that the screen protector is designed for use with the Droid 2.

- ✔ You can also find customized Droid 2 cell phone cases, belt clips, and protectors, though I've found that those add-on items are purely for decorative or fashion purposes and don't even prevent serious damage if you drop the phone.

Backing it up

A *backup* is a safety copy of the information on your Droid 2. It includes the contact information, music, photos, video, and apps you've installed, plus any settings you've made to customize your phone. Copying that information to another source is one way to keep the information safe, in case anything happens to the phone.

On your Google account, information is backed up automatically. This information includes your Contacts list, Gmail messages, and Calendar app appointments. Because the Droid 2 automatically syncs this information with the Internet, a backup is always present.

To confirm that your Google account information is being backed up, heed these steps:

1. **From the Home screen, touch the Launcher button.**

2. **Choose My Accounts.**

3. **Choose your Google account.**

4. **Ensure that a green check mark appears by every option.**

   When no check mark is there, touch the gray square to add one.

If you have more than one Google account synchronized with the Droid 2, repeat these steps for each account.

Beyond your Google account, which is automatically backed up, you can use the Verizon app Backup Assistant to create, on Verizon computers, a safety copy of *all* your phone's contact information.

To use Backup Assistant, you must configure it on your Droid 2; plus, you must create an account on the Verizon Web site.

Configure Backup Assistant by starting the app from the Applications Tray: Accept the licensing terms and conditions, create a PIN, and follow the directions to set up the account. Touch the Sync Now button to start the backup.

On a computer, you can visit the Verizon Web site to complete the process:

```
www.verizonwireless.com/backupassistant
```

Create an account by following the directions on the site. After the account is created and you log in, you can access the backup copy of the contact information on your Droid 2.

Where to find phone information

Who knows what evil lurks inside the heart of your phone? Well, the phone itself knows. You can view information about the battery, phone number, mobile network, and uptime, plus other information. To see that trivia, summon the Settings app and choose About Phone and then Status.

For specific information about your account, such as minutes used and data transmitted, you have two choices.

First, you can dial the special phone numbers included in the Contacts list to get some account usage and payment information. Contacts such as #MIN and #BAL are used to retrieve your minutes (usage) and account balance. See Chapter 8 for more information on those special contacts.

Second, you can visit the cellular service's Web site. In the United States, the Droid 2 is supported by the Verizon Wireless network at the time this book goes to press. The Web site is www.verizonwireless.com. You need to set up or access your account, which then leads you to information about your phone usage and billing and other trivia.

There's no native way to back up the data on the Droid 2 MicroSD card to your computer. That backup would include all data on your phone — even photos, videos, and music. To do this type of backup, you must manually copy the information from the MicroSD card to another location, such as your computer. That backup, or safety, copy of the information on the MicroSD card lets you restore those files to the MicroSD, in case anything bad happens to the phone.

For more information on copying the information from the MicroSD card, refer to a reference document for your computer's operating system that covers copying files. Because the Droid 2 can be mounted to your computer's storage system like an external storage device (a USB drive), the operation isn't overly complex, though it requires more explanation than I have room for in this tome.

Updating the system

Every so often, a new version of your phone's operating system becomes available. It's an *Android update* because Android is the name of the Droid 2 operating system, not because your phone thinks that it's some type of robot.

When an automatic update occurs, you see an alert or a message appear on the phone, indicating that a system upgrade is available. You have three choices:

- ✓ Install Now
- ✓ Install Later
- ✓ More Info

My advice is to choose Install Now and get it over with — unless you have something (a call, a message, or another urgent item) pending on the phone, in which case you can choose Install Later and be bothered by the message again.

You can manually check for updates: From the Settings screen, choose About Phone and then choose System Updates. When your system is up-to-date, the screen tells you so. Otherwise, you find directions for updating the system.

Help and Troubleshooting

Things aren't as bad as they were in the old days. Back then, you could try two sources for help: the atrocious manual that came with your electronic device or a phone call to the guy who wrote the atrocious manual. It was unpleasant. Today, things are better. You have many resources for solving issues with your gizmos, including the Droid 2.

Getting help

The Droid 2 comes with a modicum of assistance for your weary times of woe. Granted, its advice and delivery method aren't as informative or entertaining as the book you hold in your hands. But it's something!

To get help, open the Help Center app, found on the Applications Tray. You see four categories:

Guided Tours: Videos to help you use your phone

Tips and Tricks: Suggestions for doing things you may not know about

Users Guide: Documentation for the Droid 2

FAQs: Frequently asked questions and their answers

Choosing some of the items displays information stored on your phone. For other categories, you're whisked off to the Internet for details.

Some of the information presented is pretty good, but also pretty basic. It's also, at its core, simply what would have once been printed and bundled with the Droid 2: the dratted manual.

Fixing random and annoying problems

Aren't all problems annoying? There isn't really such a thing as a welcome problem, unless the problem is welcome because it diverts attention from another, preexisting problem. And random problems? If problems were predictable, they would serve in office. Or maybe they already are?

Here are some typical problems and my suggestions for a solution:

General trouble: For just about any problem or minor quirk, consider restarting the phone: Turn off the phone, and then turn it on again. That procedure will most likely fix a majority of the annoying and quirky problems you encounter with the Droid 2.

When restarting doesn't work, consider turning off the Droid 2 and removing its battery. Wait about 15 seconds, and then return the battery to the phone and turn on the phone again.

Check the data connection: Sometimes, the data connection drops but the phone connection stays active. Check the status bar. If you see bars, you have a phone signal. When you don't see the G, E, 3G, or Wi-Fi icon, the phone has no data signal.

Sometimes, the data signal just drops for a minute or two. Wait and it comes back around. If it doesn't, the cellular data network might be down, or you may just be in an area with lousy service. Consider changing your location.

For wireless connections, you have to ensure that the Wi-Fi is set up properly and working. That usually involves pestering the person who configured the Wi-Fi signal or made it available, such as the cheerful person in the green apron who serves you coffee.

Music begins to play while you're on the phone: I find this quirk most annoying. For some reason, you start to hear music playing while you're in a conversation on the phone. I wonder why the phone's software doesn't disable music from even being able to play while the phone is in use.

Anyway, it might seem like stopping the music is impossible. It's not: Press the Home soft button to go to the Home screen. (You might have to unlock the phone.) Pull down the notifications and choose the Music Playing notification. Press the Pause button to pause the music.

The MicroSD card is busy: Most often, the MicroSD card is busy because you've connected the Droid 2 to a computer and the computer is accessing the phone's storage system. To unbusy the MicroSD card, unmount the phone or stop the USB storage. See Chapter 13.

When the MicroSD card remains busy, consider restarting the phone, as described earlier in this section.

An app has run amok: Sometimes, apps that misbehave let you know. You see a warning on the screen announcing the app's stubborn disposition. Touch the Force Close button to shut down the errant app.

When you don't see a warning or when an app appears to be unduly obstinate, you can shut 'er down the manual way, by following these steps:

1. **From the Applications Tray, choose the Settings icon.**

2. **Choose Applications.**

3. **Choose Manage Applications.**

   If you choose the Running tab from the top of the screen, you see a list of only the apps that are running, which helps narrow your choices.

4. **Choose the application that's causing you distress.**

   For example, a program doesn't start or says that it's busy or has some other issue.

5. **Touch the Force Stop button.**

   The program stops, if it's running.

After stopping the program, try opening it again to see whether it works. If the program continues to run amok, contact its developer: Open the Market app and choose Downloads. Open the app you're having trouble with and choose the option Send Email to Developer. Send the developer a message describing the problem.

Reset the phone's software (a drastic measure): When all else fails, you can do the drastic thing and reset all the phone's software, essentially returning it to the state it was in when it first arrived. Obviously, you need not perform this step lightly. In fact, consider finding support (see the next section) before you start:

1. **From the Home screen, touch the Menu button.**

2. **Choose Settings.**

3. **Choose Privacy.**

4. **Choose Factory Data Reset.**

5. **Touch the Reset Phone button.**

6. **Touch the Erase Everything button to confirm.**

   All the information you've set or stored on the phone is purged.

Again, *do not* follow these steps unless you're certain that they will fix the problem or you're under orders to do so from someone in Tech Support.

Getting support

The easiest way to find support for the Droid 2 is to dial 611. You're greeted by a cheerful Verizon employee, or an automated robot system, who will gladly help you with various phone issues.

On the Internet, you can find support at these Web sites:

`www.motorola.com`

`market.android.com/support`

`http://support.vzw.com/clc`

Droid 2 Q&A

I love Q&A! That's because not only is it an effective way to express certain problems and solutions but some of the questions might also cover things I've been wanting to ask.

"The touchscreen doesn't work!"

A touchscreen, such as the one used on the Droid 2, requires a human finger for proper interaction. The phone interprets complicated electromagnetic physics between the human finger and the phone to determine where the touchscreen is being touched.

You cannot use the touchscreen when you're wearing gloves, unless they're specially designed gloves that claim to work on touchscreens. Batman wears this type of glove, so it probably exists in real life.

The touchscreen might also fail when the battery power is low or when the phone has been physically damaged.

"The onscreen keyboard is too small!"

It's not that the onscreen keyboard is too small — it's that you're a human being and not a marsupial. Your fingers are too big!

You can rotate the phone to landscape orientation to see a larger onscreen keyboard. Not every app may feature a landscape-orientation keyboard. When one does, you'll find typing on the wider onscreen keyboard much easier than normal.

"The battery doesn't charge"

Start from the source: Is the wall socket providing power? Is the cord plugged in? The cable may be damaged, so try another cable.

When charging from a USB port on a computer, ensure that the computer is turned on. Most computers don't provide USB power when they're turned off.

"The phone gets so hot that it turns itself off!"

Yikes! An overheating phone can be a nasty problem. Judge how hot the phone is by seeing whether you can hold it in your hand: When the phone is too hot to hold, it's too hot. If you're using the phone to warm up your coffee, the phone is too hot.

Turn off the phone. Take out the battery and let it cool.

If the overheating problem continues, have the phone looked at for potential repair. The battery might need to be replaced.

Do not continue to use a phone that's too hot! The heat damages the phone's electronics. It can also start a fire.

"The phone doesn't do Landscape mode!"

Not every app takes advantage of the Droid 2's ability to orient itself in Landscape mode. For example, the Home screen doesn't "do landscape" unless you extend the sliding keyboard. One program that definitely does Landscape mode is Browser, described in Chapter 11. So, just because an app doesn't enter Landscape mode doesn't mean that it *can* enter Landscape mode.

The Droid 2 has a setting you can check to confirm that landscape orientation is active: From the Applications Tray, choose Settings and then choose the Display category. Ensure that a check mark appears by the item Auto-Rotate Screen. If not, touch the square to put a green check mark there.

Part VI
The Part of Tens

What do you call the last part of a reference book such as *Droid 2 For Dummies?* If you call it *The Part of Afterthoughts,* it makes the topics seem trivial and unimportant. If you call it *The Part of Leftovers,* it makes people hungry. If you call it *The Part of Stuff I Had to Add Because the Publisher Said That the Book Was Too Short,* you're being transparently honest, but no one would believe you. So you end up naming it *The Part of Tens,* where you organize afterthoughts, leftovers, and space fillers into chapters that contain ten items apiece. Presto! Everyone is satisfied.

Ten Tips, Tricks, and Shortcuts

In This Chapter

▶ Accessing recent apps

▶ Formatting your email

▶ Halting unnecessary services

▶ Making the keyboard more usable

▶ Adding words to the dictionary

▶ Getting to settings and notifications quickly

▶ Adding direct-dial widgets

▶ Using sliding-keyboard menu shortcuts

▶ Finding a lost phone

▶ Creating event locations

1'd like to think that everything I mention in this book is a tip, trick, or shortcut for using your Droid 2. Given that this is a Part of Tens chapter, however, I have the freedom to simply list what I feel are ten tips, tricks, and shortcuts. These are some of the things I've learned from using the Droid 2 and from overcoming some of its more frustrating aspects.

Summon a Recently Opened App

I have to kick myself in the head every time I return to the Applications Tray to, once again, scroll the list o' icons to dig up an app I just opened. Why bother? Because I can press and hold the Home soft button to instantly see a list of recently opened apps.

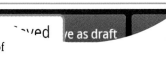

Pressing and holding the Home soft button works no matter what you're doing with the phone; you don't necessarily have to view the Home screen to see the list of recently opened apps.

Formatted Email

The email messages I receive from cell phones all have the same telltale formatting: Boring. That's because most cell phone email programs lack any formatting abilities. What you send is plain text.

```
Yawn.
```

On the Droid 2, however, you can format your email all nice and fancy. Figure 24-1 describes what's up with the email composition screen, used by the Email app.

Display Font menu

Insert happy faces

Indented bullet list

Italics

Bold   Underline

Figure 24-1: Formatting your email.

You can even create a template of sorts, kind of like preformatting your Droid 2 email messages. Follow these steps:

1. **Start the Email program.**

2. **If necessary, choose an email account.**

   For example, if you see the combined inbox, choose a specific account.

3. **Press the Menu soft button.**

4. **Choose Email Settings.**

5. **Choose Compose Options.**

   You can set the email font for all outgoing messages by making changes in the top part of the screen: Use the controls illustrated in Figure 24-2 to manipulate the preset text in the window.

6. **When you're content, touch the Done button.**

Sample (preview) text

Background color

Italics Text size

Bold Font Text color

Email signature

Save changes

Standard text-formatting toolbar

Figure 24-2: Setting the standard email text format.

Text formatting can also be applied to your email signature, as shown in Figure 24-2. In fact, you can edit your email signature as illustrated in the figure.

- ✒ Touch a format button once to turn the format on, and again to turn it off.
- ✒ Multiple formats can be applied to your text.
- ✒ When a text format has been chosen, it appears outlined in red.
- ✒ The Font menu (refer to Figure 24-1) contains four items that deal with the text font in your messages: *F* to select the font type; *Tt* to select the text size; *T* to select the text foreground color; and a paint bucket to set the background color.
- ✒ Text formatting is applied to new text you write or to selected blocks of text. See Chapter 4 for information on selecting text.
- ✒ See Chapter 10 for more information about email on your Droid 2.

Stop Unneeded Services

Some things may be going on in your Droid 2 that you don't need or even suspect. These things are computer activities, usually the monitoring of information or the phone's status. The technical term for these activities is *services.*

When a service has started that you don't want or have been requested to stop, you can halt the service. This procedure isn't one you should take lightly, and stopping a service has no amazing power to boost your Droid 2's performance (no matter what you read on the blogs).

When a service needs to be stopped, here's how it's done:

1. **While at the Home screen, press the Menu soft button.**
2. **Choose Settings.**
3. **Choose Applications.**
4. **Choose Running Services.**
5. **Touch a service to stop it.**

   Most likely, it's a service you recognize that you don't need, a service that has run amok and cannot otherwise be stopped, or a service you've been directed to disable from another source or authority.

As an example, I've stopped the Skype Mobile service from running because I don't need it. I've also stopped the Blockbuster service for the same reason.

6. **Touch the Stop button to halt the service.**

When you stop a service, you free the phone resources used by that service, including memory and processor power.

The service may start up again the next time you start the phone. If so, and if you still need to stop that service, consider uninstalling the program associated with that service.

 Do not randomly disable services. Many of them are required in order for the Droid 2 to do its job, or for programs you use to carry out their tasks. If you disable a service you don't recognize and the phone begins to act funny, turn it off and then on again to fix the problem.

Set Keyboard Feedback

Typing on a touchscreen keyboard isn't easy. Along with the screen being tiny (or your fingers being big), it's difficult to tell what you're typing. You can add some feedback to the typing process. Heed these steps:

1. **While at the Home screen, press the Menu soft button.**

2. **Choose Settings.**

3. **Choose Language & Keyboard.**

4. **Choose Multi-Touch Keyboard.**

5. **Put a check mark by the option Vibrate On Keypress.**

   This option causes physical feedback when you press a "key" on the onscreen keyboard.

6. **Put a check mark by the option Sound On Keypress.**

   The Droid 2 makes a sound when you type on the onscreen keyboard. Clackity-clack-clack.

Of the two options, I prefer Sound On Keypress. The phone makes a different sound for the character keys and the space key, which reminds me of my ancient typewriter.

- Yeah, *keypress* is two words: key press.

- Obviously, these steps don't apply to using Swype. See Chapter 4 for information on using the Swype keyboard.

Add a Word to the Dictionary

Betcha didn't know that the Droid 2 has a dictionary. The dictionary is used to keep track of words you type — words that may not be recognized as being spelled properly.

To add a word to the Droid 2 dictionary, long-press the word immediately after you type it. From the menu that appears, choose the Add *"Word"* to Dictionary command, where *Word* is the word you want to add. (Refer to Figure 4-14, in Chapter 4.)

You can also choose the word when it appears in the list of suggestions, as shown in Figure 24-3. Long-press the word, as shown in the figure, to add it to the dictionary. The confirmation that appears is your clue that the word has been added.

Confirmation

Long-press the word

Figure 24-3: Adding a word to the dictionary.

To review the contents of the dictionary, open the Settings app and choose Language & Keyboard and then User Dictionary. You see a list of words you've added. Touch a word to edit it or to delete it from the dictionary.

Quickly Access Settings and Notifications

 A Settings icon lives on the Application Tray. But, O, it's so far away. An easier choice is to press the Menu soft button while viewing the Home screen. Choose the Settings command.

Another common frustration is accessing the notifications. Though you can pull down the notifications when using any app on the phone, you can also summon the list from the Home screen by pressing the Menu soft button and choosing Notifications. I had to resort to this technique a few times when my fingertips utterly failed at pulling down the notifications and making them stick.

You can roll up the notifications by pressing the Back soft button.

Create a Direct-Dial Screen Widget

For the numbers you dial most frequently, use the Favorites list, as described in Chapter 5. For your überfavorites, you use Home screen direct-dial widgets. Here's how to create a direct-dial contact widget on the Home screen for someone you call frequently:

1. **Long-press the Home screen.**

2. **Choose Motorola Widgets.**

3. **Choose Contact Quick Task.**

4. **Choose the contact you want to direct-dial.**

5. **Choose the phone number, if the contact has multiple phones.**

   Choose the number from the top portion of the contact's information, in the Call category.

6. **Touch the Done button.**

The contact's phone number (and picture, if they have one) appears on the Home screen as a widget. Touching the phone icon on the widget summons a dialing menu; if you touch the check box, you enable one-touch dialing for that contact.

The Quick Contact widget can be resized: Long-press it and then drag the corners around with your finger to resize. You can make the Quick Contact widget as large or as small as you like. I prefer smaller, especially when the contact has an ugly picture attached.

You can also create an icon to directly text-message a contact. The difference is that you choose a phone number from the Text Message list in Step 5 rather than from the Call category.

See Chapter 9 for more information about text messaging.

Use Sliding-Keyboard Menu Shortcuts

Occasionally, you see a menu command that features a little bit of text beneath it, similar to what's shown in Figure 24-4. That's a sliding-keyboard menu shortcut. You can use these shortcuts to quickly access commands that you would otherwise have to activate by touching the screen or fumbling with the arrow keys.

Sliding-keyboard shortcut

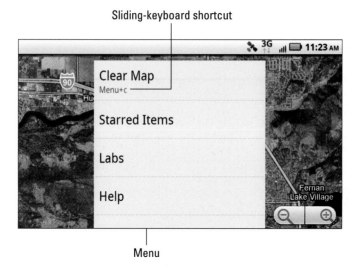

Menu

Figure 24-4: A sliding-keyboard menu shortcut.

To work a menu shortcut, press the key associated with the command. For example, in Figure 24-4, you press the C key to activate the Clear Map command.

- When there are no keyboard shortcuts, you use the sliding keyboard's arrow keys to navigate the menus. Press the OK key to choose a command.

- Lamentably, not every app features sliding-keyboard shortcuts in the commands.

Find Your Lost Cell Phone

Someday, you're going to lose your beloved Droid 2. It might be for a panic-filled few seconds, or it might be forever. The hardware solution is to weld a chain to your phone, which kind of defeats the whole mobile/wireless paradigm. The software solution is to use a cell phone locator service. Cell phone locator services take advantage of a phone's GPS ability to help find your phone wherever it's hiding (on this planet, anyway). Multiple apps, also available at the Android Market, can help you locate and, you hope, recover a wandering phone.

I've tried a few of these programs and can't recommend any in particular. Some you can try are

- ✓ LocService
- ✓ Mobile Defense
- ✓ Mobile Phone Locator Lite
- ✓ Phoning Pigeon

At the time this book goes to press, Mobile Defense is a closed beta. Hopefully, soon it will be released.

Most of these services require that you set up a Web page account to assist in locating your phone. They also enable services that send updates to the Internet. The updates assist in tracking your phone, in case it becomes lost or stolen.

Check my Wambooli Web site for any updates regarding apps that help you locate a lost phone:

```
www.wambooli.com/help/phone
```

Enter Location Information for Your Events

When you create an event for the Calendar app, be sure to enter the event's location. You can type either an address (if you know it) or the name of the location. The key is to type the text as you would in the Map app when searching for a location. That way, you can touch the event location and the Droid 2 displays it on the touchscreen. Finding an address couldn't be easier.

- ✓ See Chapter 15 for more information about the Maps app.
- ✓ See Chapter 19 for details about the Calendar.

Ten Things to Remember

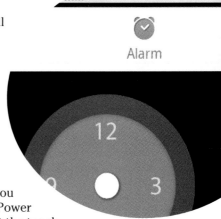

*I*t's difficult to narrow the list of all the things to remember to only ten items. So even though you'll find ten good things not to forget in this chapter, don't think for a moment that there are *only* ten. In fact, as I remember more, I'll put them on my Web site, www.wambooli.com. Check there for updates about the Droid 2, and perhaps even more things to remember.

Lock the Phone on a Call

Whether you dialed out or someone dialed in, after you start talking, you should lock your phone: Press the Power button atop the Droid 2. By doing so, you ensure that the touch-screen is disabled and the call isn't unintentionally disconnected.

Of course, the call can still be disconnected by a dropped signal or the other party getting all huffy and hanging up on you, but by locking the phone, you prevent a stray finger or your pocket from disconnecting (or muting) the phone.

Landscape Orientation

Too many times, I find myself using my phone and cursing my stubby fingers. Then I slap myself in the forehead and tilt the phone to its side. Yes, sir — landscape orientation comes to the rescue. Some applications give you a wider screen view, a larger keyboard, and more room to touch buttons in landscape orientation.

Not every app supports landscape orientation.

Use the Arrow Keys

Even though I'm a big fan of the onscreen keyboard, the sliding keyboard has something that comes in quite handy: arrow keys. You can use them to edit text better than you can stab your finger on the screen to move the cursor.

The best use of the arrow keys is for hopping between links on a Web page: Use the keys to move between links, left, right, up, or down. Press the OK key to "click" a link.

The arrow keys might also be used in certain games to move around your little man and shoot his various weapons.

Use the Keyboard Suggestions

Don't forget to take advantage of the suggestions that appear above the onscreen keyboard when you're typing text. In fact, you don't even need to touch a suggestion; to replace your text with the highlighted suggestion, simply touch the onscreen keyboard's space key. Zap! The word appears.

- ✔ The setting that directs the keyboard to make suggestions work is Show Suggestions. To ensure that the setting is active, open the Settings app and choose Language & Keyboard and then Multi-Touch Keyboard.

- ✔ Refer to Figure 4-6 (in Chapter 4) to see how the onscreen keyboard suggestions work.

Things That Consume Lots of Battery Juice

Three items on the Droid 2 suck down battery power faster than a former girlfriend updates her Facebook status to Single:

- ✔ Navigation
- ✔ Bluetooth
- ✔ Wi-Fi networking

Navigation is certainly handy, but because the phone's touchscreen is on the entire time and dictating text to you, the battery drains rapidly. If possible, try to plug the phone into the car's power socket when you're navigating. If you can't, keep an eye on the battery meter.

Both Bluetooth and Wi-Fi networking require extra power for their wireless radios. When you need that speed or connectivity, they're great! I try to plug my phone into a power source when I'm accessing Wi-Fi or using Bluetooth. Otherwise, I disconnect from those networks as soon as I'm done, to save power.

- ✔ Technically speaking, using Wi-Fi doesn't drain the battery as drastically as you would think. In fact, the Wi-Fi signal times itself out after about 15 minutes of non-use. So it's perfectly okay to leave Wi-Fi on all day — you'll experience only a modicum of battery loss because of it. Even so, I'm a stickler for turning off the Wi-Fi when I don't use it.
- ✔ See Chapter 23 for more information on managing the Droid 2 battery.

Check for Roaming

Roaming can be expensive. The last non-smartphone (dumbphone?) I owned racked up $180 in roaming charges the month before I switched to a better cellular plan. Even though you too may have a good cell plan, keep an eye on the phone's status bar. Ensure that when you're making a call, you don't see the Roaming status icon on the status bar atop the touchscreen.

Well, yes, it's okay to make a call when your phone is roaming. My advice is to remember to *check* for the icon, not to avoid it. If possible, try to make your phone calls when you're back in your cellular service's coverage area. If you can't, make the phone call but keep in mind that you will be charged roaming fees. They ain't cheap.

Use + When Dialing Internationally

I suppose most folks are careful when dialing an international number. On the Droid 2, you can use the + key to replace the country's exit code. In the United States, that code is 011. So, whenever you see an international number listed as 011-xxx-xxxxxxx, you can instead dial +xxx-xxxxxx, where the x characters represent the number to dial.

See Chapter 21 for more information on international dialing.

Properly Access the MicroSD Card

To access the Droid 2 storage area using your computer, you must properly mount the phone's MicroSD card. After the card is mounted, you can use your computer to access files — music, videos, still pictures, contacts, and other types of information — stored on your phone.

When the MicroSD card is mounted on a computer storage system, you cannot access the card by using the phone. If you try, you see a message explaining that the MicroSD card is busy.

When you're done accessing the MicroSD card from your computer, be sure to stop USB storage: Pull down the USB notification and choose Charge Only. Touch the OK button. (See Chapter 13 for more details.)

✔ Future releases of the Android operating system may change the way the USB connection is made on your Droid 2. See my Web site for more information:

    www.wambooli.com/help/phone

✔ Do not simply unplug the phone from the USB cable when the computer is accessing the MicroSD card. If you do, you can damage the MicroSD card and lose all information stored there.

Snap a Pic of That Contact

Here's something I always forget: Whenever you're near one of your contacts, take the person's picture. Sure, some people are bashful, but most folks are flattered. The idea is to build up your Contacts list so that all contacts have photos. That makes receiving a call much more interesting when you see the caller's picture displayed, especially a silly or embarrassing picture.

When taking the picture, be sure to show it to the person before you assign it to the contact. Let them decide whether it's good enough. Or, if you just want to be rude, assign a crummy-looking picture. Heck, you don't even have to do that: Just take a random picture of anything and assign it to a contact: A plant. A rock. Your cat. But, seriously, keep in mind that the phone can take a contact's picture the next time you meet up with that person.

See Chapter 16 for more information on using the Droid 2 camera and assigning a picture to a contact.

The Search Command

Google is known worldwide for its searching abilities. By gum, the word *google* is now synonymous for searching. So, please don't forget that the Droid 2, which uses the Google Android operating system, has a powerful Search command.

The Search command is not only powerful but also available all over. The Search soft button can be pressed at any time, in just about any program to search for information, locations, people — you name it. It's handy. It's everywhere. Use it.

26

Ten Worthy Apps

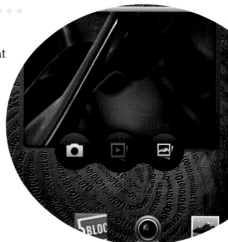

1'm taking an awful risk. It's dangerous to claim that there are only 10 worthy apps of the more than 80,000 available at the Android Market — especially when I know for certain that I haven't tried all those apps. Still, I would be remiss not to pass along a few app suggestions before concluding this book's text. Whittling the list to 10 was difficult, so — in a break with *For Dummies* tradition — this chapter contains 11 app suggestions. (Don't tell anyone!)

All these apps are free. Find them at the Android Market. See Chapter 20.

AK Notepad

 One program that the Droid 2 is missing out of the box is a notepad. A good choice for an app to fill that void is AK Notepad: You can type or dictate short messages and memos, which I find handy.

For example, before a recent visit to the hardware store, I made (dictated) a list of items I needed to buy by using AK Notepad. I also keep some important items as notes, things that I often forget or don't care to remember, such as frequent flyer numbers, my dress shirt and suit size (like I ever need that information), and other important notes I might need handy but not cluttering my brain.

Perhaps the most important note you can make is one containing your contact information. A note labeled In Case You Find This Phone on my Droid 2 contains information about me in case I ever lose my phone and someone is decent enough to search it for my information. (Also see Chapter 24 for information on finding a lost phone.)

Barcode Scanner

Many apps from the Android Market can be quickly accessed by scanning their barcode information. Scanning with what? Why, your Droid 2, of course!

By using an app such as Barcode Scanner, you can instantly read in and translate barcodes to product descriptions, Web page links, or links directly to apps in the Android Market.

Using Barcode Scanner in this chapter

Throughout this chapter, you find barcode icons. After installing Barcode Scanner (or a similar) app, use your Droid 2 to scan the barcodes. Touch the Open Browser button to download the recommended app from the Android Market.

Additional app recommendations and their barcodes are found all over the Internet, in magazines, and on my Android phone support page at www.wambooli.com/help/phone.

Though you can find similar barcode-scanning apps, I find Barcode Scanner the easiest to use: Run the app, point the phone's camera at a barcode, and, in a few moments, you see a link or an option suggesting what to do next. To get an app, the Open Browser option takes you to the Android Market, where downloading the app is just a few touches away.

Dolphin Browser

 Though I don't mind using the Browser app that comes with the Droid 2, it's despised by many Android phone owners. A better and more popular alternative is Dolphin Browser.

Like many popular computer browsers, Dolphin Browser features a tabbed interface, which works much better than the silly multiple window interface of the standard Browser app on the Droid 2.

The Dolphin Browser also sports many handy tools, which you can access by pressing the Menu soft key. Unlike in other Android apps, the tools pop up on a menu you can see on the screen.

If you grow fond of the Dolphin Browser, follow the customization directions in Chapter 22 to remove the Browser app's icon from the Home screen and place the Dolphin Browser there instead.

Google Finance

 The Google Finance app is an excellent market-tracking tool for folks who are obsessed with the stock market or want to keep an eye on their portfolios. The app offers you an overview of the market and updates to your stocks as well as links to financial news.

To get the most benefit from this app, configure Google Finance on the Web, using your computer. You can create lists of stocks to watch, which are then instantly synchronized with your Droid 2. You can visit Google Finance on the Web at

```
www.google.com/finance
```

As with other Google services, Google Finance is provided to you for free, as part of your Google account.

Movies

 The Movies app is the Droid 2 gateway to Hollywood. It lists currently running films and films that are opening, and it has links to your local theaters with showtimes and other information. The app is also tied into the popular Rotten Tomatoes Web site for reviews and feedback. If you enjoy going to the movies, you'll find the Movies app a valuable addition to your Droid 2.

MySettings

 The Droid 2 has many settings and even more places buried on the phone where you have to go to change those settings: Brightness. Volume. Bluetooth. Wi-Fi. Changing them isn't a challenge when you install the MySettings app.

The simple idea of MySettings is to place all common phone settings on one screen. You can turn settings on or off or make adjustments without having to venture down into the deep, dark recesses of the Settings screens. This app is easy to use and pure genius.

Paper Toss

 Yeah, Paper Toss is a game. The object is simple: Toss a crumpled piece of paper into a trashcan. The trashcan appears in varying locales and at different distances. Your nemesis is a circulating fan, which affects the arc of your throw. My record is ten in a row. And I love the polite "golf clapping" that takes place after each successful shot. It's a clever and addicting game.

Ringdroid

 The Ringdroid app lets you customize and create ringtones for the Droid 2. You can either snip a segment of music already on your phone or use the phone to record your own ringtone. This one-purpose app does its only job quite well.

SportsTap

 I admit to not being a sports nut, so I have difficulty identifying with the craving to have the latest scores, news, and schedules. The sports nuts in my life, however, tell me that the best app for that purpose is a handy app named SportsTap.

Rather than blather on about something I'm not into, just take my advice and obtain SportsTap. I believe you'll be thrilled.

Voice Recorder

 The Droid 2 can record your voice or other sounds, and the Voice Recorder is a good app for performing that task. It has an elegant and simple interface: Touch the big Record button to start recording. Make a note for yourself or record a friend doing his Daffy Duck impression.

Previous recordings are stored in a list on the Voice Recorder's main screen. Each recording is shown with its title, the date and time of the recording, and the recording duration.

Zedge

 Zedge is the eleventh item, but it's a good one: The Zedge program is a helpful resource for finding wallpapers and ringtones for the Droid 2. It's a sharing app, so you can access wallpapers and ringtones created by other Android phone users as well as share your own.

Zedge features an easy-to-use interface plus lots of helpful information on what it does and how it works.

Index

● S ●

Notes

Notes

Apple & Macs

iPad For Dummies
978-0-470-58027-1

iPhone For Dummies,
4th Edition
978-0-470-87870-5

MacBook For Dummies, 3rd
Edition
978-0-470-76918-8

Mac OS X Snow Leopard For
Dummies
978-0-470-43543-4

Business

Bookkeeping For Dummies
978-0-7645-9848-7

Job Interviews
For Dummies,
3rd Edition
978-0-470-17748-8

Resumes For Dummies,
5th Edition
978-0-470-08037-5

Starting an
Online Business
For Dummies,
6th Edition
978-0-470-60210-2

Stock Investing
For Dummies,
3rd Edition
978-0-470-40114-9

Successful
Time Management
For Dummies
978-0-470-29034-7

Computer Hardware

BlackBerry
For Dummies,
4th Edition
978-0-470-60700-8

Computers For Seniors
For Dummies,
2nd Edition
978-0-470-53483-0

PCs For Dummies, Windows
7 Edition
978-0-470-46542-4

Laptops For Dummies,
4th Edition
978-0-470-57829-2

Cooking & Entertaining

Cooking Basics
For Dummies,
3rd Edition
978-0-7645-7206-7

Wine For Dummies,
4th Edition
978-0-470-04579-4

Diet & Nutrition

Dieting For Dummies,
2nd Edition
978-0-7645-4149-0

Nutrition For Dummies,
4th Edition
978-0-471-79868-2

Weight Training
For Dummies,
3rd Edition
978-0-471-76845-6

Digital Photography

Digital SLR Cameras &
Photography For Dummies,
3rd Edition
978-0-470-46606-3

Photoshop Elements 8
For Dummies
978-0-470-52967-6

Gardening

Gardening Basics
For Dummies
978-0-470-03749-2

Organic Gardening
For Dummies,
2nd Edition
978-0-470-43067-5

Green/Sustainable

Raising Chickens
For Dummies
978-0-470-46544-8

Green Cleaning
For Dummies
978-0-470-39106-8

Health

Diabetes For Dummies,
3rd Edition
978-0-470-27086-8

Food Allergies
For Dummies
978-0-470-09584-3

Living Gluten-Free
For Dummies,
2nd Edition
978-0-470-58589-4

Hobbies/General

Chess For Dummies,
2nd Edition
978-0-7645-8404-6

Drawing
Cartoons & Comics
For Dummies
978-0-470-42683-8

Knitting For Dummies,
2nd Edition
978-0-470-28747-7

Organizing
For Dummies
978-0-7645-5300-4

Su Doku For Dummies
978-0-470-01892-7

Home Improvement

Home Maintenance
For Dummies,
2nd Edition
978-0-470-43063-7

Home Theater
For Dummies,
3rd Edition
978-0-470-41189-6

Living the
Country Lifestyle
All-in-One
For Dummies
978-0-470-43061-3

Solar Power Your Home
For Dummies,
2nd Edition
978-0-470-59678-4

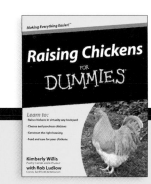

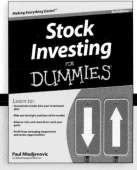

Internet

Blogging For Dummies,
3rd Edition
978-0-470-61996-4

eBay For Dummies,
6th Edition
978-0-470-49741-8

Facebook For Dummies, 3rd
Edition
978-0-470-87804-0

Web Marketing
For Dummies,
2nd Edition
978-0-470-37181-7

WordPress
For Dummies,
3rd Edition
978-0-470-59274-8

Language & Foreign Language

French For Dummies
978-0-7645-5193-2

Italian Phrases
For Dummies
978-0-7645-7203-6

Spanish For Dummies,
2nd Edition
978-0-470-87855-2

Spanish For Dummies,
Audio Set
978-0-470-09585-0

Math & Science

Algebra I For Dummies,
2nd Edition
978-0-470-55964-2

Biology For Dummies,
2nd Edition
978-0-470-59875-7

Calculus For Dummies
978-0-7645-2498-1

Chemistry For Dummies
978-0-7645-5430-8

Microsoft Office

Excel 2010 For Dummies
978-0-470-48953-6

Office 2010 All-in-One
For Dummies
978-0-470-49748-7

Office 2010 For Dummies,
Book + DVD Bundle
978-0-470-62698-6

Word 2010 For Dummies
978-0-470-48772-3

Music

Guitar For Dummies,
2nd Edition
978-0-7645-9904-0

iPod & iTunes
For Dummies,
8th Edition
978-0-470-87871-2

Piano Exercises
For Dummies
978-0-470-38765-8

Parenting & Education

Parenting For Dummies,
2nd Edition
978-0-7645-5418-6

Type 1 Diabetes
For Dummies
978-0-470-17811-9

Pets

Cats For Dummies,
2nd Edition
978-0-7645-5275-5

Dog Training For Dummies,
3rd Edition
978-0-470-60029-0

Puppies For Dummies,
2nd Edition
978-0-470-03717-1

Religion & Inspiration

The Bible For Dummies
978-0-7645-5296-0

Catholicism For Dummies
978-0-7645-5391-2

Women in the Bible
For Dummies
978-0-7645-8475-6

Self-Help & Relationship

Anger Management
For Dummies
978-0-470-03715-7

Overcoming Anxiety
For Dummies,
2nd Edition
978-0-470-57441-6

Sports

Baseball
For Dummies,
3rd Edition
978-0-7645-7537-2

Basketball
For Dummies,
2nd Edition
978-0-7645-5248-9

Golf For Dummies,
3rd Edition
978-0-471-76871-5

Web Development

Web Design
All-in-One
For Dummies
978-0-470-41796-6

Web Sites
Do-It-Yourself
For Dummies,
2nd Edition
978-0-470-56520-9

Windows 7

Windows 7
For Dummies
978-0-470-49743-2

Windows 7
For Dummies,
Book + DVD Bundle
978-0-470-52398-8

Windows 7 All-in-One
For Dummies
978-0-470-48763-1

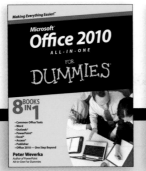
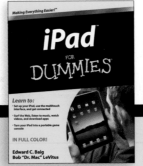
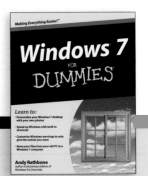

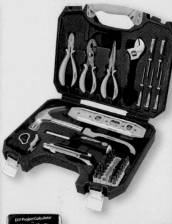